The Aural Rehabilitation Process

HERBERT J. OYER
JUDITH P. FRANKMANN
Michigan State University

The Aural Rehabilitation Process
A Conceptual Framework Analysis

HOLT, RINEHART AND WINSTON
New York Chicago San Francisco Atlanta Dallas
Montreal Toronto London Sydney

Library of Congress Cataloging in Publication Data

Oyer, Herbert J.
    The aural rehabilitation process.

    1. Deaf—Rehabilitation. I. Frankmann, Judith P.,
joint author. II. Title.
HV2380.09   362.4′2   75–1011
ISBN: 0–03–013541–9

5 6 7 8 9   059   9 8 7 6 5 4 3 2 1

To Jane and Ray

Preface

This book presents a review and critical evaluation of research literature that deals directly or indirectly with the aural rehabilitation process. In the interests of an organized approach, the presentation is made within the structure of a conceptual framework.

The conceptual framework consists of six major concepts in the rehabilitative process. To define the areas of interest and focus the literature search, questions were generated for each of the basic constructs or the subject areas under each concept. Research articles providing answers to these questions were identified from reference lists and from published abstracts. The research literature itself exerted an influence on the development of the conceptual framework. Information gleaned from the professional journals and documents helped to stimulate the development of additional constructs and questions.

The development of the Aural Rehabilitation Conceptual Framework led to the statement of six basic concepts that identify major steps in the rehabilitative process:

   I. Handicap Recognition
  II. Motivational Aspects
 III. Acquisition of Specialized Assistance
 IV. Measurement and Evaluation of Deficit and Handicap
  V. Rehabilitative Sessions
 VI. Effects of Training and Counseling

Each of the concepts subsumes a number of constructs that serve to define the concept in more detail.

Constructs were identified in the early stages of the study, and as the investigation progressed, additional questions were posed that focused on the importance of the constructs in the rehabilitation of hearing-handicapped people. Periodic review of the constructs led, in the later stages of the work, to modifications and additions in response to the data found in the literature search.

A philosophical background to the general area of aural rehabilitation is provided in Chapters One and Two. Chapter One is a general discussion of the area of rehabilitative audiology, and Chapter Two shows how the area of rehabilitative audiology can be studied through the employment of a conceptual framework. Then a chapter is devoted to each of the six basic concepts. Each of these chapters includes introductory comments, summaries and evaluations of the research, a summary of the information in the chapter, recommendations for further research, and a list of references.

The findings that have emerged from the literature search, and the evaluation of those findings, highlight the most pressing problems in the aural rehabilitation process. The authors believe that the placing of the process within a conceptual framework and their recommendations for further research constitute the most important aspects of this book.

The Aural Rehabilitation Conceptual Framework approach has provided a method for organizing the extensive and varied research literature so that (1) the work will be useful to all those who seek to know the evidence derived from research that underlies the area of aural rehabilitation; and (2), more important, the work highlights the research that must yet be undertaken if the habilitative and rehabilitative procedures employed with the hearing-handicapped population are to be more firmly based upon scientific evidence.

The authors believe that this book will be useful to students of Audiology, Special Education (including Counseling), and Otology. If it adds to the basic understanding of the aural rehabilitation process by the beginning student and stimulates much needed scientific research in the area of rehabilitative audiology, thereby helping those who are hearing handicapped, the authors will feel that their efforts have not been in vain.

ACKNOWLEDGMENTS

The original work from which this book was developed was supported by a contract between Herbert J. Oyer and the Neurological and Sensory Disease Control Program, Division of Chronic Disease Programs, Health Services and Mental Health Administration, U.S. Department of Health, Education, and Welfare, Contract No. HSM–110–69–222.

Special recognition is due Dr. William Haas for the important contributions he made to this work as a member of the project team.

Special recognition is also due Dr. Joseph L. Stewart, Project Officer, for the guidance and encouragement he provided throughout the course of the work completed under the contract with the Health Services and Mental Health Administration of the U.S. Department of Health, Education, and Welfare.

Acknowledgment is also made of the assistance of two graduate students, Richard Smith and Pamela Riedl, for their work in the early phases of the project, and for the expert secretarial services provided by Carol Remondino, Roberta Busche, and Virginia McLeod.

H.J.O.
J.P.F.

East Lansing, Michigan
February 1975

Contents

The Aural Rehabilitation Process

1
Rehabilitative Audiology

Even though the label *rehabilitative audiology* is somewhat recent, that which takes place in the process of rehabilitating those who are hearing handicapped has been a concern of society for centuries. According to earliest accounts, the process involved in ameliorating the handicap of one who suffered a loss of hearing was associated with programs for education of the deaf. As early as the seventeenth century formal programs for the hearing handicapped were getting under way in Europe. An excellent review of this very early work is found in the writings of deLand (1931, 1968) and Goldstein (1939). The primary focus of the early European programs was on teaching speech to the deaf. This objective made the stimulus input channels of immediate importance.

Methods were soon devised that provided amplification of sound to the ear. The aural or acoustic method—one of the most important methods—was greatly facilitated in its delivery of amplified sound to the ear by the invention of the vacuum tube and, more recently, by the use of germanium crystals in the production of transistors. This method provides for maximal use of residual hearing by the hearing handicapped.

Methods have also been developed for transmission of information to the hearing impaired via the visual input route. One approach utilizes lipreading and hand signs whereas another depends upon finger spelling and signing. Still another approach involves total communication, which calls for the use of both visual and aural approaches. There are well-developed arguments employed by the proponents of each approach concerning its efficacy. Regretfully, however, even though the arguments are developed and loyalties established, there is far too little scientific evidence available for any of the approaches.

Tactile reception provides still another input channel for information in aural rehabilitation, but it is in only the early stages of development. Probably the most extensive use of tactile stimulation has been made in the Verbotonal method by Guberina.

Significant developments in the area of middle-ear surgery have also proved to be of tremendous importance and of real assistance to those with hearing deficit associated with middle-ear problems.

Rehabilitative Audiology: A Definition

Inquiry into the structures and functions of the auditory system has been under way for centuries. The start of a professional field of audiology by Drs. Carhart and Canfield, however, dates back only to the 1940s.

The greatest impetus given to audiology as a professional area was brought about by the problems associated with the hearing losses suffered by World War II veterans. The great need to aid the hearing handicapped prompted establishment of programs of aural rehabilitation in military hospitals—programs that included lipreading, auditory training, and speech conservation. Because servicemen not only needed hearing aids but also made claims for compensation, the measurement of hearing became very important. The need for more highly definitive tests of hearing led to much research in pure tone and speech audiometry. The need to provide programs of aural rehabilitation led to greater expansion of such programs, but unfortunately to far too little research.

As the need to provide services of hearing testing, lipreading, auditory training, speech conservation, and rehabilitation developed, subareas of audiology emerged. Those professional workers who involved themselves principally in audiometric measurement and the determination of need for and selection of amplification devices have become known as *clinical* audiologists. Those whose efforts have been primarily directed toward (1) speech and language development and also conservation through programs that have employed techniques of auditory training, lipreading, or manual language, (2) self-adjustment, and (3) social adjustment have become known as *rehabilitative* audiologists. Those whose principal focus is in experimentation in audition are known as *experimental* audiologists. These are the broad subcategories of audiologists. However, the settings in which audiologists are found at work yield still more labels, such as military audiologist, industrial audiologist, medical audiologist, educational audiologist or hearing clinician, and hearing aid audiologist. Most certainly there are audiologists whose activities overlap several of these areas.

It is somewhat unfortunate that subcategories of audiologist have developed so rapidly, before audiology has had the opportunity to become well established as a profession. This labeling of the subcategories creates barriers among audiologists and only increases the possibility of discontinuity in services that should be rendered to the hearing handicapped. The authors would propose that all labels which refer to the subcategories of professional audiology be eliminated and that in the future the term be simply *AUDIOLOGIST*. The audiologist should be competent in all the traditional aspects of professional audiology: measurement of hearing level, determination of need for and selection of appropriate amplification devices, programs of language habilitation and educational adjustment of hearing-handicapped children, special programs with hard-of-hearing adults, all focused on improvement of communication skills as well as on self-, social, and vocational adjustment. Additionally, he should be trained in the area of physical inspection and evaluation and thus render a continuity of service to the hearing impaired who also sustain communication handicap. His work setting might preclude involvement in all these aspects, but he would be prepared by virtue of his training to function as an audiologist who is fully equipped to manage cases of hearing handicap with concomitant problems of communication.

The Aural Rehabilitation Process

Study of any process requires the observation and analysis of a flow of events that starts at some point and progresses to a logical culmination. So it is with the study of the aural rehabilitation process. Any two persons willing to describe verbally their conceptualizations of the aural rehabilitation process would undoubtedly use different labels in their descriptions. The concepts, as well as supporting constructs, might differ considerably. But any conceptualization of aural rehabilitation must include some fundamental notions concerning the process, irrespective of the terms chosen to describe them, or the ultimate uniqueness in the conceptualization of the process. The uniqueness of any conceptualization is a function of a number of variables, including the precision with which one perceives reality and the past learning and conditioning that contribute significantly to his perceptions.

The authors hope that their perceptions of the aural rehabilitation process reflect reality as perceived by others who have worked in this area and that the terms used in describing these perceptions are common enough to evoke highly similar meanings among co-workers. In order to assure this to some degree, the conceptual framework developed here has been shared with numerous colleagues at various points in its development.

The aural rehabilitation process is composed of a number of important subprocesses. The first of these is the *recognition* by someone, whether it be the client or another, that a handicap in communication exists due to hearing loss. After recognition of a handicap, something is done or is not done about it. Therefore, a second subprocess is that of *motivation.* If the motivation is lacking to the extent that nothing is done about the handicap that has been recognized, then the process of aural rehabilitation is short-circuited. If, however, something is done about the handicap, there is a third subprocess—movement involving the *identification and utilization of the knowledge, skills, and competencies of a specialist* who is prepared to render professional help. Once specialized assistance is obtained there is a fourth subprocess involved, namely, that of *precise determination of the nature and severity of the hearing deficit and the subsequent handicap(s) related to that deficit.* Not until the dimensions of the deficit and the handicap are determined can a reasonable approach be made toward the habilitation or rehabilitation of the client. The actual *clinical sessions* in which a client becomes involved comprise the fifth subprocess. The final subprocess in aural rehabilitation to which the clinician attends is that of *measuring and evaluating the effects of his work with the hearing-handicapped individual.* The kinds of improvements that have occurred and the persistence of training effects give evidence to both the client and clinician concerning the adequacy of the methods and procedures that have been employed.

Who Administers Aural Rehabilitation

History shows that aural rehabilitation was first administered by teachers of the deaf who were interested in helping deaf children to speak. In America, concern was shown by workers in hearing societies for persons needing aural rehabilitation; as a result, programs of lipreading have been carried out by workers within these agencies, and the extent of formal training of such workers has been quite varied.

The World War II veterans suffering hearing handicap received aural rehabilitation in government hospitals as well as in university clinics throughout the country. The great need for professionally trained aural rehabilitationists in the 1940s stimulated programs of professional preparation in institutions of higher education. As a result there have been courses developed that carry a variety of titles, for example, Lipreading, Speechreading, Aural Rehabilitation, Auditory Training, and so on, that are taken by students who are preparing to teach the deaf as well as those preparing for careers in audiology. There is no specific certification in aural rehabilitation; however, these courses can be applied toward certification of teachers of the deaf, toward certification by state departments of education, and also toward the Certificate of Clinical Competence in Audiology or Speech Pathology of the

American Speech and Hearing Association. Therefore, those who administer aural rehabilitation in organized programs are generally teachers of the deaf, audiologists, or speech pathologists.

Consumers of Aural Rehabilitation

The consumers receiving aural rehabilitation are of all ages. They find their way to these special programs because someone, the hearing handicapped themselves or someone near to them (teachers, physicians, or others), recognizes their handicap.

Purpose of Aural Rehabilitation

Aural rehabilitation is specifically for those who are in some way handicapped because of hearing loss. Of greatest concern are the problems of oral communication that are associated with significant loss of hearing. The handicap may also create other problems related to self-, social, school, or vocational adjustment, and it is with these problems that the audiologist deals. Those problems associated with the reception and perception of sound are dealt with directly. Related problems that are rightfully the concerns of other specialists are referred to the appropriate professional source. It is the responsibility of the audiologist to provide for the overall management of the hearing handicapped in order that the purposes of aural rehabilitation be fulfilled. Broadly conceived these are his responsibilities: moving the client toward more successful oral communication with others; helping the client to utilize nonverbal sensory stimuli more successfully in order to compensate for his auditory deficit; and assisting the client in those areas where there appears to be maladjustment (self-, social, school, vocational), or where there is performance that is considerably below his potential.

Importance of Aural Rehabilitation

The individual who deals with those suffering hearing loss does not have to be unusually perceptive to see the need for and value of aural rehabilitation. However, as one views the development of the field of audiology it is not difficult to recognize that training and research programs have stressed hearing measurement for purposes of assisting in medical diagnosis, or for purposes of recommending amplification.

Aside from the medical or physical aspect, many teachers and clinicians have sought to ameliorate other suffering that attends hearing loss by providing auditory training, practice in lipreading, speech conservation, speech rehabilitation, and language training for the handicapped. A few researchers have also attempted to discover new facts that pertain specifically to problems of the aurally handicapped for whom medical treatment, surgical intervention, or amplification through a hearing aid has not been the complete answer.[1] Both public and private funding sources have helped to support training and research in aural rehabilitation to a limited extent.

Perhaps one of the greatest professional acknowledgments of the importance of aural rehabilitation has been the establishment of the Academy of Rehabilitative Audiology. This Academy was established in 1966 at Michigan State University following a Seminar on Aural Rehabilitation (1966) supported by the Vocational Rehabilitation Services of the U.S. Department of Health, Education, and Welfare and sponsored by the Department of Audiology and Speech Sciences and the Continuing Education Service of Michigan State University.
The purposes of the Academy are—

1. to provide a forum for the exchange of ideas on, knowledge of, and experiences with habilitative and rehabilitative aspects of audiology,
2. to foster and stimulate professional education, research and interest in habilitative and rehabilitative programs for hearing-handicapped persons,
3. to correlate all aspects of this endeavor for the welfare of those so handicapped, and
4. to receive, use, hold and apply gifts, bequests, and endowments in carrying forward such purposes.

The formulation of the Academy was conceptualized by Drs. Herbert J. Oyer, John J. O'Neill, and L. Deno Reed in 1963. Following initial planning by Oyer, O'Neill, and Reed, invitations were extended to C. B. Avery, F. K. Blair, M. R. Costello, K. Frisina, R. F. Krug, F. E. McConnell, J. B. Miller, J. Rosen, and E. J. Hardick to participate in the Seminar and in the further planning of the Academy. This group of twelve persons became the charter members of the Academy, with H. J. Oyer serving as its first president for a two-year term.

At present there are approximately 100 persons who have become members of the Academy. They span the fields of education of the deaf,

[1] Chapters Three through Eight specify research that has been done pertaining to aural rehabilitation.

audiology, and otolaryngology. This group meets at least once a year to exchange information concerning research and rehabilitative programs.

Need for Broad Conceptualization

A basic need has been for the broad conceptualization of the total process involved in aural rehabilitation. There are underlying fundamental concepts and supporting constructs involved in any process, and aural rehabilitation is no exception. To view that which takes place within a conceptual framework helps one to view the process comprehensively as well as to see the relationships between and among broad concepts and supporting constructs. The needs for research then become evident. Chapter Two deals specifically with the employment of the conceptual framework approach in the study of the rehabilitative aspects of audiology.

Summary

In this chapter the area of rehabilitative audiology has been delineated. It has been pointed out that work connected with the rehabilitation of the acoustically handicapped has taken place for centuries. For many years this work was primarily a responsibility of educators of the deaf, but following World War II programs for veterans have become a responsibility of audiologists as well. Emphasis has been placed upon study of aural rehablitation as a *process*. The subprocesses of the total process have been identified as (1) recognition of the need for specialized help for the acoustically handicapped; (2) motivation to do something about the handicap created by loss of hearing; (3) identification of specialized assistance for purposes of undertaking a program of aural assessment and rehabilitation; (4) determination of the status of hearing deficit and related handicaps associated with the deficit; (5) involvement in clinical sessions in which various channels, methods, and procedures are employed in reducing the handicapping condition or conditions; and (6) the determination of effects of the rehabilitative efforts over both the short and long terms. Consumers of aural rehabilitation are frequently self-referrals but sometimes referrals come from teachers, physicians, and others.

Purposes of aural rehabilitation and the importance of the process have been discussed. There has been a continuing recognition of the importance of aural rehabilitation as witnessed by involvement of federal agencies in training and research as well as by professionals who have established an Academy of Rehabilitative Audiology.

References

deLand F. (1931, 1968). *The Story of Lip Reading.* Washington, D.C.: The Alexander Graham Bell Association for the Deaf, Inc.

Goldstein, M. (1939). *The Acoustic Method for the Training of the Deaf and Hard-of-Hearing Child.* St. Louis: Laryngoscope Press.

Oyer, H. J., and Hardick, E. J. (1966). *Aural Rehabilitation of the Acoustically Handicapped.* East Lansing: Seminar Proceedings, VRA Contract No. 66–41. SHSLR No. 266, Michigan State University.

2
A Conceptual Framework for the Study of the Aural Rehabilitation Process

The development of conceptual frameworks in the various areas of social and behavioral sciences is not new. They have been employed by scholars in the disciplines of sociology, business, home economics, and anthropology. Particularly notable is the Nye and Berardo (1966) work in family analysis in which several conceptual frameworks are presented —frameworks that were generated from areas of home economics, sociology, psychology, law, theology, economics, and anthropology. These researchers believed that this approach would lead to a far greater understanding of the dynamics of the family as a unit than the study of only *one* set of notions or concepts from *one* orientation.

The aural rehabilitative process does not lend itself to a similar kind of comparison because conceptual frameworks have not been formalized in the area of aural rehabilitation. It is imperative that overall conceptualization take place if we hope to move forward in this arena. It will be through this kind of effort that the best approaches can be determined for working toward the reduction of handicaps associated with hearing loss. Even though rehabilitation of the hard of hearing has taken place in a rather formal way since the early 1600s, there are still too few facts supporting our approaches, and very little by way of theory to which one can subscribe or disagree. Teachers of the deaf, audiologists, speech pathologists, and, more recently, language pathologists have been working and continue to work with the acoustically handicapped in their own unique ways without a common scheme within groups of specialists, to say nothing of a common scheme among the groups. This is not to say that what has taken place in classrooms and clinics has been ineffective, or without some good results. It is to say that, because we do not work within a somewhat unified conceptual structure, we cannot communicate as effectively within or among our groups. It is also to say that scientific progress toward the understanding and solving of the problems of the hearing handicapped has been greatly retarded.

We can ill afford to continue in this way, lest another century passes without the development of more scientifically based methods than those that exist today—or that existed several hundred years ago—for the alleviation of the handicaps associated with hearing loss.

The picture is not quite as bleak as it might seem, for progress has been made in alleviating deafness through the discovery and refinements of surgical techniques, through advances in biochemistry resulting in medications such as the antibiotics, and so on. There have also been engineering developments that led to the vacuum tube and transistors, which in turn have made possible the development of new and extremely important diagnostic tests.

However, in addition to the developments just cited, it is important that audiologists build conceptual structures or frameworks dealing with the process of aural rehabilitation in order that further significant advances can be made as a result of viewing the components of the process in perspective and in relationship with each other.

Purposes

The purposes of this chapter are to—

1. make a number of assumptions relative to the general area of aural rehabilitation. These assumptions might or might not square with the beliefs of some readers; however, it is mandatory to make some assumptions at the outset. Whether one does it consciously or not, one makes assumptions constantly as he works with the hearing handicapped.
2. set forth some operational definitions of terms important to both the employment of a conceptual framework and to the study of the general area of aural rehabilitation
3. suggest some needs served by the mechanism of a conceptual framework; comments will be made upon the relationships of such frameworks to research and theory
4. present in outline form the development of a conceptual framework for the study of aural rehabilitation

Assumptions

There are a number of assumptions that one must make before developing a conceptual framework for aural rehabilitation. They are as follows:

1. Aural rehabilitation is a facet of the multidisciplinary problem areas referred to as audiology (just as clinical hearing measurement or the experimental approach to the study of the normal processes of audition are facets).
2. Aural rehabilitation is a psychosocial educational process, and therefore lends itself to analysis within a conceptual framework.
3. Aural rehabilitation, as a process, must be examined as a dynamic and interrelated flow of events, and therefore cannot be studied meaningfully as events occurring in isolation.
4. Communication handicap stemming from auditory deficit can be alleviated in varying degrees through the process of aural rehabilitation.
5. Self-adjustment that has been distorted by the effects of hearing loss can be modified through the process of aural rehabilitation.
6. Social adjustment that has been adversely affected by a hearing loss can be modified through the process of aural rehabilitation.
7. Every aspect of the process of aural rehabilitation can be further clarified through rigorous empirical and experimental investigation.
8. There is at present no available well-organized conceptual framework by which to study the process of aural rehabilitation.
9. There are no extant theories of aural rehabilitation.
10. Given the proper attention through thoughtful conceptualization, pooled clinical impressions, and rigorous scientific research, the success of the aural rehabilitation process can be predicted for individuals within a specified range.

Operational Definitions of Terms

Auditory Deficit—hearing loss as measured by audiometric tests (see discussion early in Chapter Six for expansion of definition).

Auditory Handicap—problems of communication and self- and social adjustment primarily related to hearing loss.

Aural Rehabilitation—a clinical treatment process that has as its principal objective the reduction of handicaps associated with hearing deficit. (It includes habilitation here for operational purposes.)

Concept—two or more closely related constructs; a higher order abstraction than a construct.

Construct—a shorthand representation of a variety of facts. It subsumes a variety of facts under a single notion or idea. (Every area of study develops its own constructs for purposes of communication.)

Conceptual Framework—a group of related concepts that define, or place boundaries around, a process or area of study. It is a scheme of classification or taxonomy. It is a working theory.

Hypothesis—a proposition or question stated in such a manner that it permits of an answer. (It reflects the rather well-organized skepticism of science, namely, that scientists refuse to accept any statement without verification.)

Theory—meaningful ordering of related facts that permits the prediction of events. It is a statement of logical relationships among facts.

A Fact—an empirically verifiable observation.

The theory is a tool of science in three ways: (1) it defines the major orientation of a science, by defining the kinds of data that are to be abstracted; (2) it offers a conceptual scheme by which the relevant phenomena are systematized, classified, and interrelated; (3) it summarizes facts into (a) empirical generalizations and (b) systems of generalizations; (4) it predicts facts; and (5) it points to gaps in our knowledge.

On the other hand, facts are also productive of theory, in these ways: (1) facts help to initiate theories; (2) they lead to the reformulation of existing theory; (3) they cause the rejection of theories that do not fit the facts; (4) they change the focus and orientation of theory; and (5) they clarify and redefine theory (Goode and Hatt, 1952).

Some Needs Served by the Mechanism of a Conceptual Framework

A conceptual framework serves a number of needs: It defines an area of inquiry by setting up certain boundaries; by so doing it not only describes the area but also eliminates tangential related areas that are not really central to the inquiry. It highlights the research needs within an area. Thus it provides the mechanism for theory development by defining the area of inquiry and highlighting the research needs.

One might ask whether or not the conceptual framework approach is necessary for such hard-core sciences as chemistry or physics. The answer seems to be *no* for the following reasons: These disciplines have great agreement regarding terminology employed by member scientists; there seem to be rather well-established criteria for determining procedures to be followed and to judge whether or not they have been followed; there seem to be criteria for ascertaining whether or not new findings constitute a real contribution to the area (Kotzin, 1964). This is not to say that even among hard-core scientists one would not find some disagreement at levels of both procedure and theory.

The conceptual framework provides those involved in aural rehabilitation an ideal way to engage in critical introspection, to the end that they can—

1. develop a common and meaningful language
2. appraise the relative importance of components of the process
3. define the evidence available to support the components of the process
4. pinpoint the need for additional evidence
5. suggest procedure for research investigations
6. construct criteria by which to judge the importance of research contributions
7. assess the impact of the process on the behavior of the acoustically handicapped
8. determine the effects of the process upon that segment of society comprising the social milieu of the acoustically handicapped
9. describe the relationship of the effects of aural rehabilitation to educational achievement
10. interpret its needs to the larger interdisciplinary problem area of audiology, of which it is a facet, and to other relevant disciplines

Aural rehabilitation is a *practical science*—one that has as its prime objective or aim *doing,* as contrasted with the strictly theoretical sciences that have as their ultimate objectives or aims *knowledge* (irrespective of how this knowledge is put to use, or whether it is ever put to use). Engineering and medicine are also examples of practical sciences, as are soil science, urban planning, and the like. The ultimate aim of aural rehabilitation is to reduce the handicaps of the acoustically impaired, and to alter attitudes of those individuals in the immediate surrounds if this is required in order to effect better self- and social adjustment, and to improve academic achievement and/or vocational success. It is a practical science aimed at uncovering truth for purposes of *doing* something *for* the acoustically handicapped.

Kotzin (1964) suggests that there are a number of interacting features associated with practical sciences. The following points reflect some of her contentions.

1. Utilization of normative concepts, for example in medicine— health versus disease, normal versus abnormal, and so on.
   (In aural rehabilitation one uses in connection with speech reception and discrimination such terms as *adequate–inadequate,* or in self- and social status, the terms *adjusted–maladjusted.*)
2. Utilization of knowledge for purposes of achieving excellence, overcoming defects, or making improvement.
   (These are reasons why students study aural rehabilitation, not only for purposes of knowing about the process.)
3. Practical sciences are concerned with the relationships between means and ends.
   (The audiologist is guided by end results and adjusts the means to

accomplish desired ends, whereas the theoretical scientist has no concerns here—he is interested in discovering new truths irrespective of their use—witness the atomic bomb.)

4. As contrasted to theoretical sciences that deal with mathematically exact determinations and precise treatments, *a practical science deals with changing phenomena, and therefore deals in the realm of probability as regards truth.*

(In aural rehabilitation we predict outcomes at certain levels of confidence—we generalize cautiously to a specified population.)

5. *Practical sciences adjust their knowledge to individual variations and differences,* unlike the other sciences that are based squarely on mathematical precision.

(In aural rehabilitation the clinician does not, for example, deal with communication handicap in general, but employs his knowledges and skills relative to communication handicap in treating particular aspects of communication handicap of an individual client.)

In summary, it can be said that the formulation and use of conceptual frameworks are the first important step in theory building, for they serve to introduce orderliness into research processes. They are also useful in developing propositions that can be put to test. As one proponent of the conceptual framework suggests, they ". . . are necessary for the development of valid theory" (Nye and Berardo, 1966).

The remainder of this chapter is devoted to presentations of the conceptual framework that has been developed in order to derive an overall view of the process of aural rehabilitation. It is presented with the supporting constructs. Each of the remaining chapters (Three through Eight) deals separately with one of the six major concepts and its supporting constructs.

Aural Rehabilitation—A Conceptual Framework

I. *Concept: Handicap–Deficit Recognition*

Constructs
SELF-RECOGNITION
RECOGNITION BY OTHERS
SCREENING OF HANDICAP AND DEFICIT IN ADULTS
SCREENING OF HANDICAP AND DEFICIT IN CHILDREN
Screening of Hearing Handicap in Infants, Preschool, and School-Age Children
Screening for Hearing Deficit in Neonates and Infants
Screening for Hearing Deficit in Preschool and School-Age Children
INCIDENCE
BARRIERS TO RECOGNITION

II. *Concept: Motivational Aspects*

Constructs
ROLE PERFORMANCE
    Family
    Educational
    Vocational
    Social Setting
SELF-CONCEPT
VALUE-NEED RELATIONSHIP

III. *Concept: Identification and Acquisition of Professional Assistance*

Constructs
INFORMATION DISSEMINATION AND EFFECTS
    Rural Areas
    Urban Areas
    Related Professions
SELECTION OF ASSISTANCE
    Type of Service
    Propinquity
    Economic Considerations
    Personal Factors
CONTINUATION OF SERVICE

IV. *Concept: Measurement and Evaluation of Auditory Deficit and Handicap*

Constructs
AUDITORY DEFICIT
    Pure Tone Audiometry—Air Conduction
    Pure Tone Audiometry—Bone Conduction
    Speech Audiometry
    Special Tests
    Pure Tone Audiometry—Children
      Tests Based on Operant Condition
      Conventional Pure Tone Tests
      Comparisons among Behavioral Procedures
      Objective Procedures
    Speech Audiometry—Children
      Speech Reception Tests
      Speech Discrimination Tests
    Deficit Typology
    Reference Levels and Optimal Standards for Auditory Deficit Appraisal
AUDITORY HANDICAP
    Normal Hearing—Hearing Deficit Comparisons
      Intelligence
      Concept Formation and Abstraction
      Memory Processes
      Visual Perception
      Self-concept

Speech and Language
    Speech Sound Production
    Articulation Test Procedures
    Quantitative Measures of Articulation
    Voice Quality
    Language Development
    Oral Language
    Written Language
    Language Tests and Measurement
Measurement of Auditory Handicap
Auditory Handicap Typology
HANDICAP-DEFICIT ASYMMETRY
    Handicap Measuring Devices and Auditory Test Results
    Personal Variables
    Personality
    Environmental Conditions and Type of Stimulation

V.   *Concept: Rehabilitative Sessions*

Constructs
    CLINICAL METHODS
    Lipreading
        Reviews
        Speaker Variables
        Code
        Transmission Link
        Receiver
        Training Methods
    Lipreading Tests
        Examples of Tests Available
        Comparison and Evaluation
    Visual-Nonverbal
    Manual Language
    Auditory Training
        Speaker
        Code
            Consonant and Vowel Discrimination
            Word Intelligibility
            Effects of Work Context
            Transmission Link
            Receiver
    Training Methods
        Programs for Young Children
        Programs for Older Children
        Adults Discrimination Training
    Hearing Aid Selection
        Response Characteristics of Hearing Aids
        Frequency Transposition and Modification
        Audiometric Materials in Hearing Aid Selection
        Effects of Earmold Coupling on Frequency Response
        Binaural Hearing Aids

Summary

In this chapter there has been a discussion of the general use of conceptual frameworks and their potential use in studying the aural rehabilitation process. Ten assumptions were set forth relative to aural rehabilitation. It was noted that assumptions are made whether stated or not; in effect they are identified as one works with the hearing handicapped by virtue of the methods and procedures one employs. Terms were defined that are important in dealing with a conceptual framework. Needs served by using a conceptual framework include defining areas of inquiry, highlighting of research needs, and providing a mechanism for theory development. Ten ways were cited in which the use of a conceptual framework can be helpful to aural rehabilitation. Aural rehabilitation was defined as a practical science, and the features of practical sciences were discussed. The specific conceptual framework developed for the study of the aural rehabilitation process was presented along with its supporting constructs.

References

Goode, W. J., and Hatt, P. K. (1952). *Methods in Social Research*. New York: McGraw-Hill.

Kotzin, R. H. (1964). Remarks on the appropriateness and adequacy of a conceptual framework to a discipline, with special reference to home management. *Conceptual Frameworks: Process of Home Management*. Proceedings of A Home Management Conference. East Lansing, Mich.

Nye, I., and Berardo, F. M. (1966). *Emerging Conceptual Framework in Family Analysis*. New York: Macmillan.

3
Handicap–Deficit Recognition

Recognition of an auditory handicap and deficit is a necessary first step in the aural rehabilitation process; it is frequently brought about because of trauma associated with failures in oral language communication. The recognition of the handicap as such in no way assures, however, that subsequent steps will be taken to ameliorate the condition or conditions causing the hearing loss, or that habilitative or rehabilitative measures will be undertaken to reduce the handicap associated with that loss. The focus of this chapter is on those factors that bear upon aural handicap-deficit recognition.

In the discussion of the concept of handicap-deficit recognition that follows, a number of supporting constructs will be examined: self-recognition, recognition by others, screening of adults, screening of children, incidence, and barriers to recognition. Questions pertinent to each of the constructs will be raised and, wherever possible, those questions will be answered on the basis of available data.

Self-recognition

Those who have been involved clinically with the hard of hearing in testing and/or rehabilitation can testify to the fact that many who seek help do so upon self-referral. Additionally, some of those who might appear to be self-referrals are actually seeking help at the urging of a spouse, relative, or friend. Also, of course, many who seek assistance in an audiology clinic have been referred by professionals in education or medicine.

The literature reveals no data on self-recognition of handicap associated with hearing loss. Comments by Driscoll (1971), a member of the hearing aid industry, suggest that self-recognition is much less common than recognition by others. This is especially true of two types of clients, the hearing-impaired infant, necessarily identified by others, and the geriatric individual. Because of the dearth of information, some important areas require intensive investigation. These include the extent to which family, occupational, school, or other psychosocial variables are conducive to self-recognition of hearing handicap; the frequency with which self-recognition of hearing handicap-deficit leads to a request for specialized assistance as compared to the recognition by others; the characteristics of those individuals who do or do not seek specialized assistance through aural rehabilitation programs; the degree of success in programs of aural rehabilitation for those who recognized their own handicap-deficit as compared to those who did not.

Recognition by Others

Children are brought to programs of aural habilitation or rehabilitation because someone else has noticed the handicap and has sought out specialized assistance for them. It seems reasonable to assume that delay in speech and language acquisition are the alerting signs for parents, although this supposition cannot be documented by any research findings now available. To the extent that this assumption is true, it is the handicapping effect of the hearing deficit that is recognized. Clinical experiences show that parents, teachers, and physicians play a large part in the referral process. The literature, however, reveals few specific studies directed toward sources of referrals. The following table shows the results of a study conducted by Oyer, Deal, Walsh, Lashbrook, and Higgins (1971) that dealt with referral of clients who had come to Michigan State University Speech and Hearing Clinic. These results were categorized for two age groups, those up to 15 years of age and those 15 years and older. Source of referral was obtained from the clinic record for each client.

MICHIGAN STATE UNIVERSITY SPEECH
AND HEARING CLINIC REFERRAL STUDY

Age	Source of Referrals (Percentage)					
	Physician	Health Related	Self (or) Parent	Teachers	Unknown	Other
Up to 15 Years (588)	57.1	15.3	6.3	4.8	6.8	9.7
15 Years or older (958)	38.5	16.9	18.7	0.1	11.2	14.6

A study representing data that are related to the topic of handicap recognition by others was carried out several years ago by Elliott and Armbruster (1967). In this study, which dealt with the possible effects of delay in early treatment of deafness, it was found that a large majority of parents of deaf children suspected that their child had a special problem before he was 2 years of age and took the child to an examiner. Of the parents, 31 percent reported being told that "nothing was wrong" and 27 percent that the child was ". . . too young to test." Only 18 percent were told that their child had a hearing problem.

Useful information concerning recognition of hearing handicap in children has been derived by Fellendorf and Harrow (1970) from questionnaires returned by 260 parents—see table below. In this study 84 percent of the children were 2 years or younger when hearing impairment was suspected, and 54 percent were a year or younger. Just over half of the respondents were satisified with the first diagnosis. As a rule several specialists were seen before the parents were convinced about the nature of the hearing problem; 28 percent saw only one specialist, but 72 percent saw more than one. Confirmation of hearing loss, after it was first suspected, usually occurred within a year through a Speech and Hearing Center.

PERCENTAGE OF SOURCES IDENTIFYING HEARING DEFICIT IN CHILDREN

	Parents	Relatives	Physicians	Friends	Teacher/School
Percentage	70	16	7	5	2

Questions concerning the recognition of hearing handicap by others are not yet answered through systematic studies. We need to establish data as to the individual most likely to identify hearing handicap in another. Additionally, we should determine the important identifying cues and the frequency of occurrence of false identification. Of those hearing handicaps that are recognized by others, we should discover the relationships between age at onset, severity of loss, nature of loss, and time of identification, as well as the number of handicapped who eventually receive specialized assistance.

Screening of Handicap and Deficit in Adults

There have been numerous programs set up for the screening of hearing loss in adults; however, to the knowledge of the authors no screening programs have been aimed at determining the type or severity of handicap that frequently accompanies hearing loss. Screening of intelligence, social maturity, personality, motor ability, educational achievement, and hearing and vision have been suggested as important components of a screening program for hearing handicap (Myklebust, 1950).

Studies for determining auditory deficit among large adult populations were carried out by Webster (1952) and O'Neill (1956). The latter found that—

1. a higher percentage of males failed the threshold test than females
2. individuals over 40 years old failed the threshold test more frequently than individuals 39 years old or younger
3. farmers and industrial workers showed a higher incidence of hearing loss than those in other occupational classifications
4. auditory sensitivity declines with age, with the hearing loss pattern being similar for both ears (the frequency most affected was 4000 Hz)
5. males apparently had better hearing for lower frequencies while females had better hearing for the higher frequencies

Although not a research article, a monograph in the *Journal of Speech and Hearing Disorders* dealing with identification audiometry (Darley, ed., 1961) sets forth goals and procedures for identification audiometry and also discusses conservation programs for military and industrial organizations, as well as those programs used by state and local departments of health. The total thrust is upon deficit identification and management of conservation programs without dealing with problems of handicap that are so often associated with hearing loss.

Although many screening studies have been made of the hearing acuity of individuals, there has not been systematic follow-up to determine the nature of the handicaps correlated with the type and severity of hearing loss among adults. So questions remain and the areas of research become clear. First of all, we must determine the kinds of instruments to be developed as screening devices for auditory handicaps. Moreover, we need to decide how hearing-handicap screening instruments should be standardized and to determine where and when screening for hearing handicaps in adults could be most effectively carried out.

Screening of Handicap and Deficit in Children

Screening of Hearing Handicap in Infants and Preschool and School-Age Children

Although there is often an attempt made by clinicians to evaluate the potential of the hearing-handicapped child for educational placement purposes, there are no standardized instruments or sets of procedures available for use in screening for hearing handicap. There are, however, many studies that deal with the problem of screening of hearing deficit among neonates and older children.

Screening for Hearing Deficit in Neonates and Infants

From the data available on screening for hearing deficit in infants it is clearly evident that behavioral responses can be elicited by the use of acoustic stimuli at very early ages (Richmond, 1953; Hardy et al., 1959; Froding, 1960; DiCarlo and Bradley, 1961; Suzuki and Sato, 1961; Hardy et al., 1962; Miller et al., 1963; Eisenberg, 1965, 1970; Eisenberg, et al., 1964; Field et al., 1967; Downs and Sterritt, 1967; Mendel, 1968; Hoverstein and Moncur, 1969; Peck, 1970; Ling et al., 1970, 1971; Goldstein and Tait, 1971). The neonate does respond to sound stimuli; however, as evidenced by results, the accuracy of screening leaves much to be desired.

If screening is to be efficient there must be a low error rate in both false positive and false negative identifications. When the criterion for hearing deficit is relaxed, infants with normal hearing will fail the screening and the false positive rate will be high. If the criterion is high, some infants with hearing losses will pass, increasing the false negative rate. The extensive screening programs for newborn infants reported by Downs and Sterritt (1967) and Ling and his associates (1970, 1971) give evidence that no screening test is now available with acceptable error rates in both of these categories. One significant problem, that of observer reliability, contributes to unsatisfactory validity of neonate screening. More basic data on the effects of signal frequency, duration, bandwidth, and patterning are needed. When a description can be made of stimulus conditions that are reliably related to response to auditory stimulation, then observer agreement should follow. The current status of research suggests that (1) noise bands centered at the higher frequencies under 4000 Hz are more effective than pure tones, (2) patterned signals can overcome response decrement over time, and (3) accuracy of determining the presence of a response is a positive function of increasing age.

Screening for Hearing Deficit in Preschool and School-Age Children

There have been a number of rather distinct procedures established for screening the hearing of children. Likewise, there have been surveys made of various groups throughout the country. Harrington (1967) points out that nationally there are over five million children screened for hearing deficit each year. This number is approximately 9 percent of the child population of the United States between 5 and 17 years of age. The rubella epidemic, the Headstart Program, and the perinatal study of 60,000 mothers sponsored by the National Institutes of Health have all created a sharpened awareness and heightened activity in relation to the screening of hearing of children.

As could be expected, the literature in this area is diffuse. Some of it is descriptive solely of the procedures and stimuli employed. Other literature presents the results of surveys in addition to description of the procedures and stimuli employed. Still others that deal with the efficiency of hearing screening tests, their validity and reliability, will be the focus of the following discussion.

Review of the literature makes it apparent that a variety of test procedures exist for school-age children. Newby (1948) introduced the idea of using a 2 × 2 tetrachoric table to display for group and follow-up individual testing the percentages of correct judgments and mistaken judgments. The latter include both false positive errors and false negative errors. Generally, false negatives are more serious because a child will not receive the help needed if a true hearing loss exists and is not detected. Research comparing group and individual hearing testing in public schools has been reported by Newby (1947), Curry and Nagel (1959), and Hollien and Thompson (1967). As a rule group testing of children at third-grade level and above resulted in satisfactorily low error rates. Mass screening and individual sweep-check approaches are now both in use.

It is clearly evident from the literature that the use of five frequencies is superior to a single frequency (4000 Hz) test. However, there is some evidence that limited frequency screening using 4000 Hz and one other frequency is potentially useful when time is an overriding consideration. In a long line of research that peaked in the late 1950s and early 1960s, both views are represented. Those who concluded that some form of a limited frequency check has adequate validity include Glorig and House (1957), Ventry and Newby (1959), Satalof and Menduke (1959), and Hanley and Gaddie (1962). Others find the false negative rate too high with limited frequency testing (Lawrence and Rubin, 1959; Lightfoot, Buckingham, and Kelley, 1959; Miller and Bella, 1959; Norton and Lux, 1960; Stevens and Davidson, 1959; Siegenthaler and Sommers, 1959; Maxwell and Davidson, 1961). Considering the relatively little time that is saved by reducing the number of frequencies tested and the increase in errors associated with limited frequency testing, this procedure cannot be generally accepted.

Recommendations for screening procedures with school-age children were set forth by the National Conference on Identification Audiometry in 1960. The central feature of the program was screening the frequencies 500, 1000, 2000, and 6000 Hz at 10 dB and 4000 Hz at 20 dB. Applying this program to 880 school children Melnick, Eagles, and Levine (1964) compared the screening results with threshold test results. The screening program was successful in identifying children with decreased sensitivity; only 2.5 percent were incorrectly judged as normal hearing, and 1.5 percent with normal hearing failed the screening. There were, however, a number of children with otologic abnormalities who successfully passed both the screening and the complete threshold test.

The need for audiometric screening in the public schools can be demonstrated by examining studies of parent and teacher detection of hearing loss. Data reported by Kodman (1956), Geyer and Yankauer (1956), and Kodman (1969) show a very high error rate ranging from 25 to 75 percent. The most serious errors, failing to detect hearing losses, were more prominent than false negative errors.

Even though recommendations have been made concerning the periodicity of testing, there are no clear research results that indicate when children should be tested or how frequently. Although some individuals have made concerted attempts to evaluate their hearing screening programs, there are too few studies of the routine evaluation of ongoing programs of hearing screening.

Incidence

The incidence of hearing *handicap* among the population of the United States is *not known*. There are, however, various studies that present incidence of hearing *deficit*. For hearing-deficit figures to be meaningful, they must be presented along with a description of the methods and standards employed to derive them. Fortunately, these descriptions are generally available in the extant literature.

Questions concerning the incidence of hearing deficit need to be raised, namely: (1) What is the incidence among adults, school children, and preschool children? (2) Are there differences with reference to age, and sex? (3) Is the incidence different with respect to geographical area? (4) Are there differences with respect to race? (5) Are there differences between or among social classes? (6) Is educational achievement a variable of importance? (7) What types of deficits occur? (8) What is the severity of deficit that occurs? (9) Of the deficits that occur, what is the incidence of those that are medically significant; educationally significant? Unfortunately, the available literature does not fully answer these questions.

Data from the National Health Survey (*Characteristics of Persons with Impaired Hearing*, 1962–1963) reveal a number of interesting items. These data were derived from a sampling of the civilian noninstitutional population of the United States. Interviews were conducted with a representative sample of 42,000 households containing 134,000 persons. In order that a more detailed picture might be obtained of the status of those reporting a hearing loss in the initial interview, a follow-up questionnaire was sent. The response rate was approximately

93 percent of the 8005 originally reporting hearing loss. From this survey, it was estimated that *approximately eight million persons in the United States suffer hearing loss in one or both ears.* Of the persons reporting hearing loss, approximately 31 percent reported it in one ear only.

In terms of age and sex the survey revealed that the ratio of persons with binaural hearing loss increases from 3.5 per 1000 population under age 17 years to 133.0 per 1000 persons who are 65 years of age and over. About 80 percent of persons with binaural loss were 45 years of age or older, and 55 percent were 65 years of age or older.

In terms of sex and speech comprehension the survey showed that there were 25.5 males per 1000 population and 19.3 females per 1000 population with binaural losses. In terms of income and educational attainment the findings of the survey were that within each of the age and sex groups the highest number of hearing losses were among the lowest income and lowest educational attainment groups and, in general, the number of losses decreased as family income and educational attainment increased. Concerning the racial difference, the survey revealed a considerably higher rate of hearing loss among white persons (23.3 per 1000) compared with nonwhite (15.1 per 1000). These figures held true through age groups and degree of hearing loss. The survey also showed hearing losses to be lowest in the urban areas and highest in rural areas where persons 45 to 64 years of age are highest among rural farm residents. For persons 65 years of age or older, rates are highest among rural nonfarm residents. Here again, all groups showed males with more hearing loss than females. Throughout all age groups, the rates of hearing loss were lowest for the north and east sections of the country and highest for the south and west.

The National Health Survey of 1962–1963 cited earlier comes closest to answering the nine questions posed at the beginning of this section. However, the data presented are *based upon interviews and not upon actual hearing testing.* The other literature reveals, in the main, percentage figures of losses of specified populations that range from approximately .70 percent to 10 percent. In India, the average loss was much higher, that is, 16.3 to 18.6 percent.

Barriers to Recognition

Individuals are delayed in recognizing their hearing handicap-deficits for one or more reasons. One factor that probably looms large in nonrecognition is the inability to provide screening programs for the vast majority of the population throughout the United States. The authors

The following table presents some selected cross-cultural comparative figures of the incidence of hearing deficit.

CROSS-CULTURAL COMPARATIVE FIGURES
OF INCIDENCE OF HEARING DEFICIT

	Percent with Deficit
Fay et al., 1970 (Severely disabled children—U.S.A.)	19.8
Kodman & Sperrazzo, 1959 (Public School Children—U.S.A.)	5.0
Proctor, 1963 (School Children—U.S.A.)	7.0 – 10.0
Connor, 1961 (U.S.A.)	0.7 – 5.0
Kapur, 1965 (School Children—India)	16.3 – 18.6
Scottish Ed. Dept., 1950 (Scotland)	5.0 – 8.0
Livingstone, 1964 (England)	2.0
Fabritius, 1964 (Denmark)	3.4
Van Laar, 1965 (Netherlands)	9.0

know of no reliable data that reveal the percentage of the population that actually participate in hearing screening throughout the country. Variables related to the barriers preventing recognition of hearing handicap and deficit that require additional research are the influence of ignorance, social status, and economic status; neglect; age, sex, and occupation; and awareness of screening programs.

The literature reveals some of the causes for late identification of hearing handicap-deficit. In a study of causes of late recognition of deafness in Czechoslovakia, Ferdinand (1966) pointed out that some delay is caused by physicians who recommend to parents that they wait to determine hearing status until the child is older. Another cause identified was the inaccessibility to facilities in which proper hearing appraisal can be made. Still another cause for delay is that the hearing problem is only a part of a constellation of other factors—mental retardation as just one example. Ferdinand points out that in his study of two schools for the deaf, two thirds of the time deafness was recognized by parents and one third of the time by physicians. Ferdinand reports that parents had immediate diagnosis made in 41.4 percent of the cases, but had up to six months to have diagnoses made in 8.3 percent of the cases. He adds that incorrect procedures by the physician caused delay of identification fifty-five times, or in 27 percent of the cases.

The method employed in the identification process itself might prove to be a barrier to recognition of hearing handicap and deficit.

In studies directed toward determining efficiency of teacher judgment in identifying children with hearing loss, Geyer and Yankauer (1956) found that teachers missed identifying 62 percent of those actually found to have hearing loss by the survey, and Curry (1950) found teachers identified only 7.6 percent of the children.

In a study of hearing loss among school children as related to socioeconomic settings, Talbe-Hansen (1954) determined that 15.5 percent of the pupils came from socially poor sections whereas only 9.7 percent came from schools located in more socially favorable sections. This finding suggests that lower socioeconomic level might function as a barrier in recognition of hearing handicap.

Still another barrier, as suggested in a study made by Kodman and colleagues (1962) in Kentucky, was that 34 percent of the children who were screened and needed follow-up could not receive it because parents were not interested in follow-up service.

Some barriers to recognition have been identified through studies that recognize ignorance, socioeconomic status, and neglect as contributing factors. No data are available, however, that relate age, sex, and occupation to recognition of hearing handicap-deficits. More importantly there is no evidence available in the literature that identifies programs which have as their objective the reduction of barriers to recognition of hearing handicap-deficit.

Summary

The concept of handicap and deficit recognition and the supporting constructs (involving self-recognition, recognition by others, hearing screening of infants, children, and adults, incidence studies of hearing loss, and barriers that prevent identification of those who are suffering from hearing deficit and handicap) indicate that some of the supporting constructs under that concept have virtually no data to validate them, whereas others have a substantial amount, and thus the following summary statements appear to be in order.

There are no hard data that describe how many individuals recognize the handicap they sustain as a result of hearing deficit. Likewise, there are no studies that describe the dynamics involved in self-recognition of hearing handicap-deficits. The fact that many adults seek out audiological assistance indicates that there is a recognition of handicap, but there are no reports that present systematic appraisal of the process.

Two studies focus on the problem of handicap recognition by others.

The term *handicap* is used because recognition probably is related to delay in speech and language acquisition rather than to detection of hearing deficit per se. From these studies it becomes apparent that parents were able in many instances to detect hearing handicap before the child was 2 years of age, but when they sought out specialized assistance, 58 percent were told that the child was either too young to test or that nothing was wrong; only 18 percent were told that their child had a hearing loss. In terms of referral sources, the systematic study of seven years of records of one speech and hearing clinic disclosed that over 40 percent of the referrals of children, and over 60 percent of referrals of adults, were made by nonmedical sources.

There appears to be no research that relates screening results specifically to handicaps associated with hearing deficit. There are numerous studies, however, that deal with tests designed for determining hearing deficit. Screening tests and procedures are available that are appropriate for adults. Statistics show that males are found with hearing deficit more often than are females. More adults over 40 years of age fail hearing tests than those under age 40. Farm and industrial workers sustain hearing deficits more frequently than others.

The same situation exists for children as for adults concerning studies of handicap, namely, there are no systematic studies that give results of screening for handicaps associated with hearing deficit.

Studies have been carried out on the hearing screening of infants. Interobserver reliability in infant testing has not proved to be very high, and false negative or false positive errors have been unacceptable. The accuracy of hearing screening of neonates leaves much to be desired, for identification of hearing deficit that depends upon behavioral response is quite crude. As a matter of fact, mass neonatal screening programs are not endorsed by medical authorities.

There are available a number of hearing screening tests for children, and there is a procedure for making comparison of group and individual tests to determine the efficiency of the group testing procedures. Procedures vary in terms of frequencies employed and responses that are demanded of children. It has been shown that *teachers do not function effectively in referral* of children with suspected hearing loss. Of those children teachers do refer, the percentage sustaining hearing deficit is quite high; however, they fail to refer many who do sustain deficits. Insofar as limited frequency testing is concerned, there are somewhat conflicting results. Some studies show that 4000 Hz combined with another lower frequency is a valid indicator of losses.

Incidence figures of *handicap* associated with hearing deficit in the United States are not known. There is great variability in the estimates made of incidence of hearing *deficit* in the United States as well as variability in estimates among countries. From National Health Survey results it can be estimated that there are eight million persons in the United States suffering hearing deficit, with approximately 31 percent reporting unilateral losses. The Survey showed also that, among adults with binaural losses, more males than females sustain hearing deficit, the frequency of hearing deficit increases with age, lower socioeconomic levels report more hearing deficit than higher levels, deficit is higher among whites than nonwhites, and rural areas show greater losses for those over 65 years of age than urban areas. Actual screening results among school children show variation in incidence between .70 and 10 percent. In India, however, the reports show incidence of loss to range between 16.3 and 18.6 percent.

The literature provides little information concerning barriers to recognition of handicap associated with hearing deficit. Factors set forth in a few studies as contributing to the delay in recognition are inaccessibility to hearing test facilities, inadequate methods, ignorance, and neglect.

RECOMMENDATIONS

The following recommendations for research are made in view of the need for study in areas where the literature provides no data or inadequate data. Research efforts should be directed toward the determination of—

1. handicap that accompanies hearing deficit in relation to age, sex, vocational involvement, and attitude
2. the barriers that prevent discovery of hearing handicap
3. the factors that cause one to recognize he has a handicapping condition and interaction of these factors
4. age, sex, nature and extent of hearing deficit, educational level, socioeconomic level, position in family, status in school, intelligence, and vocational demands upon self-recognition of handicap
5. the frequency of self-recognition as a factor in acquisition of specialized assistance
6 the characteristics of those individuals who recognize they are handicapped and do not seek specialized assistance
7. the degree of success individuals experience in programs of aural rehabilitation, and whether or not success can be predicted on the basis of self-recognition of handicap and self-referral
8. the factors that contribute to the recognition of a handicapping

condition associated with hearing deficit in another individual and the pattern of interaction of these factors

9. factors that play a significant role in recognition of handicap by others, namely age, sex, nature and extent of loss, educational level, socioeconomic level, position in family, intelligence, and vocational demands

10. whether or not recognition by others of a hearing handicap leads to acquisition of specialized assistance, and if so with what relative frequency as compared with those who seek assistance through the process of self-recognition of hearing handicap

11. the characteristics of those individuals who are made aware of their handicap but refuse to seek or accept specialized assistance

References

Belkin, M., Suchman, E. A., Bergman, M., Rosenblatt, D., and Jacobziner, H. (1964). A demonstration program for conducting hearing tests in day care centers. *J. Speech Hearing Dis.*, 29, 335–338.

Connor, L. E. (1961). Determining the prevalence of hearing impaired children. *Except. Children*, 27, 337–343.

Curry, E. T. (1950). The efficiency of teacher referrals in a school hearing testing program. *J. Speech Hearing Dis.*, 15, 211–214.

Curry, E. T., and Nagel, R. F. (1959). An evaluation of group hearing test methods. *Except. Children*, 25, 199–201.

Darley, F. L. (ed.), (1961). Identification audiometry. *J. Speech Hearing Dis. Monogr. Suppl.*, 9.

DiCarlo L., and Bradley W. (1961). A simplified auditory test for infants and young children. *Laryngoscope*, 71, 628–646.

Downs, M. P., and Sterritt, G. M. (1967). A guide to newborn and infant hearing screening programs. *Arch. Otolaryng.*, 85, 15–22.

Driscoll, H. F. (1971). Personal communication. Chicago: Beltone Electronics Corporation.

Eagles, E. (1961). Hearing levels in children and implifications for identification audiometry. *J. Speech Hearing Dis. Monogr. Suppl.*, 9, 52–62.

Eagles, E., and Doerfler, L. G. (1961). Hearing in children: Acoustic environment and audiometer performance. *J. Speech Hearing Res.*, 4, 149–163.

Eagles, E., and Wishik, S. (1961). A study of hearing in children. *Trans. Amer. Acad. Ophthal. Otolaryng.*, 64, 261–296.

Eisenberg, R. B. (1965). Auditory behavior in the human neonate. I

Methodologic problems and the logical design of research-procedures. *J. Aud. Res.,* 5, 159–177.

Eisenberg, R. B. (1970). The development of hearing in man: An assessment of current status. *Asha,* 12, 119–123.

Eisenberg, R. B., Griffin, E. R., Coursin, D. B., and Hunter, M. A. (1964). Auditory behavior in the human neonate: A preliminary report. *J. Speech Hearing Res.,* 7, 245–271.

Elliott, L. L., and Armbruster, V. B. (1967). Some possible effects of the delay of early treatment of deafness. *J. Speech Hearing Res.,* 10, 209–224.

Fabritius, H. F. (1964). Nine years examination of the hearing in school children in North Trondelag. *Acta Oto-Laryng. Suppl.,* 188, 351–361.

Fay, T. H., Hochberg, I., Smith, C. R., Rees, N. S., and Halpern, H. (1970). Audiologic and otologic screening of disadvantaged children. *Arch Otolaryng.,* 91, 336–370.

Fellendorf, G. W., and Harrow, I. (1970). Parent counseling. *Volta Rev.,* 72, 51–57.

Ferdinand, O. (1966). Causes of late recognition of deafness in children. *Volta Rev.,* 68, 547–551.

Field, H., Copack, P., Derbyshire, A. J., Driessen, G. J., and Marcus, R. E. (1967). Responses of newborns to auditory stimulation. *J. Aud. Res.,* 7, 271–285.

Froding, C. A. (1960). Acoustic investigation of newborn infants. *Acta Oto-Laryng.,* 52, 31–40.

Geyer, M. L., and Yankauer, A. (1956). Teacher judgment of hearing loss in children. *J. Speech Hearing Dis.,* 21, 482–486.

Glorig, A., and House, H. P. (1957). A new concept of auditory screening. *Arch Otolaryng.,* 66, 228–232.

Goldstein, R., and Tait, C. (1971). Critique of neonatal hearing evaluation. *J. Speech Hearing Dis.,* 36, 3–18.

Griffing, T. S., Simonton, K. M., and Hedgecock, L. D. (1967). Verbal auditory screening for preschool children. *Trans. Amer. Acad. Ophthal. Otolaryng.,* 71, 105–110.

Hanley, C. N., and Gaddie, G. B. (1962). The use of single frequency audiometry in the screening of school children. *J. Speech Hearing Dis.,* 27, 258–264.

Hardy, J. B., Dougherty, A., and Hardy, W. G. (1959). Hearing responses and audiologic screening in infants. *J. Pediatrics,* 55, 382–390.

Hardy, W. G., Hardy, J. B., Brinker, C. H., Frazier, T. M., and Dougherty, A. (1962). Auditory screening of infants. *Ann. Otol. Rhinol. Laryng.,* 71, 759–766.

Harrington, D. A. (1967). Hearing conservation in the United States—status and trends. *Int. Aud.,* 6, 163–166.

Hollien, H., and Thompson, D. L. (1967). A group screening test of hearing. *J. Aud. Res., 7*, 85–92.

Hoverstein, G. H., and Moncur, J. P. (1969). Stimuli and intensity factors in testing infants. *J. Speech Hearing Res., 12*, 687–702.

Johnston, P. W. (1952). An efficient group screening test. *J. Speech Hearing Dis., 17*, 8–12.

Kapur, Y. P. (1965). A study of hearing loss in children in India. *J. Speech Hearing Dis., 30*, 225–233.

Kodman, F. (1956). Identification of hearing loss by the classroom teacher. *Laryngoscope, 66*, 1346–1349.

Kodman, F. (1969). Identification of hearing loss by parents and teachers versus audiometry. *Audecibel, 18*, 168–172.

Kodman, F., Fraser, H., Acuff, C., and Hood, J. A. (1962). Hearing conservation. *Arch. Otolaryng., 75*, 226–230.

Kodman, F., and Sperrazzo, G. (1959). An analysis of one thousand cases of hearing loss in children. *Ann. Otol. Rhinol. Laryng., 68*, 227–233.

Lawrence, C. F., and Rubin, W. (1959). The efficiency of limited frequency audiometric screening in a school hearing conservation program. *Arch. Otolaryng., 69*, 606–611.

Lightfoot, C., Buckingham, R. A., and Kelley, M. N. (1959). A check on Oto-Chek. *Arch. Otolaryng., 70*, 103–113.

Ling, D., Heaney, C., and Doehring, D. G. (1971). The use of alternative stimuli to reduce response decrement in the auditory testing of newborn infants. *J. Speech Hearing Res., 14*, 531–534.

Ling, D., Ling, A. H., and Doehring, D. G. (1970). Stimulus, response, and observer variables in the auditory screening of newborn infants. *J. Speech Hearing Res., 13*, 9–18.

Livingstone, G. (1964). The deaf child. *Practioner, 192*, 461–469.

Lutz, K. R. (1955). Seasonal variations in hearing screening results. *Except. Children, 22*, 67–68.

Maxwell W. R., and Davidson, G. D. (1961). Limited frequency screening and ear pathology. *J. Speech and Hearing Dis., 26*, 122–125.

Melnick, W., Eagles, E., and Levine, H. (1964). Evaluation of a recommended program of identification audiometry with school age children. *J. Speech Hearing Dis., 29*, 3–13.

Mencher, G. T., and McCulloch, B. F. (1970). Auditory screening of kindergarten children using the VASC. *J. Speech Hearing Dis., 35*, 241–247.

Mendel, M. I. (1968). Infant responses to recorded sounds. *J. Speech Hearing Res., 11*, 811–816.

Miller, J., deSchweinitz, L., and Goetzinger, C. P. (1963). How infants three, four, and five months of age respond to sound. *Except. Children, 30*, 149–154.

Miller, M. H., and Bella, J. L. (1959). Limitations of selected frequency audiometry in the public schools. *J. Speech Hearing Dis.*, 24, 402–407.

Myklebust, H. R. (1950). The use of clinical psychological screening techniques by audiologists and speech pathologists. *J. Speech Hearing Dis.*, 15, 129–134.

National Center for Health Statistics (1967). Characteristics of persons with impaired hearing, United States—July 1962–June 1963. *Vital and Health Statistics.* PHS Pub. No. 1000–Series 10–No. 35. Public Health Service. Washington, D.C.: U.S. Government Printing Office.

Newby, H. A. (1947). Group pure-tone hearing testing the public schools. *J. Speech Dis.*, 12, 357–362.

Newby, H. A. (1948). Evaluating the efficiency of group tests of hearing. *J. Speech Hearing Dis.*, 13, 236–240.

Norton, M. C., and Lux, E. (1960). Double frequency auditory screening in public schools. *J. Speech Hearing Dis.*, 25, 293–299.

O'Neill, J. J. (1956). Ohio County Fair hearing survey. *J. Speech Hearing Dis.*, 21, 188–197.

Oyer, H. J., Deal, L. V., Walsh, P. S., Lashbrook, W. B., and Higgins, J. M. (1971). Computer based information retrieval system for a Speech and Hearing Clinic. Unpublished report.

Peck, J. E. (1970). The use of bottle-feeding during infant hearing testing. *J. Speech Hearing Dis.*, 35, 364–369.

Proctor, D. F. (1963). *The Conservation of Hearing and Speech and Problems of Communicology, The Nose, Paranasal Sinuses and Ears in Childhood.* Springfield, Ill.: Charles C. Thomas.

Richmond, J. B. (1953). A hearing test for newborn infants. *Pediatrics*, 11, 634–638.

Sataloff, J., and Menduke, H. (1959). Single and double-frequency screening in school children. *Arch. Otolaryng.*, 70, 624–626.

Scottish Education Department (1950). *Pupils Who Are Defective in Hearing: Report of the Advisory Council on Education in Scotland.* Cmd. 7866. Edinburg: Her Majesty's Stationery Office.

Siegenthaler, B. M., and Sommers, R. K. (1959). Abbreviated sweep-check procedures for school hearing testing. *J. Speech Hearing Dis.*, 24, 249–257.

Stevens, D. A., and Davidson, G. D. (1959). Screening tests of hearing. *J. Speech Hearing Dis.*, 24, 258–261.

Subcommittee on Human Communication and Its Disorders (R. Carhart, Chairman), (1969). *Human Communication and Its Disorders—An Overview.* Bethesda, Md.: National Advisory Neurological Diseases and Stroke Council, National Institute of Neurological Diseases and Stroke.

Suzuki, T., and Sato, I. (1961). Free field startle response audiometry. *Ann. Otol. Rhinol. Laryng.*, 70, 997–1007.

Talbe-Hansen, J. (1954). Hardness of hearing in school children. *Acta Oto-Laryng.,* 44, 157–160.

van Laar, F. (1965). Audiometry in preschool children. *Int. Aud.,* 4, 201–206.

Ventry, I. J., and Newby, H. A. (1959). Validity of the one frequency screening principle for public school children. *J. Speech Hearing Res.,* 2, 147–151.

Webster, J. C. (1952). A recorded warble tone audiometer test suitable for group administration over loudspeakers. *J. Speech Hearing Dis.,* 17, 213–223.

4
Motivational Aspects

As we pointed out in Chapter Three, the first step in the aural rehabilitation process is recognition that an auditory handicap-deficit exists. However, in order that the necessary specialized assistance is acquired, there must be motivation on the part of someone to acquire it. It might be the individual suffering the handicap-deficit, a parent, a spouse, a relative, or a friend. The purpose of this chapter is to consider the factors that are important in motivating an individual who has an auditory handicap to seek help.

When examining the concept of motivation in relation to the aural rehabilitation process, we find several supporting constructs and sub-constructs to consider: role performance (family, vocational, educational, social), self-concept, and value-need relationship. The discussion that follows is based upon questions that have been raised relative to the supporting constructs.

Role Performance

For the most part, every individual performs several roles. For example, at home the father plays the role of father and additionally the role of husband. At work he might be the plant manager, teacher, law enforcement officer, or physician. In the social world outside the boundaries of home and work he is called upon to interact with people and thus is responsible for fulfilling several roles. And so it is for mother as for father. She, too, may play several different roles in the course of a day. And children are sons, daughters, students and playmates. With each role that the individual is called upon to fulfill, there are certain role expectations generated by the individual himself and by those with whom he interacts. When role expectations are met or fulfilled, a social equilibrium is maintained. If, however, for some reason or reasons the role expectancies of self or others are not satisfied, one can expect a condition of disequilibrium. This can generate conflict, disappointment, unhappiness, and ultimately failure.

If, because of a deficit of hearing, an individual fails to live up to his own expectancies or to the expectancies of others in certain situations, the individual or those around him might be motivated to seek specialized help to reduce the handicap, thereby assisting the hearing-handicapped person to become more successful. Therefore, a general question arises: "What part do role performance demands play in motivating the client to seek assistance for his aural handicap?" One can only speculate as to the answer to this question, for a thorough search of the literature reveals no data that shed light in this area.

Family

In the attempt to define the behavioral failures within the family unit that motivate an individual to seek specialized assistance for his hearing handicap, one must consider carefully the position of the individual within the organization of the family. If, for example, a man is having difficulty holding his job or being promoted because of his aural handicap, the penalties are far greater if he has a wife and several children to support than if he is single and has responsibilities for no one but himself. If his children and other adults are penalized because of his failure, the motivation to do something about his problem will probably be greater than if only he suffers. If, on the other hand, he is in the father role but there are several other sources of support in the family, the motivation to acquire help for a hearing handicap that prevents him from being more successful might not be as high.

The social norms that are adhered to by the family are another factor in motivation to seek specialized assistance. These differ, of course, from family to family and to some extent from person to person within families. If within a family unit the expectation is that children must go to college, and perhaps even on into graduate or professional schools, then an aural handicap that makes this difficult or impossible for a child would be viewed as the cause for failure. The fear of failure could provide the necessary motivation on the part of the parents to seek aid. It no doubt would be their belief that such aid would reduce the handicap that prevents son or daughter from pursuing the education deemed so important by parents. If, on the other hand, the family does not consider higher education important in the lives of children, acceptance of the aural handicap might be somewhat easier, and an attempt might be made to seek vocational placement for the child as soon as possible. With such expectancies the responsible adults might never be motivated to alter the conditions of the hearing-handicapped son or daughter and thereby might never seek out specialized assistance. Thus position within families and social norms established within families are seen as factors that have a significant effect upon the motivation to seek help for, or by, one with aural handicap. Campanelli (1968) speculates that geriatric patients come for help because they are coerced by immediate family members who have become desperate because of the problems that are associated with the loss of hearing of a parent.

If one were to collect all the clinical interviews and then abstract the factors that motivated individuals to seek help for themselves or others, one would undoubtedly find a multitude of different factors. Those who work clinically can attest to this. However, at this time there are no survey research results available to answer a number of pertinent questions. For example, there is a need to know which failures of performance in family roles cause the hearing handicapped to seek specialized assistance. Another need is to determine the manner in which age, sex, family position, and social norms within the family relate to motivation for seeking aid by the hearing handicapped. Still another need is to identify the circumstances under which some other members of the family seek aid for the hearing-handicapped relative.

Educational

As we indicated in the previous chapter, many schools have regular programs of screening for hearing and thereby identify children who sustain losses of hearing. The effects of failures in the educational setting due to hearing handicap frequently motivate referral by teachers, parents, counselors, or the students themselves, for specialized help. There are, however, no reports of systematic studies available that present the relative importance of such factors within the educational setting as teacher attitudes, peer relationships, academic achievement, counseling programs, and so on, that serve to motivate someone to seek out specialized assistance for the hearing-handicapped student. We must examine the extent to which teachers are informed concerning the effects of hearing loss on school adjustment and achievement, and determine the bases upon which a hearing-handicapped child's school placement is made. The extent to which the recommendation of a specialist in audiology is followed in such placement would be of particular interest. The effectiveness or lack of effectiveness of present activities of the school counselor, psychologist, or special educator in motivating the hearing-handicapped student or his parents to seek specialized assistance is not known. Nor do we know the extent to which peer relationships have an influence on motivating the hearing handicapped to seek help.

Vocational

Although hearing tests are included in preemployment practices in some vocational settings and some employers make periodic checks thereafter, the literature does not provide studies that reveal how factors within the vocational setting serve to motivate hearing-handicapped individuals to seek specialized help. The authors have performed audiological evaluations of individuals who have sought assistance because they were experiencing failure in certain aspects of their work. This is not unusual, and undoubtedly many audiologists elsewhere have had similar self-referrals. We need to learn how the work environment alerts the hearing handicapped to seek help, and how important the vocational associates are in helping to motivate a hard-of-hearing person to seek help. Those factors in self-evaluation of vocational success that motivate a hearing-handicapped individual to seek specialized help, and the importance of hearing handicap in relation to fulfilling the demands of vocations, are also considerations that require investigation.

Social Setting

Even though a hard-of-hearing individual might experience little or no failure within the family, or in his vocation because of the nature of his work, he might experience considerable failure in other social situations. His reduced effectiveness at church, in the club, in shopping, and in other situations might be a salient force in getting him to seek specialized help. It is not unusual to learn in interviews with hearing-handicapped individuals that they are withdrawing from those social situations that are not vital to their existence because of failures related to hearing loss.

Oyer and Paolucci (1970) found that homemakers with hearing losses belonged to only one half as many organizations outside the home as did the normal-hearing comparison group. Additionally, they attended less than one half as many meetings outside the home as did the normal-hearing homemakers.

The nature of those social situations apart from work, school, and family settings in which hard-of-hearing persons feel penalized and are motivated to seek specialized assistance should be studied. Personality features of those who are motivated to seek specialized assistance, as compared to those who choose to withdraw, require further definition, along with the compensatory behaviors that are evident in those who are failing in social interactions due to hearing handicap and who choose neither to seek specialized help nor to withdraw.

Self-concept

In a study of self-concept, Hardick (1964) found that when hearing loss in adults is so severe as to interfere with communication, the hearing-handicapped person feels *less capable* than does a normal-hearing person of the same age, sex, and level of education. The way in which one views himself is greatly influenced by his perception of the responses he elicits from those with whom he interacts. The conception of self is a determining factor in the way the individual responds to those about him. Therefore the perception of responses of others is a salient factor in behavior.

If, for example, the hard-of-hearing individual is not very successful in his oral communication with others, and perceives the responses of others in a way that suggests to him that he is failing in oral communication situations, his self-concept and subsequent behavior will be influenced accordingly. If, on the other hand, the hearing-handicapped person does not perceive himself as a failure in the eyes of others, his response patterns should also reflect this. One can only speculate as to whether the individual who perceives himself as failing in the eyes of others will be more highly motivated to seek specialized audiological assistance than the individual who has problems in communication but does not perceive himself as failing. The literature surveyed does not offer data that answer these questions. It might be hypothesized that those who perceive themselves as failures would, of course, be highly motivated to seek assistance. However, on the basis of the authors' experiences, this is not necessarily so, for these persons often decide to withdraw from social situations that demand oral communication rather than to seek help on their own. We need to explore further the relationship of hearing handicap, self-concept, and the motivation to acquire special assistance. Similarly, we need more scientifically derived information concerning the interaction of such variables as age, sex, educational level, occupation, socioeconomic status, position in the family, and the self-concept of hearing-handicapped individuals and their motivation to seek specialized assistance.

Value–Need Relationship

Still another factor in motivating hard-of-hearing persons to seek help from a specialist is the value that they place upon success in communication as related to the need they feel stemming from their own failures in communication. Values have a strong effect upon behavior and are in a large measure the principal governing influence upon behavior. Generally, the greater the importance placed upon success in oral communication, the greater the perceived need for assistance if communication breakdowns are occurring frequently.

Informational items that we need in this area include the effect that social class has upon the value placed upon success in oral communication by the hearing handicapped; the extent to which age, sex, educational level, occupation, and position in the family modify the ordering of desired success in oral communication situations—if such successes were to be scaled by the hard of hearing; the degree to which value and need would each be scaled by the hard of hearing in relation to success in oral communication situations, and the degree to which these relationships would remain constant across the variables of age, sex, educational level, occupation, socioeconomic status, and position in the family; and the nature of the felt need that is generated when value is placed upon success in oral communication situations by the hard-of-hearing person.

Summary

As yet we are without research data that provide answers to questions concerning the motivating factors that prompt hard-of-hearing individuals to seek specialized assistance. Unless the necessary information can be derived from research studies concerning important motivating factors, we will continue to face difficulties in predicting the effects of role performance demands, self-concept, and value-need relationships upon the decisions that hard-of-hearing individuals make concerning the need for specialized help. With this information at hand, however, the counseling of the hearing handicapped could be carried out much more intelligently, thus averting needless suffering and crises.

RECOMMENDATIONS

The following recommendations are based upon the need that exists for data that would provide information concerning those factors which motivate hard-of-hearing individuals to seek specialized assistance. Research efforts should be directed toward determination of—

1. the failures of performance in family roles that cause the hearing-handicapped person to seek specialized assistance
2. the relationship of age, sex, position within the family, and

social norms within the family to motivation for seeking aid by the hearing-handicapped person

3. those circumstances under which another member of the family seeks aid for the hearing-handicapped relative
4. the information teachers have concerning the effects hearing loss can have on school adjustment and achievement
5. the frequency with which school placements of hearing-handicapped children are based upon evaluations and recommendations of persons who are competent to make them
6. the effectiveness of the present activities of the school counselor, psychologist, or special educator in motivating the hearing-handicapped student or his parents to seek specialized assistance
7. the influence of peer relationships in motivating the hearing-handicapped individual to seek specialized help and the extent to which they are influential
8. the features of the work environment that alert the hearing-handicapped person to seek help
9. those factors in the self-evaluation of vocational success that motivate a hearing-handicapped individual to seek out specialized help
10. the relative importance of vocational associates in helping to motivate a hard-of-hearing person to seek help
11. the types of employers that exert a significant influence upon hard-of-hearing employees to get them to seek specialized help
12. the importance of hearing handicap in relation to fulfilling the demands of occupations
13. the nature of those social situations apart from the work, school, and family settings in which hard-of-hearing persons feel penalized and are motivated to seek specialized assistance
14. the personality features of those who are motivated to seek specialized assistance as compared to those who choose to withdraw
15. the compensatory behaviors that are evident in those who are failing in social interactions due to hearing handicaps who choose neither to seek specialized help nor to withdraw
16. whether a hearing handicap affects self-concept unfavorably and thus motivates one to acquire special assistance
17. how the variables of age, sex, educational level, occupation, socioeconomic status, and position in the family interact with self-concept of the hearing-handicapped individuals and their motivation to seek specialized assistance
18. the effects of social class upon the value placed on success in oral communication by the handicapped
19. those variations that occur as a function of age, sex, educational

level, occupation, and position in the family if value placed upon success in oral communication were to be rated by the hearing handicapped
20. the relationships across the variables of age, sex, educational level, occupation, socioeconomic status, and position in the family if value and need were each rated by the hearing handicapped in relation to success in oral communication
21. the nature of the felt need that is generated when sufficient value is placed upon success in oral communication situations by the hard-of-hearing person that he is motivated to seek specialized assistance

References

Campanelli, P. A. (1968). Audiological perspectives in presbycusis. *EENT Monthly,* 47, 3–10, 81–86.

Hardick, E. J. (1964). The self-concept of hard-of-hearing adults as measured by the semantic differential technique. Unpublished Doctoral dissertation, Michigan State University.

Oyer, E. J., and Paolucci, B. (1970). Homemakers' hearing losses and family integration. *J. Home Econ.,* 62, 257–262.

5

Identification and Acquisition of Professional Assistance by the Hearing Handicapped

When recognition of the aural handicap has occurred and the handicapped individual or other responsible person has become motivated sufficiently to seek specialized assistance, a great stride has been taken toward eventual habilitation or rehabilitation. However, unless there is identification and acquisition of professional help, the process of aural rehabilitation breaks down.

One of the most logical sources for aurally handicapped persons to seek help from is the family physician, who may treat them or refer them on to an otolaryngologist or audiologist. If the factors causing the hearing deficit can be remedied by medical treatment or surgical procedures, the hearing-handicapped individual has been successful in identifying and acquiring professional assistance. If, on the other hand, the problem is not amenable to medicine or surgery but is one that calls for a differential diagnosis—to be followed by language training procedures, hearing aid evaluation, lipreading and/or auditory training —the hearing-handicapped individual should identify or be helped to identify an audiologist certified by the American Speech and Hearing Association.

This chapter is centered upon identification and acquisition of specialized assistance as it pertains to the services of the audiologist. Constructs and subconstructs to be dealt with are (1) information dissemination (rural, urban, related professions), (2) selection of assistance (propinquity, type of service, economic considerations, personal fators), and (3) continuation of service. Pertinent questions are raised concerning the constructs and, where possible, answers made on the basis of data.

Information Dissemination and Effects

For years some public agencies and private organizations have taken the responsibility for making the public aware of the effects of hearing loss and the programs that focus primary attention upon diagnostic and counseling services for children and adults. State and federal departments of public health and education have published information in the form of brochures and booklets that have given advice to hard-of-hearing individuals and also to parents of the hearing handicapped. These materials have been distributed through schools, physicians' offices, and the like. Two private organizations in the United States that have as one of their chief objectives the dissemination of information concerning hearing loss are the Alexander Graham Bell Association and the National Association of Hearing and Speech Agencies, formerly called the American Hearing Association. Both of these organizations have headquarters in Washington, D.C. The messages of the Alexander Graham Bell Association extend beyond the borders of the United States, thus providing information to individuals in foreign countries as well. In addition to these two organizations there have been local groups such as the New York League for the Hard of Hearing, clinics, and schools for the deaf that disseminate information in one way or another concerning the help that can be obtained by those suffering hearing loss. The John Tracy Clinic in Los Angeles, California, is a notable example. This clinic provides an outstanding service in its dessemination of information to the public and in addition makes its correspondence course available to parents of deaf children throughout the United States and beyond. Speech and hearing clinics within colleges, universities, hospitals, and community centers, as well as departments of health and education, continue to disseminate information via printed materials, radio, and television. However, with all this dissemination of information, many who need help are still unaware of the services available to them.

Search of the literature offers little information concerning the methods employed by agencies and organizations in the process of disseminating information. Likewise, there are no data that show how effective the programs of dissemination have been. There is no way of knowing whether those living in urban areas are more or less aware of available services for the hard of hearing than those living in rural areas. The writers are frequently impressed by those persons living in close proximity to well-established clinics who confess that they have not known of the services the clinics have available for the hearing handicapped.

Downs (1961) shows that in the United States within 38 states there are 166 hearing rehabilitation centers with the following distribution:

Universities	46
Medical Schools	48
Hearing Societies	35
Federal Agencies	17
State Agencies	5
Public Agencies	9
Private Agencies	6

Individual institutions have carried on special programs that are effective in disseminating information; for example, Miller (1964) describes an institute she sponsored for deaf children and their parents in Oletha, Kansas, at the School for the Deaf. Parents attended lectures and engaged in discussions concerning the development of communication and the problems attending it.

One must assume that as a result of such programs many people, friends of those who attended, and others, were made aware of opportunities available to the deaf child. The following discussion deals specifically with questions concerning the dissemination of information to persons in rural and urban areas and also to professions related to audiology.

Rural Areas

In the past, those living in rural areas were more isolated than they are today. Now, through radio and television, messages of importance can be transmitted to even the most remote areas. However, because of fewer personal contacts, one would expect that dissemination of information by word of mouth would be more restricted than in urban areas.

The literature does not provide data with respect to the acquisition of specialized assistance by the hearing handicapped as a function of a program of information dissemination. In order to plan for such a program, a number of questions must be answered. These follow the discussion of the dissemination of information in urban areas.

Urban Areas

Because large hospitals, specialized medical facilities, and specialized programs for the handicapped are most frequently located in urban areas, one might assume that usually the urban dweller would know of these programs and thus acquire necessary services. However, there are no research data that would support such an assumption. There are questions that need to be answered for both the rural and urban settings concerning the dissemination of information to the hearing handicapped, if indeed we wish to understand more fully the decisions that are made relative to acquisition of specialized assistance. Answers to the questions that follow should also provide us with greater understanding of the approach that should be made to the problem of informing the hearing handicapped in both rural and urban settings of the services that are available to them. These are the questions:

1. What sources or potential sources are there throughout the United States that could disseminate information at local levels to the hearing handicapped that would apprise them of the nearest specialized assistance available to them?
2. What specific responsibilities are assumed by the relevant federal and state governmental agencies, voluntary agencies and organizations, and professionals in making the hearing-handicapped population aware of specialized assistance available to them?
3. How effective are the current efforts that are being made to inform the hearing handicapped of specialized assistance in rural and urban areas?
4. Should there be a difference in the approach employed to disseminate information to the hearing handicapped in relation to age, sex, urban or rural settings, and geographical areas of the country?

Related Professions

Success in getting the hearing handicapped to avail themselves of services is in part contingent upon how well audiologists and others dealing with the hearing impaired communicate with other relevant professionals. These other professionals include social workers, nurses, physicians, teachers, principals and superintendents of schools, counselors, and special educators.

Garrett (1963) notes that one of the projects sponsored by the then Vocational Rehabilitation Administration resulted in the publication of a *Directory of Social Services for the Deaf of Metropolitan Washington, D.C.* This directory lists the organizations and community resources available in that area to meet the needs of the deaf population. This represents a real step ahead in attempting to disseminate important information to the hearing handicapped in that particular community.

Much of the information passed to other professionals is by word of mouth or by brief announcements of audiological services available that are published by clinics. In some training institutions there are, for example, attempts made to inform the health educators, medical students, nurses, and special educators of the problems associated with hearing loss. In the past, professional associations at local, state, and national levels have made possible the transmission of information concerning the hearing handicapped. The literature, however, provides no study of the effectiveness of those various approaches made to the related professions.

We must assess the present status of communication between those who deal professionally with the hearing handicapped and other relevant professionals, and we must determine how the related professionals get information about services available to the hearing handicapped. In addition, we need to discover how related professionals respond to the information they receive concerning services to the hearing handicapped. Until systematic study is made, the status of the communication between those primarily responsible for the hearing handicapped and other important related professionals will be unknown except for isolated local instances. Planning for more intelligent communication could, however, be accomplished if the facts were known.

Selection of Assistance

There are several factors of importance in relation to the selection of professional assistance by the hearing handicapped. These factors include type of service desired, propinquity of service, economic considerations, and personal biases. Survey of the literature provides no data concerning these factors. Therefore, at this time we can only raise questions, with the hope that answers will be forthcoming in the future.

Type of Service

The type of service sought out by the hearing handicapped is undoubtedly linked with a number of factors, which include the nearness to a source of help, knowledge concerning the professionals that deal with problems of hearing, and also the desire to have a complete and thorough appraisal made of the problem. Whether first contacts are most frequently made with the family physician, otologist, audiologist, or the hearing aid salesman is not revealed by data from the literature. Nor is there any clue from survey research as to how hearing-handicapped individuals evaluate the types of services available to them. Therefore, in order to be able to carry out the most intelligent program of public education it would be helpful to investigate several obvious concerns: the ordering of the sources of assistance or types of service with respect to which is the first contact that is made by the hard of hearing; the basis used by the hearing handicapped to evaluate the types of services available to them; and the status of the relationship among those who provide services to the hearing-handicapped population.

Propinquity

The literature sheds no light on the factor of propinquity. However, it is quite obvious to those in hearing clinics that it is not unusual for people to be willing to drive many miles for an audiological evaluation yet be unwilling to drive the same number of miles to participate in a program of rehabilitation. A logical question arises: "What are the facts with respect to the factor of distance that an individual must travel for professional assistance and the utilization of such assistance by the hearing-handicapped individual?" The answer to this question should provide useful information in comprehensive planning for professional audiological assistance for the hard-of-hearing population.

Economic Considerations

Cost is an important factor in the selection of professional assistance. Because of economic status some are compelled to seek the least expensive way to derive assistance. With the ever-increasing costs of professional service, it is mandatory to determine the manner in which cost factors influence the type of service selected by the hearing handicapped; the relationship between the economic status of the hearing-handicapped individual and his use of specific types of service; and the relationship, if any, between the cost of services and the completeness of services rendered the hearing-handicapped individual.

Personal Factors

In addition to the factors just discussed there can be some personal factors that also operate in the selection of specialized assistance. It would seem that general educational level would be related in some way to the use of specialized assistance by the hearing handicapped. One might hypothesize that the higher the educational level, the greater the use of the finest of resources available. Still another potential personal factor is that of personal bias with respect to seeking help for a handicapping condition. Although this is the twentieth century, there are still those who believe that handicapping conditions are meant *to be,* and feel that seeking specialized assistance for one's infirmity is not in the best interests of the handicapped individual. Several questions need to be answered:

1. Is the utilization of specialized assistance related to the educational level of the hearing-handicapped individual or his family?
2. Are personal biases important factors in the selection of specialized assistance by the hearing-handicapped person?
3. Who decides that the hearing-handicapped individual needs specialized assistance and initiates contact for help?

Again, the literature does not provide data that answer these questions.

Continuation of Service

There are those who with high motivation seek out specialized assistance, and, following evaluation of their problems, embark upon a program of rehabilitation. Some continue in the program until they derive a maximum benefit from the rehabilitation procedures, but there are those who discontinue the program prematurely. Research should focus on the identifiable characteristics of those who, after hearing evaluation, never embark upon a recommended program of rehabilitation; the identifiable characteristics of those who embark upon and continue within a program of aural rehabilitation; the identifiable characteristics of those who discontinue a program of aural rehabilitation prematurely; and the factors that contribute to the success of a program of aural rehabilitation.

Summary

A review and an evaluation of the literature make evident that there are virtually no studies made that deal specifically with the topic of how professional assistance is identified and acquired by the hearing-handicapped population. If such data were available, a much more intelligent approach could be made to programs of public education concerning hearing loss and its ramifications, and also to individual programs of counseling. This chapter has also dealt with factors involved in information dissemination to and its effects on persons in rural and urban settings, and to professions related to audiology. It also has considered the problem of selection of assistance and such influencing factors as the type of service, propinquity, economic consideration, and personal bias. Last, the topic of continuation of service has been discussed. Following are our recommendations relative to questions that should be answered through research.

RECOMMENDATIONS

It is recommended that research efforts should be directed toward determination of—

1. those sources or potential sources throughout the United States that could disseminate information most effectively at local levels to the hearing handicapped that would apprise them of the nearest specialized assistance available
2. the responsibilities that are assumed by federal and state governmental agencies, voluntary agencies and organizations, and professionals in making the hearing-handicapped population aware of specialized assistance available
3. effectiveness of the current efforts that are being made to inform the hearing handicapped of specialized assistance in rural and urban areas
4. the approaches that should be employed to disseminate information to the hearing handicapped in relation to age, sex, urban or rural settings, and geographical area of the country
5. the present status of communication between those who deal professionally with the hearing handicapped and other relevant professionals
6. the way in which related professionals get information about services available to the hearing handicapped
7. how related professionals respond to the information they receive concerning services to the hearing handicapped
8. how the sources of assistance or types of service rank with respect to the order in which they are contacted by hard-of-hearing individuals
9. criteria by which the hearing handicapped evaluate the types of services available to them
10. the status of the relationship among those who provide services to the hearing-handicapped population
11. the facts with respect to distance from the source of the professional assistance and the utilization of such assistance by the hearing-handicapped individual
12. how cost factors influence the type of service selected by the hearing-handicapped individual
13. the relationship between the economic status of the hearing-handicapped individual and his use of specific types of services

52 IDENTIFICATION AND ACQUISITION OF PROFESSIONAL ASSISTANCE

14. whether or not there is a relationship between the cost of services and the completeness of services rendered the hearing-handicapped individual
15. the utilization of specialized assistance as related to the educational level of the hearing-handicapped individual or his family
16. importance of personal biases in the selection of specialized assistance by the hearing-handicapped person
17. who it is that decides that the hearing-handicapped individual needs specialized assistance and initiates contact for assistance
18. the identifiable characteristics of those who embark upon and continue within a program of aural rehabilitation
19. the identifiable characteristics of those who never undertake a recommended program of aural rehabilitation or who discontinue a program of aural rehabilitation prematurely
20. the factors that contribute to the success of a program of aural rehabilitation and how these factors rank in importance

References

Downs, M. P. (1961). Hearing rehabilitation centers in the United States. *Arch. Otolaryng., 73*, 419–443.

Garrett, J. F. (1963). Vocational Rehabilitation Administration Research and Training Programs for the rehabilitation of the deaf. In *Orientation of Social Workers to the Problems of Deaf Persons* (Beryl Godfrey, ed.). Washington, D.C.: U.S. Department of Health, Education, and Welfare, Vocational Rehabilitation Association.

Miller, J. (1964). Institute for parents and their deaf children. *Volta Rev., 66*, 185–197.

6
Measurement and Evaluation of Auditory Deficit and Handicap

After specialized assistance has been identified and acquired, the next step in the aural rehabilitation process is that of determining the extent of the auditory deficit and the degree to which the deficit is a handicap to the individual. Current diagnostic testing in the United States has three main thrusts: determining the extent of auditory deficit for pure tone and speech stimuli, identifying the site of lesion, and hearing aid evaluation. It is not surprising, then, to find an extensive research literature concerned with these issues. Well-recognized procedures are available to measure the function of the auditory system. This is not the case, however, as regards the measurement of handicap. In contrast to deficit measurement, there is only a small body of research that explores the extent to which an individual is able to meet the communicative requirements of daily life. Deficit and handicap are not mutually exclusive, to be sure, but the effects of auditory deficit can vary from one individual to the next depending upon the communicative settings that are encountered at home, in school, at work, and in social activities.

Throughout this chapter four major constructs will be discussed with reference to the data available in the literature. Questions will be raised and answers will be presented insofar as is possible through evidence provided by research studies. The constructs that will be discussed are auditory deficit, standards for deficit measurement, auditory handicap, and deficit-handicap asymmetry.

Auditory Deficit

The concept of auditory deficit could be defined in several ways but, for the sake of the discussion here, it shall be defined as hearing level that is outside the range of normal, as determined by measurements of pure tone air- and bone-conduction thresholds, speech reception thresholds, and measures of speech discrimination. Several questions arise immediately with reference to the concept of auditory deficit as related to standards, namely: (1) Are there scientifically based tests available for the measurement of auditory function? (2) What standards are there for normal hearing by air conduction, bone conduction, and for speech? (3) Is there an established typology for levels of auditory receptive function?

Pure Tone Audiometry—Air Conduction

Over the past fifty years, following the development of the vacuum tube and the audiometer, many test procedures have been developed for the measurement of hearing threshold via both air and bone conduction. Air-conduction thresholds are usually the first measures obtained in a clinical evaluation. From the audiogram, which depicts these threshold values as a function of frequency, one can see the extent and configuration of hearing loss without amplification. In the total test battery these threshold measures also serve as a comparison for bone-conducted thresholds and as baseline levels for material presented according to sensation level. Among those techniques that have been used clinically we found the Hughson-Westlake procedure to be the one most often chosen for measuring air-conducted threshold. Threshold measurement calls for ascending with pure tone test stimuli from levels of inaudibility to audibility (Hughson and Westlake, 1944). Carhart and Jerger (1959) compared this procedure with two others and recommended the Hughson-Westlake for general use when 5-dB steps are being employed because of the consistent measures it yielded of the unadapted level of hearing acuity. (In the experiment thirty-six young adults with normal hearing served as subjects. A 5-dB step was employed for all threshold measurements and three positive responses served as criterion for threshold). The Hughson-Westlake procedure also has had endorsement by the Committee on Conservation of Hearing of the American Academy of Ophthalmology and Otolaryngology.

In a 1971 report Martin and Pennington summarized the results of a questionnaire study on actual practices of over 300 clinicians. The Hughson-Westlake procedure and a bracketing method of threshold determination were each commonly used, accounting for over 85 percent of the sample.

Pure Tone Audiometry—Bone Conduction

On some occasions when test signals are introduced through bone conduction the resulting threshold measures indicate a better hearing level than air-conducted thresholds. When there is evidence of such an air-bone gap the hearing loss is classified as conductive, indicating a problem in either the external or middle ear. Medical procedures are often effective in treating conductive disorders, so that aural rehabilitation is rarely required, but hearing aids are sometimes recommended.

In bone-conduction testing there are a variety of techniques that can be employed in the determination of hearing thresholds. The reviews of Hood (1957, 1962) give a comprehensive discussion of the theoretical issues and clinical techniques in bone-conduction audiometry. A procedure that Hood describes has been accepted in many clinics and illustrates the traditional approach. A pure tone test signal is introduced through a bone vibrator placed on either the mastoid process or the forehead while a masking noise is simultaneously presented to the nontest ear. After the detection threshold is determined for the ear under test, the level of the masking noise is successively increased by 10-dB steps. With each increment in noise level a new threshold determination is made at the test ear until the threshold value remains unchanged; that is, there is no further increase in threshold when the noise level increases. The intensity of the pure tone test signal when this plateau is reached is the bone-conducted threshold for the ear under test.

An alternative procedure suggested by Rainville (1959) has prompted the M–R, or Modified Rainville, test reported by Lightfoot (1960) and the Sensorineural Acuity Level (SAL) test introduced by Jerger and Tillman (1960). The SAL modification is described here. Air-conducted thresholds were first determined for the frequency range from 250 to 4000 Hz. Then a second set of measures was made, over the same set of frequencies, with a constant level white noise delivered to an oscillator placed in the middle of the forehead. The Sensorineural Acuity Level was determined by subtracting the standard shift in air-conducted threshold that occurred with normal hearing subjects under comparable conditions from the shift exhibited by the subject under test. Upon further investigation, Tillman (1963) found that for subjects with sensorineural loss at the frequencies above 1000 Hz, the bone-conduction measures were lower than for the conventional bone-conduction testing, and for those with conductive losses, the SAL test gave higher thresholds below 1000 Hz. Because of these findings he suggests that the SAL test cannot replace the ordinary bone-conduction test.

Unresolved issues continue to attract research on procedures for bone-conducted threshold measurement. Masking is one such issue studied by, among others, Lightfoot, Carhart, and Gaeth (1956), Carter and Kryter (1962), Goetzinger, Proud, and Embrey (1962), Palva and Palva (1962), König (1963), Sanders and Rintelmann (1964), and Studebaker (1964, 1967). These investigations suggest a consensus that narrow band masking centered at the test tone frequency is best. Another line of research has considered the optimal placement of the bone vibrator, for example, Rainville (1959), Feldman (1961), Palva and Palva (1962), Studebaker (1962), Hoops and Curry (1963), Dirks (1964), Tronczynska (1964), Martin and Wittich (1966), Hurley and Berger (1970).

In the routine application as part of the general audiometric battery, forehead placement of the vibrator is the preferred location. The survey of Martin and Pennington (1971) found that 91 percent of their respondents placed the vibrator on the mastoid process, despite the research evidence favoring a forehead location. They also reported that the traditional method of threshold determination predominated with only one fourth of the sample reporting use of the SAL test.

Speech Audiometry

Two measures of speech hearing are included routinely in audiometric evaluations, the speech reception threshold (SRT) and speech discrimination. The relationship to handicap of speech audiometric data will be discussed in a later section when handicap measurement is introduced. At this point significant steps in the development of our current speech tests will be summarized.

Historically, Carhart (1951) singles out four events that have contributed to modern speech audiometry: the development of speech tests at the Psycho-Acoustics Laboratory (PAL) at Harvard in the 1940s, the early work of Fletcher, aural rehabilitation programs following World War II, and the refinement of test lists and procedures at the Central Institute for the Deaf (CID).

Early stimulus materials for obtaining the speech reception threshold (SRT) were developed at the Harvard Psycho-Acoustics Laboratory for applied use in the evaluation of military communication systems. Methods of articulation testing described by Egan (1948) were general enough to find application in speech hearing evaluation. Later Hirsh et al. (1952), at the Central Institute for the Deaf, refined the PAL tests 9 and 12 for clinical purposes. From this work there emerged the CID W-1 and W-2 tests of speech reception consisting of words with spondaic stress patterns.

Fletcher (1950a,b) related the SRT to pure tone audiometric results. His rationale was based upon studies of loudness, including the determination of the relative contributions of different frequency regions to the audibility of speech near threshold. A formula for estimating speech hearing loss resulted, namely, the average of the pure tone threshold values at 500, 1000, and 2000 Hz. Following Fletcher's early research on prediction of speech threshold from pure tone data, investigation has continued, for example, Quiggle et al. (1957), Dahle et al. (1968), and Carhart and Porter (1971).

Speech discrimination testing also had its beginning in the early work at Harvard. In connection with the evaluation of communication systems for military use lists of phonetically balanced test words, PB-50 Word Lists were developed. Although the original 50 word lists are still in use, a derived test, the W-22 lists, constructed at the Central Institute for the Deaf (Hirsh et al., 1952) is more commonly found in current practice. The CID W-22 test maintained a phonetic balance within lists, but the vocabulary of the PB-50 lists was modified to include more familiar words.

Not all speech discrimination tests are predicated on the concept of phonetically balanced word lists. Mention should be made of such alternatives as the Fairbanks Rhyme Test (Fairbanks, 1958), the Semi-Diagnostic Test constructed by Hutton et al. (1959), a nonspeech discrimination test proposed by Niswander (1968), the Modified Rhyme Test (Kreul et al., 1968), Synthetic Sentence Identification (Jerger et al., 1968), and N.U. Auditory Test No. 6 developed by Tillman and Carhart as reported in Rintelmann et al. (1973).

Frequency statistics on clinical usage (Martin and Pennington, 1971) find the CID Test W-1, for SRT, and Test W-22, for speech discrimination, cited most often. Only a small percentage of clinicians employ the Harvard PAL Test 9 and PB-50 lists to measure SRT and speech discrimination, respectively.

Special Tests

Within the total audiometric battery, special tests are included to further delineate both auditory function and site of lesion. Those tests that measure recruitment (the abnormal growth of loudness in a pathological ear) are of particular interest to audiologists in recommending hearing aids.

Jerger, Shedd, and Harford (1959) describe the development of a clinical test of sensorineural impairment based on recruitment. The SISI (short increment sensitivity index) test presents a series of very small intensity increments imposed upon a steady-state pure tone stimulus. An ear exhibiting recruitment can detect these increments, which are not detectable by a normal ear. Two other widely accepted procedures for measuring recruitment are the Alternate Binaural Loudness Balance Test (ABLB) and the Monaural Bifrequency Equal Loudness Balance Test (MBFLB). The ABLB test presents a reference tone to one ear, usually the better ear, and then requires the observer to determine when the test tone in the opposite ear sounds equally loud. The MBFLB alternates the presentation of tones at two frequencies introduced to the poorer ear. Again the observer must state when there is a balance in the loudness of the test frequency and the reference frequency.

At least 80 percent of respondents to the Pennington and Martin

(1972) questionnaire on audiometric practices included loudness balance tests and the SISI test in their audiometric battery. The questionnaire focused on tests for site of lesion, but the same tests can serve as guides for hearing aid evaluation, a topic that will be considered in detail in the next chapter.

Pure Tone Audiometry—Children

The hearing testing of children, particularly young children, has proved to be no simple task as evidenced by reports found in the literature. As with the testing of adults, there have been numerous studies carried out, the most significant of which will be cited in this section. By reason of methodologies employed, the literature can be viewed as it relates to (1) conventional methods of testing, (2) behavioral methods based on operant conditioning principles, and (3) objective methods of testing that do not demand overt responses on the part of the child. There are also accounts of comparisons of various techniques that employ pure tones as test stimuli.

Conventional pure tone tests. Informal reports from clinicians indicate that the conventional approach can be successful with cooperative children of ages 3 years and older. This procedure calls for delivering stimuli systematically through earphones and eliciting an overt response for determination of threshold. Since conventional pure tone testing has served as a reference for determining the effectiveness of other approaches to threshold measurement, the reliability of this technique is an important consideration.

Many variables can affect the reliability of threshold determination including those related to the clinician, the child, and the amount of hearing deficit. A report by Rapin and Costa (1969) suggests that when children have severe and profound hearing losses test-retest reliability can be low. Using successive audiograms of children in a school for the deaf, the testers compared threshold values at the frequencies 500, 1000, 2000, and 4000 Hz. Considering differences of 20 dB or more as unreliable, they found that almost half of the audiograms had two or more differences that failed this criterion. Unreliability was related to several sources, including the experience of the clinician and the type and extent of loss. Data are not available that allow a full description of circumstances under which conventional testing of children yields reliable results.

Tests based on operant conditioning. Over twenty years ago Dix and Hallpike (1947) described a peep-show technique for hearing testing of children employing a visual reinforcement. A child was shown a set of characters on a stage through a small peephole in a box when he responded appropriately to a pure tone presented to him via earphones.

If the child depressed a switch when the tone was present, the characters were illuminated; if he depressed the switch without the presence of the tone, there was no illumination of the characters. Thus, the child was conditioned through a contingent reinforcement procedure. Since this early application of operant conditioning, many variations have appeared in the literature (Green, 1958; Liden and Kankkunen, 1959; Guilford and Haug, 1952, 1960).

When edible food follows a response or when the child is able to choose a toy or other physical reward, this variation of conditioning is referred to as tangible reinforcement in operant conditioning audiometry, known by the acronym TROCA. Studies such as Meyerson and Michael (1964) and Lloyd, Spradlen, and Reid (1968) illustrate the procedure. Fulton and Lloyd (1969) discuss TROCA and related procedures in some detail.

Play audiometry differs from the other operant techniques in that no visual or tangible reinforcement follows the correct response. Instead the child is allowed to complete a response that is intrinsically rewarding. An experiment by Lowell et al. (1956) describes one procedure. Children were trained to make simple motor responses with a toy when the auditory signal was presented. Initially a drumbeat served as the stimulus that was heard, seen, and felt. After this preliminary training a pure tone was substituted for the drumbeat. Reliability data collected on forty-three children from 3 to 3½ years old showed that this procedure is as reliable as conventional techniques.

Comparisons among behavioral procedures. Several research investigations comparing techniques of pure tone testing with children have been productive in clarifying the relative merits of procedures available to audiologists. The following table displays the results of these experiments.

When conventional audiometry was compared with play and modified peep-show techniques the latter two were preferred. The study by Barr (1955) recommended an objective procedure, the psychogalvanic skin response (PGSR or simply GSR), if play audiometry was not successful, but results of later research have eliminated this procedure from most clinics. The next section will consider briefly various objective procedures.

Objective procedures. For years audiologists have attempted to design audiometric tests that are objective and do not rely upon overt responses of the subject being tested. Three approaches to testing have stimulated considerable interest. One approach utilizes electrodermal responses, the second electroencephalography, and the third impedance measures.

Early work on electrodermal audiometry was carried out at Johns

COMPARATIVE STUDIES OF PURE TONE TECHNIQUES WITH CHILDREN

Test Procedure	Barr (1955)	Siegenthaler & Kaplan (1958)	O'Neill, Oyer, & Hillis (1961)
Conventional		X	X
Peep-Show Type		X	X
Play	X		X
PGSR	X		X
Reliability	Yes	Yes	No
Subjects			
Ages	Under 7 Yrs	3.5 to 6.75 Yrs	Mean of 64 Mos
Number	324	39	58
Preferred	Play/PGSR if	Modified	Play
Procedure	Needed	Peep Show	for under 4 Yrs
			Peep Show
			for over 4 Yrs

Hopkins University by Hardy and Bordley (1951). To illustrate the technique we will briefly describe their experiment comparing the galvanic skin response (GSR) and conventional thresholds. A conditioning procedure was employed in which pure tones were paired with weak electric shock. When conditioning occurred, substantial skin resistance changes took place in anticipation of the shock. The least intense tone that produced the conditioned response defined the threshold value. Threshold measures obtained for subjects ranging from 4 to 18 years old were compared to conventional threshold measures. Over the frequency range 500 to 2000 Hz approximately two thirds of the difference scores were within 5 dB. Test-retest reliability scores found that absolute differences were within 5 dB from 55 to 62 percent of the time for the frequencies 500, 1000, 2000, and 4000 Hz.

Although a whole body of research on GSR audiometry has accumulated, it is not a widely used procedure for children for it calls for cooperation to the point where the child will remain quiet during the test period. In addition, the GSR response adapts quite rapidly with repeated stimulation.

Electroencephalography (EEG) makes use of the electrical activity of the brain in an attempt to obtain measures of hearing thresholds. In the earliest stages of its development, threshold determinations were extremely difficult because single evoked responses to auditory stimuli are masked by "noise" that arises from spontaneous activity of the brain, muscular responses, and other aperiodic sources. With the advent of computer techniques for averaging evoked responses over time, the presence of responses associated with stimulus onset has become more readily detected.

Evoked response audiometry (ERA) is potentially promising for threshold measurement of difficult-to-test subjects. Cost factors and the need for specially trained personnel usually rule out ERA as a preferred method when behavioral procedures can provide the necessary audiometric data. Selected articles will illustrate research applications with children, primary targets of ERA.

Price and Goldstein (1966) tested seventy children ranging in age from 2 months to 13 years. On the basis of past records children were categorized as normal hearing, impaired auditory sensitivity only, impaired auditory sensitivity plus some other disorder, or other than impaired auditory sensitivity. Agreement between ERA measures and behavioral threshold values was good for the normal hearing and those with only auditory impairment. Threshold scores were underestimated with ERA in approximately half of the children in the other two categories.

At CID, Davis, Hirsh, Shelnutt, and Bowers (1967) tested the student population, which yielded 162 complete records over a three-year period. Primary variables were the three frequency pure tone average and ERA averages. Distributions of difference scores between ERA pure tone averages and laboratory behavioral pure tone averages showed occasional differences of 20 dB, but the average *absolute* difference between ERA and behavioral thresholds averaged 4.9 dB by individual subject. Limitations pointed out in the report include the masking effects of background electrical activity in the brain, latency and waveform variations of the evoked potential both between and within subjects (especially those under 7 years old), and the need for the subject to remain quiet during the recording intervals. Subjects who were difficult to test by behavioral methods were also those for whom ERA was less successful.

It is beyond the scope of this book to survey the extensive literature covering threshold applications, parameters of the test situation, and diagnostic implications derived from ERA measurements. Reviews of this subject area by Cody, Griffing, and Taylor (1968) and Goldstein (1967) cover the development of cortical audiometry, descriptions of the details of the test situation, and a discussion of the usefulness of ERA in the clinical situation.

A special test developed for measurement of pathology of the middle ear, originally described by Zwislocki (1963) and Feldman (1964), shows promise as an objective procedure for testing both children and adults. The test determines, through the use of an acoustic bridge, the impedance of the middle ear. Routine clinical application of impedance audiometry appears to be increasing. For example, Jerger (1970) obtained three measures for 400 consecutive clients: compliance of the tympanic membrane, acoustic impedance measures, and threshold levels for the acoustic reflex. Although any single measure did not exhibit adequate validity, patterns appeared for different diagnostic categories. These were especially useful for confirming unilateral and bilateral conductive and sensorineural hearing losses in young children.

Reaction time to auditory stimuli also has been proposed as a sensitive measure of auditory acuity in a recent study by Rapin and Steinberg (1970). They reported a direct relationship between reaction time and signal intensity when deaf children aged 5½ years and older were tested. In order to obtain threshold measures of reaction time, tones at 500, 1000, and 2000 Hz were presented at decreasing intensities. Subjects were asked to press a key when they detected the signal. Reaction time plotted as a function of intensity showed a sudden increase in latency when intensity approached the threshold value on the audiogram obtained by conventional methods.

Of the obective measures described in this section, impedance audiometry is becoming the most widely used because of its relatively low cost and its application to children. ERA audiometry continues to stimulate research as part of the special test battery rather than as a threshold procedure.

Speech Audiometry—Children

Testing speech-hearing in children is generally agreed to be a difficult task because of age-related factors that can obscure auditory sensitivity. Lack of cooperation in the test situation, variability in development and maturation of speech and language, and inability to obtain reliable pure tone measures all contribute to the difficulties of test construction and administration. Efforts to overcome these extraneous variables have been reported in the literature and there are now available several tests for speech reception threshold and speech discrimination.

Speech reception tests. When a child is old enough to make consistent motor, verbal, or written responses to commands, the speech reception threshold (SRT) can be particularly useful as a complement to pure tone threshold measures. Three speech reception threshold tests calling for picture identification will be described here.

The earliest account of a test for children was reported by Keaster (1947). Twenty nouns from the International Kindergarten Word List were spoken by the examiner, through a calibrated amplification system. Words were used within the context of a direction given to the child. The speech reception threshold was defined as the lowest level at which the child was able to follow three directions.

The Threshold by Identification Pictures Test (TIP) reported by Siegenthaler et al. (1954) and Siegenthaler and Haspiel (1966) has been standardized on a group of normal-hearing children from 3 to 8 years of age. Each test card contains a set of five pictured representations of monosyllabic words selected on the basis of familiarity to children, unambiguity of name, and degree of audibility. For the preschool and school-age children tested, reliability was satisfactory. The standard error predicted that two thirds of test-retest scores would fall within a 3-dB range.

Meyerson (1958) later developed the Verbal Audiometric Test (VAT) consisting of words with spondiac stress pattern that are equated for audibility, familiarity, and speech sound distribution. Young children make a picture identification response while older children give written responses. Data from over 700 ears, kindergarten through sixth grade, found high test-retest reliability. When pure tone threshold measures were compared with VAT scores, those children having impaired hearing for pure tones usually showed impaired hearing for speech. However, the reverse was not found, for many of the children showing impaired hearing on the VAT did not show significant loss for pure tones.

Available tests appear to measure adequately the SRT for children. Additional research relating SRT scores to pure tone thresholds would be welcome to determine whether the same relationships apply that have been demonstrated for adults. No comparative studies were found that would aid in a decision about the appropriateness of each test for different subject populations. Meyerson's evidence relating pure tone thresholds to SRT scores has shown some agreement, but it is less than perfect. If both pure tone and SRT measures are available, inconsistencies may alert the clinician to problems unrelated to pure tone sensitivity or, alternately, agreement between the two measures can confirm threshold data. In either case SRT measures are useful, especially in view of the limited number of tests developed for clinical diagnosis of children's hearing status.

Speech discrimination tests. Formal speech discrimination testing of children has received comparatively little attention in the research literature. For adults speech discrimination measures are used extensively as a part of both the routine audiometric battery and in hearing aid evaluation. Experimental investigations with children were found only with regard to test development.

One approach has utilized adult tests for assessing the child's discrimination ability, but none of the research supports this practice. Data reported by McNamee (1960) and Nielson (1961) show that CID W-22 lists are not appropriate for testing below the ninth-grade level. Sanderson (1972) found lower scores and greater variability within groups of subjects up to age 11½ when the Northwestern N.U. Auditory Test No. 6 for adults was compared to other tests developed for children.

A second type of test parallels adult test procedures, but the vocabulary has been modified for children. Haskins (1949) adapted the PAL PB-50 lists for use with children by simplifying the vocabulary with words selected from the International Kindergarten Union List. Measures of list difficulty and test-retest reliability for the PBK-50 test were obtained from a sample of normal-hearing adults; no data were reported for children. Adults showed some improvement from test to retest, indicating that practice effects were operating for this age group.

A third procedure for discrimination testing has emphasized test material developed specifically for children. The Word Intelligibility by Picture Identification (WIPI) test eliminated the requirement of a verbal response. Basic research by Myatt and Landes (1963) and Lerman, Ross, and McLaughlin (1965) led to the final version published by Ross and Lerman (1970). Test stimuli consist of twenty-five color plates, each containing six pictures. On each plate four pictures correspond to a word on each of four lists; the remaining two pictures are foils. Final evaluation of the test was based on responses of sixty-one hearing-impaired children ranging in age from 4 years and 7 months to 13 years and 9 months. Stimulus words were delivered at a 40-dB sensation level on each of two different occasions. Mean discrimination scores improved from the first to the second presentation, averaging 3 percent. Reliability was high, however, and the test differentiated among children according to hearing level.

Only one experiment was found that compared children's performance on these different types of tests. Sanderson (1972) obtained articulation functions for the WIPI, the PBK-50, and N.U. Auditory Test No. 6. Subjects included twelve children from each of the age groups 3½, 5½, 7½, 9½, and 11½. For the youngest children, 3½ years old, the WIPI (picture identification) test was clearly the test of choice. The PBK-50 (verbal response) test for children yielded discrimination scores of over 95 percent for all groups 5½ and older at the highest sensation level of 32 dB. Thus, if a child has normal speech and language and is at least 5½ years old, the PBK-50 is appropriate. Otherwise the WIPI might be preferred. Consistently lower scores were found with N.U. Auditory Test No. 6 and variability within groups was larger than for the other two tests. Generally the greatest discrepancies in performance between age groups were associated with the younger children. As age increased, discrimination scores for adjacent age groups were more similar.

Compared to the extensive literature on adult discrimination tests there are very few directed toward children's tests. Topics that need special emphasis are basic data on the performance of hearing-impaired children and normative data for tests administered in a test environment similar to the usual clinical evaluation.

Deficit Typology

Audiometric tests yield useful information for both medical diagnosis and rehabilitation. We use the term *deficit typology* to refer to diagnostic categories developed for medical purposes, categories that usually have been organized around the anatomical site of impairment. Classifications based on severity of loss are discussed under the section "Handicap Typology" later in this chapter.

Newby and Molyneaux (1951) worked out a schema for diagnosis based on measures of pure tone threshold, air-bone gap, speech reception, speech discrimination, and audiometric pattern. Audiometric patterns were classified according to the change in threshold between the pairs of frequencies 500–1000 Hz and 1000–2000 Hz. Threshold levels were designated as flat (F), gradually increasing (G), markedly increasing (M), or decreasing (R) over each of the two frequency intervals. A sample of 500 subjects 6 to 89 years old provided data for studying the relationship between audiometric results and diagnosis of impairment. Diagnostic categories included nerve deafness, otosclerosis, otosclerosis plus nerve involvement, otitis media, and congenital deafness. Some consistent patterns were found. For example, nerve deafness was associated with minimum air-bone gap, poor articulation scores and audiometric configurations G, G–M, and M–F. Otosclerosis, on the other hand, was characterized by significant air-bone gap, good articulation scores and the audiometric configurations F–R, F, G–R, and R–F.

A refined classification system has been described by Davis (1962) and Davis and Goldstein (1970). Strategies are outlined for detecting impaired function originating in the middle ear, inner ear, auditory nerve, and the central nervous system. Recommended tests for diagnosing malfunction of the middle ear associated with conductive hearing loss include a personal interview, air- and bone-conducted audiograms, SRT, PB maximum, and impedance measures. Inner-ear disorders, categorized as sensorineural hearing losses, are investigated by these same tests plus the additional information obtained from Bekesy audiometry, the SISI test, measures of recruitment by loudness balances, acoustic reflex threshold data, impedance audiometry, and assessment of tone quality. Similar detail is provided for functional hearing loss and impairment of the VIII nerve and the central nervous system.

Jerger (1968) discussed the same categories in a more recent review. Test batteries appropriate for distinguishing conductive and cochlear sites of impairment are very similar to those described above. Suggestions are offered for areas of diagnostic procedure that need further work, for example, the aural overload test and adaptive procedures based on signal detection models for threshold testing. Jerger (1970) contributed to the differential diagnosis of children by studying impedance audiometry as part of the routine clinical battery for over 400 patients. He concluded that the pattern of results yielded by measures of tympanometry, acoustic impedance, and acoustic reflex threshold can be extremely useful for confirming unilateral or bilateral conductive and sensorineural hearing loss.

A different diagnostic problem arises when the goal is to differentiate peripheral auditory impairment from other types of disorder such as asphasia, mental retardation, or emotional disturbance encountered frequently in childhood diagnosis. Goldstein, Kendall, and Arick (1963) used ERA to distinguish children with problems of purely auditory sensitivity from those exhibiting at least one nonperipheral factor. Two measures were particularly sensitive to this distinction: a more regular increase in mean scores with increasing sound intensity and shorter latency periods were noted for children with peripheral auditory impairment. Price and Goldstein (1966) continued to study ERA as a diagnostic tool in a study of seventy children aged 2 months to 13 years. Normal-hearing children and those with only auditory sensitivity impairment showed good agreement between ERA and conventional behavioral methods. For children with some nonperipheral factor, approximately half of those tested showed lower thresholds for ERA than for behavioral audiometry. The discrepancy between behavioral threshold and averaged evoked response threshold is a useful test, especially for children with perceptual problems not due to impairment of peripheral auditory sensitivity.

Language performance and other behavioral measures have also been used diagnostically. Olson (1961) found that on four subtests of the ITPA (Illinois Test of Psycholinguistic Ability), hearing-impaired children were superior to sensory aphasic children. Myklebust (1964) points to the fact that differentiating cues for peripheral and nonperipheral auditory disorders include those of consistency of response, integration of function, and performance on language tests.

Reichstein and Rosenstein (1964) in a review of the literature on differential diagnosis noted that diagnostic categories for central nervous system disorders are not well defined and disagreement among workers in the field is common. Consistency of response to auditory stimuli was frequently found to differentiate deaf children from those with aphasia, but this variable has not been systematically studied.

As yet there is no agreed-upon battery for differential diagnosis of children. Many special tests can be administered to adults, leading to a more refined classification. Even for this group, however, greater precision in defining the locus of impairment can be expected as new tests become standardized for clinical use.

Reference Levels and Optimal Standards for Auditory Deficit Appraisal

The matter of reference levels and standards has been a continuing concern of audiologists and otologists for many years. Field tests as well as laboratory tests of hearing have contributed threshold data as a function of age and environmental conditions. Acuity for pure tones via air conduction and bone conduction are central to the question of levels and standards as is the performance of listeners on speech materials. The American Standards Association (ASA) in 1951 developed norms that were adhered to in the United States until the development of a new standard by the International Standards Organization (ISO) in 1964. The ASA standard values, based on a USPHS population survey, are approximately 10 dB poorer than the ISO values, a discrepancy that may be accounted for by differences in test procedures. In an effort to make the transition to the ISO standards easier, a formula for an exact translation between the two standards and an approximate rule for the speech range frequencies were recommended by the working group of the NAS-NRC Committee on Hearing, Bioacoustics and Biomechanics (CHABA). Their recommendation follows:

	Frequency (Hz)							
	250	*500*	*1000*	*2000*	*3000*	*4000*	*6000*	*8000*
Add to ASA (dB)	15	14	10	8.5	8.5	6	9.5	11.5
Approximate (dB)	15		10			6	10	

The American National Standards Institute includes these translations from ASA to ISO in its report (1970) on specifications for audiometers. Reference threshold sound pressure levels for pure tones and speech are also provided. The speech reference threshold level is based on the 50 percent intelligibility of spondee words, 20 dB SPL for the TDH–39 earphone commonly used in the clinic.

Auditory Handicap

An auditory handicap is the extent to which an individual is disadvantaged by the hearing loss he sustains. One normally thinks of auditory handicap in relation to oral language communication and perhaps rightfully so. However, auditory handicap can and does extend beyond oral communication situations. For example, a body of research comparing cognitive functioning of deaf and normal-hearing children finds differences in performance on a variety of verbally dependent tasks.

For the adult, psychosocial effects of hearing loss can impose a handicap in family, vocational, and social adjustment. Idenification of these behaviors can guide the audiologist and educator to more effective rehabilitation and educational training.

Under the concept of auditory handicap we consider these topics: (1) comparisons of children with normal hearing and those with hearing deficits, (2) speech and language, (3) measurement of auditory handicap, and (4) handicap-deficit asymmetry.

Normal Hearing—Hearing Deficit Comparisons

When an individual has an auditory deficit there are often observable effects on behavior beyond those directly related to auditory sensitivity. Perhaps the most easily recognized evidence that auditory deficit imposes limitations in basic processes other than strictly auditory ones is found in (1) the retardation in academic achievement typical among children with congenital or prelingual hearing losses, and (2) the restricted social and vocational status of adults. Poorly developed communicative skills in both receptive and expressive language appear to be the most serious barriers. Before addressing the question of speech and language development directly we will examine here some basic cognitive processes that play a part in language acquisition. Unfortunately, the role of such processes as memory, concept formation and abstraction, and visual perception in the overall growth of language and other communicative skills is not understood either in children with normal development or in children with auditory deficits. However, on a heuristic basis one could contend that memory and perception underlie both oral and written forms of language production and comprehension. Similarly the ability to categorize, form concepts, and think abstractly appears necessary for effective control over the symbolic aspects of language.

Although we cannot portray adequately the interactions of language and cognition, we can present the evidence available at this time, including (1) intelligence, (2) concept formation and abstraction, (3) visual perception, (4) memory, and (5) self-concept.

Intelligence. One might hypothesize that the retarded academic achievement of hearing-impaired children is the result of reduced general intelligence. But reviews of numerous studies of hard-of-hearing and deaf children have concluded that they are similar or equal to hearing children in the distribution of intelligence (Berlinsky, 1952; Levine, 1963; Ives, 1967; Vernon, 1969). Although the potential for learning appears similar in the two populations, there is reason to believe that the interaction of abilities differs. Both Levine (1963) and Farrant (1964) characterized the cognitive processes of hearing-impaired subjects as less well integrated than in the hearing population. In Farrant's experiment a factor analysis of scores on a battery of intelligence and achievement tests found less intercorrelation among abilities in the hearing-impaired sample.

Test batteries recommended for hearing-impaired children at various age levels were reported by Vernon and Brown (1964). Their review covered tests of intelligence, personality, and brain damage designed for preschool children, children in kindergarten up to age nine, 9 to 15-year-olds, and age 16 through graduation. Since hearing-impaired children are penalized on verbal tests of intelligence because of their poor linguistic skills, performance tests were preferred.

Concept formation and abstraction. One of the cognitive skills included in many intelligence tests is the ability to form concepts. Developmentally children tend to progress from the more concrete to the more abstract, allowing categorization of lower-order concepts into superordinate groupings. The development and transfer of concepts is thought to depend upon both language and nonverbal experiences derived from interaction with the environment. Various investigators place different emphasis on these two factors. Whether concept attainment requires language or simply is facilitated by language is an unresolved issue. Furth (1966) reviewed some thirty experiments on conceptual thinking where the tasks did not call directly for verbalization. His interpretation of this research emphasized the similarity of thinking processes of deaf and hearing children when the tasks were nonverbal. Lower achievement levels of deaf children on many tasks were attributed to slower development arising from restricted social and experiential opportunities. In support of this position Furth summarized a training program to develop logical thinking in deaf children. After four days of teaching, the children were able to manipulate abstract symbols logically without the introduction of linguistic rules. Kohl (1967) takes issue with Furth's position, arguing that knowledge of sign language may serve as a mediator in concept formation tasks. He believed that cognitive limitations in deaf children should be attributed to the inadequacies of sign language and to educational methods.

Whatever the reason, deaf children do not perform as well as hearing children in many instances. For example, Hughes (1961) presented deaf students from 10 to 14 years old with a task that involved sorting pictured equivalents of familiar words into concept categories. Comparisons of deaf subjects with hearing subjects disclosed that the hearing children knew more individual percepts and concepts, and they were able to sort a greater proportion of the percepts into the appropriate concepts. Although deaf children recognized 163 of the 241 individual percepts, they sorted only 46 of them correctly. Hughes advocated early training on low-order concepts and more adequate teaching of the discriminations required to determine what is *not* included under a concept as well as what is included.

Two tests of conceptualization have been reported in the literature. An Experimental Concept Formation Test for preschool deaf children was developed by Lowell and Metfessel (1961). Children 2 to 5 years old were instructed to isolate the test item that was most different from other items in a set. One of the simplest problems required the subject to isolate a white card from two black cards. Correct responses were followed by a candy reinforcement. Validation of the test against teacher ratings of ability found moderate correlations of about 0.50. Test reliability was adequate and the test was found to discriminate among the ages represented in the study.

Silverman (1967) administered the Triple Mode Test of Categorization to deaf and hearing children between 7 and 14 years old. The test considers three types of categorization. Superordinacy refers to grouping things under a common label, such as different items of furniture. A second type is associative categorizing, in which two items such as a book and a bookcase are related. The third kind is functional, pairing a chair with a person standing. As age increased, deaf children's usage of superordinate and associative responding decreased while functional categorization increased. In contrast, the hearing children increased superordinate responding, decreased associative responding, and maintained the same level of functional responding.

Considering the number of experiments on concept formation, we have surprisingly little information on the process by which concepts are acquired and the sequence of acquisition. There is also a need for applied research on methods of accelerating the growth of conceptual thinking in deaf children. Since daily experience is rarely under experimental control, structured programs are needed for application in clinical and educational settings. Guidelines for program content require an empirical base that may be provided by further systematic research.

Memory processes. Although the role of memory processes in communication is not well understood, it is certain that both short- and long-term memory are involved. Whether a message is presented visually or auditorily, sequential processing of the incoming signal is required in the immediate instance, and the assignment of meaning to the message requires recall of information previously learned and stored.

Furth (1961) studied nonverbal memory processes using a visual paired-associate task with 180 deaf and 180 normal-hearing children ranging in age from 7 to 12 years. Up to age 10 there were no differences in learning between deaf and hearing children. At the 11- and 12-year age levels, however, hearing children showed rapid improvement in performance, a shift not paralleled by the deaf children. Since the two groups were comparable during the younger years, it seems reasonable to conclude that the difficulty was not in their basic capacity for visual memory. Rather, their problems in later years should be attributed, Furth suggested, to restricted experience and training. This argument reflects the same rationale he offered in his examination of research on concept formation.

Blake, Ainsworth, and Williams (1971) reported that the performance of 15-year-old deaf subjects on a word-digit paired-associate learning task was similar to the performance of 12-year-old hearing subjects. This result complements Furth's finding of a gap at older age levels.

Furth's suggestion that lack of training was at least in part the reason for poorer performance of older deaf children was followed up by Espeseth (1969). His subjects were thirty-six deaf children from 6 to 12 years old. Experimental subjects underwent a training program consisting of half-hour sessions, four days a week, for a total of forty sessions. Training sessions emphasized reproduction of designs formed by bead-stringing and flannel-board picture sequences. Control subjects were seen at the same number of sessions but they were not given this type of training. Eight criterion measures of visual sequential memory were administered prior to the training and at the end of training to evaluate changes in performance. Three tests were of primary interest: the Visual-Motor Sequencing subtest of the ITPA, a Picture Span Test, and a Digit Span Test. After training, the group that underwent training improved on the ITPA subtest and the Picture Span Test, but not on the Digit Span Test. Improvement occurred on tests with items very similar to exercises used in training. This seems to imply that transfer of training is relatively specific.

Several investigators have explored the effects of verbal mediation on memory and verbal learning. Putnam, Iscoe, and Young (1962) employed a verbal discrimination task that required subjects to learn the "correct" word in each item of a fourteen-pair list. Seven of the word pairs had two members with identical sign equivalents; the other seven had low similarity sign equivalents. Deaf subjects learned the discrimination more rapidly than hearing subjects, and high-similarity word pairs were learned more easily than pairs with low similarity. Odom, Blanton, and McIntyre (1970) investigated the effects of sign equivalence in paired-associate learning in deaf and hearing children. Subjects were forty deaf students with an average age of 16 and a reading level of grade five, and forty hearing subjects averaging 10 years old. A sixteen-pair word-number list was presented eight times during training, using a study recall method. Within the list eight words had sign equivalents and eight did not. Separate analyses of words correct were carried out for the two types of items. Deaf subjects showed consistently better learning over the eight trials when words had sign equivalents. Learning rates of hearing subjects were lower on both types of words, and similar to learning rates of deaf subjects on words without signs. Both experiments suggest that signs may serve as mediators for deaf children. However, since words with no sign equivalents may occur less frequently and words with similar signs are often similar semantically, the effects of sign equivalents may not have been completely isolated.

Chovan and McGettigan (1971) hypothesized that vocal labels would aid hearing children on the Visual-Motor Sequencing subtest of the ITPA, but would interfere with performance of deaf children. Subjects were divided into two groups according to mental age with 7 years and 2 months as the cutoff. Half of the deaf subjects were given vocal labels for the design arrangement task; all hearing subjects were supplied with labels. No performance differences were found among the younger children. At the older level, hearing children were superior to deaf children in both groups, those with and without labels. Among the deaf groups, older subjects trained without labels were superior to younger deaf subjects, but they were not significantly different from the older group with labels. The effect of vocal labeling on performance of deaf children was weak.

Conrad and Rush (1965) sought to determine whether deaf and hearing subjects use the same type of acoustic coding for simple verbal material. They employed a forced guessing procedure where a letter had to be placed in each of five positions following each stimulus presentation. If a letter was wrong for the position in which it was placed, an error was counted. Confusion matrices of errors were constructed with particular attention being paid to whether the error was related to the correct letter in some systematic way. The normal-hearing subjects made considerably fewer errors, 13.6 percent, compared to the deaf subjects, who made 40.5 percent errors. When the fifteen best experimental subjects and the sixteen worst performing normal-hearing (control) subjects were considered as subsamples, it was found that hearing children made errors based on acoustic confusion but deaf children did not. There was a consistent type of error made by the deaf, but the underlying basis of the encoding procedure could not be determined from the data.

Subsequent research by Conrad (1971, 1973) has shown that within a group of deaf subjects, different coding strategies may be employed. In these memory-recall experiments sets of consonants were presented visually one by one. Immediately after each sequence, subjects wrote down the set they had seen. Confusion error matrices were then constructed to determine the basis for their errors. One group of deaf subjects exhibited a pattern of errors similar to hearing controls. Conrad interpreted this as evidence for speech-based coding, perhaps articulatory, without an acoustic element since all subjects were profoundly deaf. For the second group of deaf subjects, errors were related to shape confusions, suggesting a visual coding of letters. Data from the 1971 study showed that reading the sequences aloud had no effect on the articulatory coding group, but led to more errors in the visual coding group. Both types of coding differ from that employed by hearing subjects, who apparently use a phonological code that includes acoustic as well as articulatory information in memory tasks.

Sequential presentation of stimuli and delayed recall of stimuli both have been found to effect short-term memory. Withrow (1968) compared a simultaneous method of presentation of visual material with a sequential presentation of material. His main finding was that whereas there were no differences between a deaf and a hearing group under simultaneous presentation, there were differences for sequential presentation. Normal-hearing subjects were superior to three groups of hearing-impaired subjects: an oral group, a manually trained group, and a special group of CID students who had hearing problems and language learning problems. Hartman and Elliott (1965) reported similar findings on the inability of deaf subjects to encode sequential information auditorily. Ling (1971) found that deaf children had difficulties both with short-term memory and with sequential processing in a dichotic listening situation. In one condition sets of digits were presented monaurally. In a second condition different digits were presented to each ear simultaneously. Superior performance of hearing subjects on the monaural task was attributed to short-term memory and better auditory discrimination. On the dichotic task hearing-impaired children appeared to have difficulty processing the simultaneous auditory information. Very seldom did hearing-impaired children recall both members of a pair presented dichotically. In contrast, normal-hearing children recalled almost all digits in two-digit sequences and approximately two thirds of the three-digit sequences.

Goetzinger and Huber (1964) studied immediate and delayed visual retention in deaf and hearing adolescent subjects. Memory processes were studied by means of the Benton Visual Retention Test for geometric figures. Three forms of the test vary in the following manner: Form A has a 10-second exposure and immediate reproduction, Form B uses 5-second exposure and immediate reproduction, and Form C has a 10-second exposure followed by a 15-second delay before reproduction. Performance of the deaf students was equivalent to that of hearing subjects on tests of immediate recall but the delay condition led to significantly inferior performance on the part of the deaf.

It has been demonstrated rather convincingly that short-term memory in deaf children is inferior to that in normal hearing-children in three types of situations: (1) sequential presentation of visual and auditory stimuli, (2) simultaneous dichotic presentation of auditory stimuli, and (3) delayed recall following visual stimulus presentation. The nature of the encoding and decoding memory process needs further experimental attention.

Visual perception. Because of their decreased auditory sensitivity, hearing-impaired children often depend on visual perception in the communication process to a greater extent than do hearing children. Several comparisons of hearing and deaf children appear in the literature.

Binnie, Elkind, and Stewart (1966) used Piaget's suggested developmental stages as a basis for selecting perceptual tasks. According to Piaget the child's perception initially is focused on dominant figures in the visual field—it is "centered." As development proceeds, the child gains the ability to shift from one perceptual configuration to another. This is referred to as "decentering." A test designed to measure this behavior was included in the experimental battery. In addition, a second test measured part-whole integration of visual stimuli. A diamond illusion test completed the battery. Standardized norms for normal-hearing children are available for each of the tests. Participating subjects were eighty children with hearing levels of at least 65 dB in the better ear. Hearing-impaired subjects made fewer part-whole integrations than hearing subjects and were less mature in decentering. None of the children achieved a score above the first-grade level norm for hearing subjects on the diamond illusion test, which compares sizes of squares and diamonds. Older subjects, 7, 8, and 13 years old, obtained scores at or near the first-grade level.

Doehring and Rosenstein (1969) investigated the ability of fifty deaf and fifty hearing children to locate relevant test stimuli embedded in a context of irrelevent stimuli. Stimulus material varied in complexity and in the degree to which it was based on verbal material. Since all tests had time limits, speed of visual perception was a primary variable. Hearing children scored significantly higher than deaf children on nine of the thirteen tasks. Analysis of the tasks led the authors to postulate a greater usage of symbolic cues on the part of hearing children.

Although our information is fragmentary at best, some restrictions in visual perception have been identified. Whether this reflects a delay and slowing of maturity or a different sequence of development is not known.

Self-concept. In addition to the negative effects of hearing impairment on communication and on certain cognitive functions there is also an influence on how a person views himself. Rutledge (1954) compared fifty-two young teen-age deaf children from the Minnesota School for the Deaf with fifty-two normal-hearing children who were also institutionalized. Two tests were used to determine level of aspiration and the discrepancy between aspiration level and the level actually achieved. Analysis of scores on the Heath Railwalking Test, a test of balance, showed that the performance of deaf children was actually inferior to the performance of the hearing subjects. On the Aspiration Board Test there were no significant differences between the experimental and the control group. In terms of goal discrepancies, when aspiration level was compared with actual performance, deaf boys and girls set their levels of aspiration below their past performance on the test of balance in which they were indeed handicapped. Goal discrepancies were not found for other tasks, however.

A later study of self-concept by Craig (1965) considered institutionalization an important variable in development of self-concept. The experiment investigated self-ratings of deaf institutional subjects, deaf noninstitutional children, and children who were neither deaf nor institutionalized. Significant differences were found between the deaf groups and the nondeaf group in the accuracy with which they rated themselves. Deaf children were less accurate in predicting how others would rate them. The self-acceptance of the deaf institutional group was higher than either of the noninstitutional groups. Craig suggests that the self-concept of the deaf child is inaccurate because of his language deficit, regardless of his place of residence, home or institution. The tendency of high acceptance of self and others in the "in group" of the residential school was regarded as a different factor, dependent more on institutional living than on deafness itself.

Hardick (1964) found the semantic differential a reliable instrument in quantifying the attitudes of adult hard-of-hearing persons about themselves and for comparing their attitudes with those of normal-hearing persons. The most striking difference between the two subject groups was found in the Capability dimension. Hard-of-hearing subjects rated themselves as somewhat less capable than their normal-hearing counterparts.

Both children and adults who are hearing handicapped have been shown to differ in some respect from normal-hearing individuals in assessing themselves and their abilities. To the extent that these attitudes are realistic they reflect an objective view. When they underestimate ability there may be a need for, or at least interest in, counseling.

Speech and Language

Since the development of receptive and expressive language is normally associated with auditory exposure in a linguistic environment, one can expect that hearing loss will interfere. The extent to which language is affected, however, is an imperfect function of the nature and severity of the hearing loss. In this section those studies that deal with speech and language problems of both hard-of-hearing and deaf children are reviewed. Matters of speech intelligibility, articulation, voice, and language development are discussed.

Speech sound production. Hirsh (1950) emphasized that during the critical years of language development profoundly deaf children lack a monitoring system to provide auditory feedback, although there is some possibility that cues from the kinesthetic sense can serve as a substitute for this feedback role. Evidence arising from the deterioration of intelligibility in adult speech and the difficulty that congenitally deaf children have in developing language both point to the central importance of auditory feedback in maintaining and acquiring precision in speech skills. Hirsh suggests that in terms of intelligibility alone, the importance of defective speech is not too great, but when one considers social acceptance, pleasantness, and other such characteristics, then a speech defect really warrants professional attention.

Spontaneous vocalizations of infants are the precursors of later systematic differentiation of speech sounds and the single-word utterances usually observed by the end of the first year in normal-hearing children. Several persons have studied the phonetic content of speech sounds emitted by deaf children in relation to phonetic distributions found in the speech of normal-hearing children at different age levels. One of the earliest experiments came from the Clarke School for the Deaf where Heider and Heider (1940b) transcribed phonetically the spontaneous vocalizations of fourteen deaf and severely hard-of-hearing children who ranged in age from 3 years and 10 months to 6 years and 10 months. For vowels, which accounted for two thirds of all utterances, almost half occurred as isolated speech sounds. Middle vowels were observed more frequently than the extreme front or back vowels. Consonants rarely occurred alone but rather were uttered in combination with a vowel, usually in the initial position. The labials /b/ and /m/ were most frequent, and voiced sounds were represented more often than unvoiced. Hearing level affected the variety of speech sounds rather than the distribution of occurrence. Children with more residual hearing produced an average of thirteen consonants while profoundly deaf children averaged nine consonants. Profoundly deaf children favored sounds that are most easily produced. Carr (1953) reported similar results in an investigation of 5-year-old untrained deaf children. Relative frequencies of vowel sounds produced by deaf children at age 5 were similar to those of much younger hearing children in the age range 11 to 12 months. The deaf children used vowels more frequently than consonants, and the front vowels were more often found than back vowels. Profiles of frequency of usage for consonant data were unlike those of hearing children at any one age. In comparison to the hearing children the *deaf had more voiced consonants than voiceless, and the front consonants were represented more often than back consonants.* This latter measure showed a higher preponderance of front consonants than for any age category of the hearing group. The author suggests that deaf babies vocalize and babble in much the same manner during the first year as do normal-hearing infants, but then, deaf children fail to develop more speech sounds because they are not able to imitate the sounds of speech around them. Carr recommends that the spontaneous speech sounds of children be recorded and incorporated into daily activities with deaf youngsters so that these sounds are retained and then can be used as a basis for further teaching of speech.

A study that related speech production of deaf children to age and to degree of hearing loss was reported by Nober (1967). His interest centered on (1) comparisons of articulation errors made by deaf children and normal-hearing children of the same age, and (2) investigation of the nature of articulation problems at different levels of hearing loss. Subjects were forty-six deaf children with sensorineural losses covering an age range from 3 to 15 years, divided into five age groups. Each age group was further divided into four hearing levels ranging from 61–70 dB HL in the least severe category to greater than or equal to 91 db HL. Both the Templin-Darley Screening Test and the full-range Diagnostic Test of Articulation were administered to each child while he was wearing his individual hearing aid. Four judges were employed to identify the speech output of each subject, relying on auditory cues only. There was only a small effect of degree of hearing loss and of age on articulation scores. When hearing loss was less than 81 dB, articulation scores of the older children exceeded those of the younger children; but when the loss was in excess of 81 dB, no subject obtained an articulation score equal to 3 years, regardless of his chronological age. Speech sounds that are visible were ranked highest in intelligibility, which suggests that the *visual reinforcement the children are able to obtain has an important influence.* Phonetic power of the speech sound and frequency of usage were apparently effective variables in increasing intelligibility. A list of consonants ranked according to intelligibility was also provided. Nober concluded that the *visibility of the sound is a most important parameter in determining correct articulation of a consonant.* The frequency-intensity parameters are of secondary importance.

The three experiments by Heider and Heider, Carr, and Nober are complementary in showing that the most intelligible speech sounds and the speech sounds most frequently used by deaf children are also the sounds produced with greatest visibility. Both usage and intelligibility decrease as place of production moves from front to back.

Penn (1955) studied short-term effects of acquired hearing loss on subjects with conductive or sensorineural hearing losses. On the basis of subjective rating scale measures, patterns of articulatory errors emerged. Sensorineural loss was characterized by general vowel confusion and omission of high-frequency consonants. Subjects with conductive losses showed a different pattern of unvoiced, weak, or omitted consonants, and consonant deviations for /m/ and /n/. The number of voice and speech deviations was related more closely to type of hearing loss than to intensity of loss or years of education.

Efforts to determine factors underlying articulatory errors have identified several variables. Bradley (1959) studied the relationship between pitch discrimination and speech production. He hypothesized that the inability of the deaf child to discriminate fine changes in pitch perhaps had a negative influence on his discrimination of certain sounds, thus limiting his ability to imitate speech accurately. This study compared three groups of subjects: normal-hearing and speaking children, children having articulation defects only, and children with both hearing and speech impairment. When difference limens were obtained for reference tones at 500 Hz, 1000 Hz, and 2000 Hz, all groups exhibited an increase as frequency of the reference tone increased. Difference limens were larger for the defective articulation group compared with the normal developmental group. However, the defective-hearing subjects were markedly inferior to both of the other groups of subjects. This was taken as evidence that pitch discrimination is a contributing factor in speech development.

Locke (1969) studied the learning of new sounds by seventy-five normal-hearing first-grade children in order to identify the variables important to the natural development of articulation. He related the ease of learning to imitate three German phrases to auditory memory and oral stereognosis ability. A sequence of three sets of four digits served as stimuli for the memory task. In the oral stereogonosis task he required subjects to associate the shape of haptic forms felt by the tongue with the correct pictures of the shapes. Children who had the highest scores for oral perception and those who had the longest memory spans showed an initial superiority in articulating the German phrases and they maintained a higher level throughout training.

The search for operative variables underlying correct articulation and those related to the faulty articulation of hearing-impaired people should be fruitful in suggesting possible training procedures to improve speech sound production. Analysis of speech sound production of hearing-impaired children as a process throughout the first years would be particularly useful.

Articulation test procedures. One of the problems of articulation testing with children concerns the format of the test itself. Should the examiner try to elicit spontaneous samples of speech or should a more structured imitative approach be chosen? Siegel, Winitz, and Conkey (1963) employed an imitative and a spontaneous method of presenting word stimuli to 100 normal-hearing kindergarten children. Under the imitative procedure the child was asked to repeat each of forty stimulus words; under the spontaneous method the response was to name a picture representing each stimulus word. It was found that eight of the forty sounds were produced correctly by significantly more children in the imitative than in the spontaneous condition. No subject performed better on the spontaneous method than on the imitative method of presentation. Although an imitative procedure may lead to higher performance levels, Johnson, Darley, and Spriestersbach (1963) recommend the spontaneous method as more valid for assessing natural usage.

Method of presentation of test material also was studied by Vargo (1968) with a hearing-impaired group. Adolescent residents of a state school for the deaf were tested under five conditions of stimulus presentation (1) a printed word, (2) a printed word and a word spoken through an auditory trainer with a face mask covering the speaker, (3) visual presentation with no auditory stimulation—subjects could view the speaker's mouth, (4) audiovisual, where the word was shown and then the auditory trainer was used with visual lipreading, or (5) a color picture was shown. Eighty college students evaluated the intelligibility of the adolescents' responses under two scoring conditions. Either they had an open set of possible responses where they only knew that the word was monosyllabic, or they had a closed set for scoring in a multiple-choice procedure. No differences in intelligibility resulted from the five variations in stimulus presentation. In general, higher scores were obtained under the closed-set method of scoring. Under open-set scoring subjects with some residual hearing achieved approximately 30 percent intelligibility and profoundly deaf subjects less than 10 percent. With closed-set scoring residual-hearing subjects were scored 60–70 percent correct, and the deaf subjects 45–55 percent, a substantial increase over the open-set condition.

Quantitative measures of articulation. For diagnostic value a descriptive analysis of articulatory errors is necessary, but there are occasions when a quantitative measure of articulation may be useful. A case in point is when articulation ability is related statistically to other behavioral measures. A quantitative description of vowel articulation has been developed by Stevens and House (1955). Parameters of this description give information on the position of the tongue constriction, the size of the constriction formed by the tongue, and the dimensions in the vicinity of the mouth opening. An experiment was carried out to determine the applicability of the model. Stimuli were recorded outputs of configurations on an electrical vocal tract analog where the output was specified by means of three numbers: (1) the position of the point of greatest constriction, (2) the degree of constriction at that point, and (3) the size of the mouth opening. Subjects with experience in phonetic transcription listened to the stimuli and were instructed to make their response selections from one of nine vowel categories; or under a second condition, the response set included an additional non-vowel response as well. Results of the phonetic transcription procedure allowed a matching of the configurations based on the model with their corresponding vowel identification. When the ranges of configurations identified as a given vowel were plotted by contours, they showed good agreement with previous studies.

Barker (1960) has proposed two numerical measures of articulation that are based on the relative frequency with which each speech sound occurs in the English language. One measure equally prorates the consonant values for all positions (initial, medial, and final) in which speech sounds are found in American speech. An alternative score considers only the initial and final syllabic positions of the consonant involved. Values for vowels and diphthongs are scored in the same way in each procedure. Confirming the utility of these measures, forty-five children with a wide range of articulation performance were given an articulation test and assigned articulation scores. Correlating their scores with ratings by trained judges yielded a coefficient of 0.94. Articulation scores were similar under both scoring procedures whether the three consonant positions were considered or whether the initial and final syllable positions were used. In an updating of this measure of articulation, Barker and England (1962) reported using the simplified method. On the recording form for this test, speech sounds are arranged in developmental order to provide an indication of articulation age. Adminstration time requires less than one minute.

Voice quality. Aside from problems of articulation, many hard-of-hearing people and most of the deaf population exhibit voicing disorders such as lack of loudness control, nasality, inappropriate pitch, and incorrect timing.

Two studies were found that evaluated voice quality of hard-of-hearing subjects. Penn (1955) reported that the voices of people with short-term sensorineural losses exhibited excessive volume, poor articulatory movement, stridency, monotonous pitch, rapid rate, and audible breathing. Subjects having conductive losses had fewer difficulties but they showed nasal quality and weak volume. Carlin (1968) studied the relationship between visual representation of speech by spectrographic presentation and the vocal quality of partially-hearing school children. The second formant was used as a determinant of their voice quality. For purposes of the study, inefficient voices were described as those that could not be used for communication with a minimum of effort and that were not appropriate for the age and sex of the child; 37 percent of the subjects were judged to be in this category. Inefficient voices had the following characteristics on the sonogram: (1) more irregular striations, (2) greater variability in distance between peaks, (3) greater variability in the height of the peaks, and (4) more variation in the size of the troughs. For the hard-of-hearing subjects under study, the central frequency of the phoneme /i/ varied from 1600 Hz to 3200 Hz and the duration from 40 milliseconds to 640 milliseconds, with a mean of 322 milliseconds. Carlin suggests that a computer analysis of large samples could lead to standards in measurement of vocal quality.

Typically, voice disorders of deaf individuals are widespread and many faceted. The following articles illustrate deviations in formant frequencies, duration of phonemes, and nasality. Angelocci (1962) and Angelocci et al. (1964) compared vowel formants produced by deaf and normal-hearing teen-age boys using the sound spectrograph for measurement. The deaf subjects had an average hearing level of 60 decibels over the frequency range from 250 Hz through 4000 Hz. Ten vowel sounds spoken in an "h-d" context served as stimulus material for tape-recorded speech samples obtained from the eighteen subjects in each group. Frequencies and amplitudes of the fundamental and the first three formants were measured to determine differences between utterances of the deaf and the hearing subjects. Recorded stimuli were also presented to thirty-four college students for judgment of intelligiblity. Results showed three characteristic deviations for the deaf subjects: the fundamental frequency was higher, formant frequency positions were more widely scattered, and the first formant/second formant relationship of one vowel to the next was more distorted compared with control voices. Pooling intelligibility scores, deaf speakers averaged 32 percent intelligibility compared to normal-hearing subjects, who averaged 81 percent. The least identified vowel of the normal-hearing subjects was still more intelligible than the most intelligible vowel of the deaf.

Calvert (1962a, 1962b 1964) studied five profoundly deaf and five normal-hearing subjects in terms of speech sound duration. Deaf speakers were found to distort the duration of the phonemes in two main ways. First they extended the duration several times over that of hearing speakers, and second, they did not follow the relative differences in duration for voicing of consonants or for the effect of one sound upon another that one usually finds in normal-hearing speakers. In another study, using the same subjects, Calvert had speech samples played for ten experienced teachers of the deaf who felt that deaf speakers could be identified on the basis of voice quality. The alternatives for the listeners to choose among were (1) a deaf speaker, (2) a normal speaker, and (3) a speaker simulating a voice defect. A fairly high speaker identification score of 70 percent was obtained when sentence samples were rated by the listener judges, but when smaller units, such as simple vowels in isolation, were the stimuli, only 5 percent of the deaf and normal samples were identified correctly.

Colton and Cooker (1968) compared observer judgments of nasality of speech samples spoken by deaf and normal-hearing young adult subjects. Experienced speech clinicians first rated the samples for nasality on a nine-point equal appearing interval scale. This provided a criterion for selecting a speech sample of moderate nasality based on high observer agreement which could serve as a standard stimulus in the second phase of the experiment. In this phase thirty college students judged speech samples in relation to the standard by a method of direct magnitude estimation. Speech samples of deaf subjects had higher nasality ratings than those of hearing subjects even when the control speakers read the passage in a word-by-word manner similar to the tempo of the deaf speakers.

The relative importance and frequency of different voicing problems require additional investigation. Systematic research is needed on patterns or combinations of voicing disorders as they relate to severity and duration of hearing loss and to speech intelligibility.

Language development. Deficiencies in language development place limits on the later academic achievement of congenitally hearing-impaired children and pose a barrier to adequate social and vocational adjustment. The comprehension and production of language by hearing-impaired children have been the subjects of investigation over many years. Some trends can be identified. First, as remarked by Presnell (1973), the study of oral language has received relatively little attention, perhaps because of the difficulty in recording accurately the oral output of deaf children, which is often unintelligible. Poor speech production prevents the potential linguistic response. Comprehension of oral languages presents a parallel difficulty, separating auditory discrimination and comprehension of the linguistic message. In any event, the investigation of written language has been the more thorough.

A second trend reflects the influence of transformational grammar on methods of investigation. Research emphasis has shifted from the study of word counts, vocabulary, and use of word classes to the grammatical aspects of language reflected in syntactic usage.

The following discussion reviews research on oral and written language. Methods of language training are considered in the next chapter.

Oral language. Experiments by Goda (1959) and Simmons (1962) compared oral and written language samples of deaf children. Goda obtained measures of lipreading, reading, and quality of sentence structure rated on an eleven-point scale, ranging from unintelligible to elaborated sentences with two or more clauses. In absolute terms, sentence quality ratings averaged less than five on the eleven-point scale. Within the sample, children who scored high on one measure tended to score high on others as well. Simmons analyzed language samples of deaf and hearing children as a function of age. When the Type-Token Ratio (TTR) was applied, TTR values for written and spoken language of hearing subjects remained stable over age and were similar for the two modes of production. Deaf subjects had a somewhat higher TTR in speaking than in writing and their TTR scores were lower than for hearing subjects. Their sentences were characterized as simple, redundant, and stereotyped.

Two related experiments by Brannon and Murray (1966) and Brannon (1968) examined the distribution of word classes in the spoken language of normal-hearing, hard-of-hearing, and deaf children. Thirty normal-hearing children were drawn from a junior high school. Fifteen hard-of-hearing children and fifteen deaf children, 8.7 to 18.5 years old, were drawn from their special classes in the public schools. Language samples of fifty sentences in response to picture stimuli were obtained for each child. In the earlier study Brannon and Murray derived a syntax score from errors of addition, omission, substitution, and word order. Each of the three groups differed significantly from each other in the expected order of syntactic ability. Extent of hearing loss showed a moderate correlation with total word output, but it was more highly correlated with measures of syntax. The later study added more detailed information about usage of particular word classes. Generally the distribution of word classes for hard-of-hearing children was more like that of the normal-hearing group than the deaf group. However, hard-of-hearing children used fewer adverbs, pronouns, and auxiliaries. Deaf children used even fewer words in those classes and, in addition, they had a reduced output of prepositions, quantifiers, and indefinites. An earlier study by Hardy, Pauls, and Haskins (1958) also focused on children with moderate hearing losses. Twenty children with an average SRT for the better ear of 46 dB (ASA) ranged in age from 6 to 15 years. A control group of normal-hearing children was matched closely for age and socioeconomic environment (but control subjects had higher intelligence quotients). Tasks required of the children included sentence imitation, spontaneous sentence production, and storytelling. Experimental judges noted differences in language production for the two groups, especially in connected discourse. Language production of the normal-hearing group was smoother and sentences were more complex, reflecting greater usage of connectives and modifiers.

Applying the newer approach to language acquisition, Presnell (1973) investigated the comprehension and production of syntax of deaf children from ages 5 to 13 years. The Northwestern Syntax Screening Test (NSST) was administered to forty-seven children with moderate to profound hearing losses. Two subtests of the NSST include measures of comprehension of sentences by picture identification, and sentence production using a repetition technique. A spontaneous language sample of fifty sentences was also elicited. Although some improvement was found with increasing age on both the receptive and expressive subtests of the NSST, the rate of change was less than for normal-hearing children reported by Lee (1970). Variability of scores within age levels was also larger than for hearing children. When Lee and Canter's (1971) Developmental Sentence Scoring technique was applied to the spontaneous language samples, no improvement was observed as a function of age. Use of main verbs contributed most to low sentence scores. The only background variable to correlate significantly with linguistic performance was age/degree of impairment. Presnell concluded that hearing impaired children are less proficient than hearing children and apparently follow a different sequence of acquisition. She related these differences to the sequence of teaching in their language curriculum.

We still know little about the process of oral language acquisition in hearing-impaired children. Looking to the future, our opportunity to gain further knowledge becomes more favorable as information accumulates regarding normal language acquisition. When the sequence of acquisition is clarified in the normal development of language, more effective training programs can be anticipated for hearing-impaired children.

Written language. An extensive analysis of written sentence structure was reported in a monograph by Heider and Heider (1940a). Deaf children aged 11 to 17 and normal-hearing children aged 8 to 14 wrote over 1000 compositions about a short motion picture. A measure of sentence length in words showed increases over age for both hearing and deaf children. However, the oldest deaf children had the same average number of words as 8-year-old hearing children. The Heiders then examined the structure of the written sentences to clarify differences in production. The relative frequency of simple and compound sentences provided at least a partial explanation. At younger ages both deaf and hearing children produced more simple sentences than compound ones. Within the hearing group the relation was reversed at age 11, when compound sentences began to predominate. This shift never occurred for deaf children; at age 17 simple sentences were still somewhat more frequent. By age 10 the sentence structure of hearing children was as complex as that of 17-year-old deaf children. Comparisons of subordinate clauses and different forms of subordination are described in detail in the monograph. Walter (1959) also analyzed sentence structure, but sentence production was not considered as a function of age.

Several experiments have employed a sentence fill-in-the-blank test format as a method of studying ability to use different word classes (Hart and Rosenstein, 1964; MacGinitie, 1964; Odom, et al., 1967). In this research the performance of deaf children was consistently below that of hearing children. Choice of function words and use of morphological and syntactic rules were particularly difficult for the hearing-impaired subjects. Templin (1966) identified further problem areas in vocabulary knowledge and usage. Compared to the performance of hearing children, there were delays of up to eight years on an analogies test, a test of words with more than one meaning, and synonym recognition.

As with oral language acquisition, recent research reflects the influence of modern linguistics. Power and Quigley (1973) employed a transformational approach to the investigation of comprehension and production of the passive voice. Deaf subjects covering five age ranges from 9 to 18 years had hearing levels of at least 85 dB in the better ear. Several tests were employed. A test of comprehension of reversible and nonreversible passive sentences required subjects to manipulate toys demonstrating the action of the test sentence. In an agent-deleted sentence task, subjects selected one of two pictures that represented action in the passive voice. Production was tested by having subjects fill in the verb form of incomplete sentences such as, "The boy ——— the girl." Pictures represented the intended meaning and a choice of verb forms was available. Comprehension of the passive voice was significantly better than production, except for agent-deleted passives, in which case scores were similar. For the three types of sentence used to test comprehension, performance was highest on nonreversible passives, intermediate on reversibles, and lowest on agent-deleted passives. Comprehension of reversible and nonreversible passives exceeded production and it appeared that only children who had high comprehension scores were able to produce passive sentences correctly. Several age-related differences were found. Between 11 to 12 and 13 to 14 years there was a significant increase in comprehension; production scores of the oldest children, 17 to 18 years, were significantly higher than those of the 9 to 10-year age group. Over the age range studied, comprehension improved more than production. However, even the oldest deaf children were severely delayed in both aspects of performance. As a group, their highest comprehension score was 65 percent, and for production, 40 percent correct. Similar data for hearing children attributed to Schmitt (1968) showed equivalent levels of comprehension and production by age 6.

Empirical evidence indicates serious delay in language acquisition associated with reduced auditory sensitivity in hearing-impaired children. Since language skills are prerequisite for learning in many academic and vocational fields, the negative effects can hardly be overestimated. What remains to be determined is whether language training alone can solve the problem. Perhaps simultaneous or sequential training in memory, perception, and concept formation are also required.

Language tests and measurement. In clinical and educational settings quantitative measures of language often are needed for diagnostic and rehabilitative purposes. This is also true in research when language ability is related to other variables or when changes in language ability are used to evaluate training programs.

Several language scales for infants and young children yield scores that define the developmental level of language skill. Mecham and his colleagues (1959, 1967) have published two related tests of language ability designed for both normal and handicapped children. The earlier Verbal Language Development Scale an extension of Vineland Social Maturity Scale, uses an interview approach, questioning someone close to the child about his language behavior. A corresponding direct test of ability (the Utah Test of Language Ability) was published in 1967. Test scores can be expressed in terms of *language age* or as a *language quotient* when chronological age is taken into account. A quite different approach, which compares linguistic growth to other aspects of maturational development, has been described by Ewing (1963). The Watson-Pickles Scale divides language production into 10 developmental levels. At level 1 there is no vocalization; at level 10 the child talks freely. Each language level is related to maturational stages for normal children as described by Gessell and others. Boone (1966) summarized in tabular form a speech and development scale for infants from 1 month to 24 months. Parallel columns refer to development of comprehension and production of language. Statements within the table refer to original research articles from which the data were derived.

Some of these tests were discussed at a conference on early training of deaf infants from 0 to 3 years, chaired by McConnell (1968). In training programs across the country the following instruments were in use: Boone's Language Scale, the Watson-Pickles Scale, Doll's Vineland Social Maturity Scale and his Preschool Attainment Scale. Indirect assessment of changes due to training was attempted by testing parents. We quote from the report an evaluation of this technique:

> Several scales have been used by participants of this group, mainly the John Tracy Clinic Parent Attitude Scale, the only one designed specifically for the deaf; the Tennessee Self-Concept Scale by William Fitts; the Perry Scale of Parent Attitudes, which was developed by the Rochester Speech and Hearing Center; and the Schontz Scale of Psychological Reaction to Crises. Pre- and post-training reports from the use of most of these scales seemed to indicate that the scales do not successfully measure parent attitude changes which were observed by those working directly with the parents and the child. . . . In the Rochester Scale, parents are asked to check certain lists. The teacher then rated the child's progress. Comparing these, it was discovered that the parent's and the child's progress seemed unrelated insofar as parent information was concerned. The Tracy Attitude Scale has not given the kind of information that was expected and is no longer used by the Tracy group.

For preschool and older children, the Illinois Test of Psycholinguistic Abilities (ITPA) developed by McCarthy and Kirk (1961) has been employed diagnostically and in research. The test, based on Osgood's model, is diagnostic for nine psycholinguistic abilities and has been standardized in a group of 700 children aged 2½ to 9 years. Each subtest can be specified by three dimensions of Osgood's model: level of organization is either representational or automatic-sequential; psycholinguistic process includes decoding, encoding, and association; channel of communication for reception is either auditory or visual, and on the response side the channel is vocal or motor. Briefly sampling the types of skills covered we find Auditory Decoding with items such as, "Do pincushions cheer?"; Vocal Encoding calls for oral descriptions of simple objects; and Visual-Motor Sequencing requires reproduction of designs or picure sequences.

Two recently developed techniques for assessing syntactic development were described by Lee (1970) and Lee and Canter (1971). The first article reviews the status of tests of syntax and then describes a new screening test for comprehension and production of language. Comprehension is measured by picture identification; an imitation procedure is used to assess production. Test items are paired sentences that differ in one language structure, for example, "The cat is under the chair," or "The cat is behind the chair." Medians, quartiles, and 90th and 10th percentile scores are reported for 242 middle-class children between 3 and 8 years old. Lee and Canter's later article describes a more elaborate evaluation procedure for analyzing spontaneous speech samples. Developmental Sentence Scoring (DSS) is applied to a sample of fifty complete, different, consecutive, intelligible, nonecholalic sentences elicited in conversation. Eight features of language assessed by the sentence scoring procedure include indefinite pronouns and noun modifiers, personal pronouns, main verbs, secondary verbs, negatives, conjunctions, interrogative reversals, and Wh-questions. Within each of these categories specific responses are weighted according to degree of difficulty on a scale ranging from one to as high as eight, depending on the category. Very detailed directions and examples are given in the text. An additional point is awarded for a complete grammatical sentence. Percentile scores are provided for successive six-month age groups.

For the most part the tests described above measure oral language comprehension and production. As far as we could determine, the reliability and validity of these tests have not been determined for hearing-impaired children. Presnell (1973), however, has successfully applied Lee's screening test and the sentence scoring technique to deaf and hard-of-hearing children, as described earlier.

In a search for indices sensitive to growth in written language maturity, Marshall and Quigley (1970) analyzed written language samples of deaf subjects at each age level from 10 to 18 years. This research is extensive in its evaluation of measures of growth and also is directly applied to the written production of deaf students. While many indices were quanitified, there were two that were recommended as most sensitive to changes taking place over the full age range. One was the Subordination Ratio, initially proposed by La Brant (1933) and later modified by Hunt (1965). Hunt's definition, used by Marshall and Quigley, defines the Subordination Ratio as the ratio of the number of dependent clauses to all clauses in the sample, where a clause consists of a subject and a predicate, either of which may be coordinated. The second measure was Length of T-Unit, based on the concept of the minimal terminable syntactic unit or T-Unit. The T-Unit, as defined by Hunt, is a segment of written language consisting of a main clause and all subordinate clauses related to it as modifiers, complements, or substitutes. Length of T-Unit in Words can increase by expansion of the main clause or by the addition of subordinate clauses. Further analyses of the data identified a number of language structures that accounted for observed increases in Length of T-Unit with increasing age.

There are a number of difficulties in designing language tests. Insufficient information about the process and stages of language acquisition is a major one. In assessing infants' language, for instance, linquists tend to believe that early cooing and babbling are not stages in the acquisition process, but a reflection of vocal play. According to this view, the late babbling stage, when a phonological system begins to emerge, is the real beginning of language. In support of this position it is pointed out that infants must be able to perceive or discriminate speech sounds before they can begin to organize them. Other data on the distribution of speech sounds in infant vocalizations also bears on this issue. Another difficulty arises when one tries to assess comprehension in infants. It is fairly well established that comprehension precedes production in the acquisition of phonology, syntax, and semantics and therefore it is a more direct reflection of language competence than production. Methods of testing comprehension usually depend upon the cooperation of the child, which becomes more difficult to obtain with decreasing age. If one looks only at production, he cannot determine when comprehension was achieved. These problems are accentuated in the case of hearing-impaired children because of their reduced auditory receptive ability.

Measurement of Auditory Handicap

A great deal of effort has been directed toward the appraisal of hearing deficit. Only a limited amount of effort has been directed toward determination of the psychosocial effects that hearing loss imposes upon the individual. This discussion will seek to answer two questions: (1) Have scientifically based instruments been devised for purposes of measuring auditory handicap? (2) Is there an established typology for auditory handicap?

The best known measuring instrument is undoubtedly the Hearing Handiap Scale (HHS) devised by High, Fairbanks, and Glorig (1964). This is a five-point self-rating scale with items that indicate the frequency with which a particular activity causes problems of communication for the rater. The content areas include speech perception, localization, telephone communication, and settings with multiple voices or noise. The scale was administered to 100 subjects in the age range 18 to 65, with a mean hearing level if approximately 30 dB in the better ear and 45 dB in the poorer ear. Discrimination scores for the group averaged 88 percent, a fairly small loss for speech. When correlations between HHS scores and various audiometric measures were computed, measures based on pure tone frequencies in the speech range and SRT scores correlated highly with the Handicap Scale. However, speech discrimination scores were not significantly correlated with the HHS scores. The investigators referred to the restricted range of speech discrimination scores which could well produce a small correlation.

Giolas (1970) noted an advantage of the scale that derived from the content of the items. The audiologist would be able to identify problem areas that occur infrequently or that do not apply to the clinical setting. Self-rating items might yield information that otherwise would require extensive observation of the client over a period of time. A major limitation of the scale, in his view,. was the narrow content of the items that related primarily to sensitivity difficulties. Giolas recommended more emphasis on vocational status and the client's general attitude toward his handicap. In this connection, the original article by

High, Fairbanks, and Glorig pointed out that in a predevelopment survey a number of otolaryngologists and audiologists suggested these areas be limited. Giolas advocated more detailed collection of information on whether the hearing loss has been a handicap for the client. If so, a refined analysis should be made of the problem areas, perhaps in the form of a profile that would allow a customized rehabilitative treatment program. He favored emphasis on diagnostic information relevant to rehabilitative prescription instead of an audiometric data aimed more at prognosis. Several subtests, each concerned with a different problem area, were recommended.

A self-rating scale similar to the HHS has been developed in Norway by Quist-Hanssen (1966). Again the test subjects were quite homogeneous with good speech discrimination. According to the ratings, communication problems first arose in church and the theater, in group conversations, and lastly on the telephone.

Several reports in the literature have looked for audiometric measures that correlate with ability to communicate in everyday life. One of the earliest efforts to predict everyday communicative effectiveness from clinical measures was the Social Adequacy Index (SAI) introduced by Davis (1948). The SAI score was based on two variables, the individual's hearing loss for speech obtained from a threshold value for spondee words, sentences, or other speech material, and his discrimination loss obtained in a suprathreshold level. The SAI could take on values from 0 to 100, with 94–100 considered the range of normal hearing. A score of 67 indicated the beginning of social difficulty; an SAI of 33 was the threshold of social adequacy. Schoenkerman (1965) found a strong relationship between SAI scores and the average discrimination score of normal hearing subjects tested with CID W-22 word lists at 33 dB, 48 dB, and 63 dB. Giolas (1966) compared SAI values resulting from a Harvard PB-50 list, a CID W-22 list, and a CID Sentence list, with performance scores obtained on a sample of continuous discourse. The CID Sentence list was found to yield the highest SAI scores and to best represent ability to understand continuous discourse. Monosyllabic words produced lower SAI scores, particularly the PB-50 list.

Research by Kryter (1963), Webster (1964), and Harris (1965) investigated the relationship between pure tone threshold measures and the intelligibility of everyday speech. All of these investigators concluded that estimates of impairment for everyday speech could be evaluated more accurately by thresholds at 1000, 2000, and 3000 Hz than at 500, 1000, and 2000 Hz, the combination adopted by the American Academy of Ophthalmology and Otolaryngology.

Carhart (1968), in discussing the future of audiological diagnostic procedures, cited the need for tests that measure listening efficiency under difficult conditions, if one is concerned with evaluating handicap in social situations. He noted that the tendency in clinical evaluation of hearing impairment is to ignore the everyday communication aspects. He also observed that there are really only two fairly well-standardized and commonly used speech tests, namely, the SRT and the monosyllabic word test. The kinds of tests that he offered as valuable additions included accelerated speech and competing message tests.

The Semi-Diagnostic Test materials developed by Hutton et al. (1959) broaden the usual concept of deficit measurement by the inclusion of visual and auditory-visual stimulus material in addition to the traditional auditory test. In clinical application, multiple-choice word lists are presented under three different conditions: auditory only, visual only (lipreading), and combined auditory and visual cues. The testers administered the test to both normal-hearing and hard-of-hearing subjects. The thirty hearing-impaired subjects, spanning the ages from 8 to 71, were assigned to one of these three classifications: primarily conductive loss, mixed loss, or sensorineural loss. Semi-Diagnostic test scores differentiated among classifications more effectively than CID W-22 scores. Although visual scores were all low, the sensorineural group had considerably higher scores than the conductive subjects. It was concluded that the approach seemed sensitive to distinctions among subjects within groups as well as between groups.

Frisina (1967) suggested a classification that included background information and selected cognitive functions in his schema for selecting among various rehabilitative treatments. He advocated a description of the client in terms of his ability to handle information input, storage, and retrieval. Each of the three major categories was viewed as a continuum on which each client could be ranked, with a score of 1 representing the least severe problem and 4 the most severe. Expanding somewhat, the code for input was based upon the past history of the client, the availability of varied experiences to him, his socioeconomic status, and the integrity of his sensory system and overall physical condition. Storage of information processing related to central nervous system functioning and how the material, once it had been received, was stored for future use. The third dimension, retrieval, was related to short-term and long-term memory processes, abstraction, and expressive output of the client. Frisina indicated that after initial evaluation of these three dimensions and the assignment of a three-numbered profile, the ratings would have to be reassessed frequently as the process of rehabilitation proceeded.

Thus, there are a number of different approaches to dealing with the broader notion of handicap as compared to auditory deficit while still remaining in the general area of receptive auditory performance.

No scheme has been accepted clinically, however, and empirical validation of those procedures suggested is necessary.

Auditory Handicap Typology

There have been some attempts to classify hearing handicap, prompted by those responsible for the special education of children, by those making surveys of hearing handicap, and by the military. In the following discussion these questions will be raised: (1) What are the classifications of handicap associated with hearing loss? (2) Are the classifications of hearing handicap based upon research?

The U.S. Department of Health, Education, and Welfare (1965), using an interview survey technique, reported the development of a scale to measure functional hearing ability. This report concluded that the hearing scale as developed is a satisfactory measure, for statistical purposes, of the degree of hearing loss in the population. Several samples of persons were processed with the instrument. The survey results led to four suggested classifications of hearing impairment:

Category 1—unable to hear and understand speech (persons assert they cannot hear or understand without a hearing aid although they may just be able to distinguish speech from other sounds).

Category 2—limited speech perception where persons can hear and understand only a little of what is said.

Category 3—can hear and understand most speech, which can be considered a slight hearing impairment.

Category 4—unilateral hearing loss has separate mention.

An additional group of persons in the sample could not be classified because of the nature of their responses.

Davis and Silverman (1970) discussed in detail the principles and procedures for handicap classification and evaluation recommended by the Committee on Conservation of Hearing of the American Academy of Ophthalmology and Otolaryngology. They state that

Ideally, hearing handicap should be evaluated in terms of ability to hear everyday speech under everyday conditions. The ability to hear sentences and repeat them correctly in a quiet environment is taken as satisfactory evidence of correct hearing for everyday speech. However, because of present limitations of speech audiometry, the preferred procedure is to *estimate the hearing-threshold level for speech from air-conduction measurements made with a pure-tone audiometer.* For this estimate the Committee on Conservation of Hearing recommends *the simple average of the hearing-threshold levels (in decibels) at the three frequencies 500, 1000, and 2000 Hz.*

Recommendations for calculating percentage of handicap are stated as follows:

For every decibel that the estimated hearing-threshold level for speech exceeds 26 dB (ISO), or 15 dB by the American Standard of 1951, allow one-and-one-half percent in handicap of hearing, up to a maximum of 100 percent. This maximum is reached at 93 dB (ISO) or at 82 dB by the American Standard of 1951.

The Committee further recommends that any method for the evaluation of hearing handicap should include an appropriate formula for binaural hearing which will be based on the hearing-threshold levels in each ear tested separately. Specifically, the Committee recommends the following formula: The percentage of handicap of hearing in the better ear is multiplied by five (5). The resulting figure is added to the percentage of handicap of hearing in the poorer ear, and the sum is divided by six (6). The final percentage represents the binaural evaluation of hearing handicap.

Although these procedures have been accepted by the American Academy of Ophthalmology and Otolaryngology, they have not been utilized by practicing clinicians and later research has supported a different combination of frequencies. We would contend also that ability to comprehend everyday speech, although a major concern, is but one aspect of handicap associated with hearing loss.

Handicap–Deficit Asymmetry

Because of the uniqueness of each individual and the special demands made by the psychosocial milieu in which he lives, the handicap resulting from a hearing loss will vary among individuals. Such factors as age of the individual, age of onset of the hearing loss, personality characteristics, vocational demands, and family dynamics, as well as the interaction among these variables, all can be important in determining the extent to which a hearing loss handicaps a person. There are well-developed methods for measuring hearing loss, but not for measurement of handicap. There have been, however, some experiments that relate difficulty in communication to various external conditions and to characteristics of the individual.

The following section discusses the relationship of deficit to handicap and seeks to answer several questions: (1) Are there studies that specifically relate measures derived from instruments used to measure handicap and auditory test results? (2) What evidence is there with respect to personal variables that affect the relationships between handicap and deficit? (3) Do stimulus material and environmental conditions affect deficit and handicap relationships?

Handicap Measuring Devices and Auditory Test Results

It was noted that High, Fairbanks, and Glorig (1964) found that scores on the Hearing Handicap Scale (HHS) did not correlate highly with speech discrimination scores. The relationship was stronger between HHS and pure tone thresholds. The close relationship between HHS and measures of pure tone sensitivity has been demonstrated with a variety of different subject groups. Blumenfeld, Bergman, and Millner (1969) administered the Hearing Handicap Scale to an aging population in order to compare scores on the scale with speech discrimination scores based on the Rhyme Test. The experimental sample of fifty-five subjects had a mean age of 58.7 years and a range from 25 to 84 years. Each subject responded to discrimination word lists in conditions of quiet and noise. Scores on the HHS Form A and Form B were correlated with scores on the Rhyme Test for conditions of quiet and noise separately. For the entire sample of subjects correlations ranged from r = −0.51 for HHS Form A and Rhyme Test in noise to r = −0.32 for HHS Form B and Rhyme Test in quiet. Correlations were then recomputed with subjects divided into the two age groups, the younger ages 27 to 59 years, and older ages from 60 to 82 years. Generally, the relationship between HHS scores and Rhyme Test measures were stronger for the older group; the largest correlation was r = −0.55 for Rhyme Test Form A presented in noise and the lowest was r = −0.29 for Form B in noise. This indicates that even when one restricts the sample to the elderly, their ability to discriminate speech stimuli accounts for only a moderate portion of the variability found on the Hearing Handicap Scale.

Berkowitz and Hochberg (1970) also studied the relationship between the Hearing Handicap Scale and audiometric measures in the aged. Audiometric measures included pure tone average (PTA), SRT, discrimination of half-lists of CID W-22 words, and CID Sentence List B. The 100 subjects were categorized into three age ranges, 60 to 69, 70 to 79, and 80 to 89. Significant correlations were found between both HHS–PTA and HHS–SRT except for the 80 to 89-year age group. Only in the 60 to 69-year group was HHS significantly related to speech discrimination. Correlations between HHS and pure tone measures were always considerably stronger than corresponding correlations of HHS and speech measures.

Bode and Oyer (1970) administered the Hearing Handicap Scale to adult subjects with sensorineural losses who were participating in an auditory training experiment. Subjects were divided into high- and low-handicap groups. Although the group with less handicap showed somewhat better discrimination in noise, 69 percent compared to 66 percent, and a lower average SRT, 28 dB versus 32 dB, correlations were very low between HHS scores and these measures. Predictive power for individuals was negligible. The authors suggested that the homogeneous nature of hearing losses in their sample might have obscured the relationship to some extent.

Speaks et al. (1970) tested a varied group of subjects in an investigation of the relationship between pure tone average, sentence identification, word discrimination, and handicap in everyday communication. The sample exhibited a wide range of HHS scores that indicated handicap levels from 6 percent to 100 percent. Sensitivity measures correlated most highly with HHS scores; the highest was the correlation between HHS and PTA, r = –0.72. Discrimination measures were always less closely related to HHS. No combination of sensitivity and discrimination measures provided better predictive value than sensitivity measures alone. The authors suggested the need for a more sensitive measure of handicap.

If we assume that speech discrimination performance is related to handicap more closely than are pure tone threshold measures, it is clear that the Hearing Handicap Scale measures deficit rather than handicap. Since sentence discrimination has been found to predict intelligibility of continuous discourse in studies reported earlier, the results of Speaks et al. are particularly interesting. HHS scores were related more closely to pure tone average than to Synthetic Sentence Identification scores, rather convincing evidence that HHS does not tap communicative effectiveness.

Personal Variables

Clinicians are aware of the fact that elderly people tend to require more time to process incoming speech signals and they also recognize that speech discrimination in the elderly is not as good as one would expect on the basis of pure tone measures. Gaeth (1948) coined the term *phonemic regression* to describe this condition. Later research has substantiated these observations. Pestalozza and Shore (1955) found that a group of elderly people, all over age 60, showed poorer speech discrimination than one would expect according to the degree of hearing loss. The discrimination loss appeared to be independent of the slope of the audiogram; their discrimination scores, which ranged from 10 percent to 58 percent, were always poorer than those of a younger age group with the same degree of hearing loss.

Harbert et al. (1966) investigated discrimination ability in the aged under difficult speech listening conditions. They found that discrimination for distorted speech was much poorer for presbycusics and that distortion had a greater effect on their discrimination performance than it did for either normal-hearing subjects or nonprogressive congenitally hard-of-hearing persons, all of whom had similar audiometric configurations, but who were younger.

In a study by Blumenfeld, Bergman, and Millner (1969) performance on the Rhyme Test was analyzed as a function of age. The authors concluded that there is a tendency for increasing age to be associated with lower scores on the speech discrimination Rhyme Test in quiet.

When noise was introduced, responses became variable and correlations were considerably lower.

In terms of the concept of handicap, it would seem that given the same needs for receptive communication, the elderly person often experiences a handicap greater than a younger person for a given degree of hearing. This is reflected in speech discrimination deficiencies and possibly psychological emotional problems for the more severe cases of impairment.

Personality. The handicap-deficit asymmetry shows itself in several separate, but related, responses of hearing-impaired persons. First, regarding hearing aid adjustment, Pauls and Hardy (1948) hypothesized that clients with hearing levels in the 35–70 dB range would be most receptive to hearing aid usage and training because their handicap is self-evident. Contrary to this reasoning, they found that those with moderate losses actually exhibited great difficulty in adjustment to amplification. They attributed this to the need to adapt to constantly changing situations and to overoptimistic anticipation of benefits from amplified sound. In related research, Myklebust (1963) reported that the hard of hearing, in a self-rating situation, considered their handicap greater than deaf respondents.

Pauls and Hardy (1948) also mentioned type of personality as a factor in degree of resistance to disrupted communication associated with hearing deficit. They stated that individuals with stable personalities could more easily readjust through rehabilitative treatment than persons of unstable personality, who might suffer depression and other side effects. This could lead in some cases to suspicion and hypersensitivity, with accompanying feelings of lack of self-confidence. Although the hard of hearing may in some situations experience greater difficulty in adjusting to their handicap, Myklebust (1963) found that the greater the degree of hearing loss, the more emotional problems there were. Social maturity, the ability to care for oneself, was less well developed in the deaf, and this was more marked for adults than children.

Research on personality variables is characterized generally by a lack of quantitative measures, which contributes to the difficulty in comparing one study with another. At this point, the safest conclusion seems to be that the personality structure of the deaf and hard of hearing may affect their reaction to hearing impairment, but one cannot specify as yet the precise relationship.

Environmental Conditions and Type of Stimulation

The relationship that exists between deficit and handicap should not be thought of as static. On the contrary, it is a relationship that is dynamic and that varies as a function of the stimuli which the hard of hearing are called upon to utilize in communicative situations. Additionally, the setting in which communication is attempted has a direct bearing upon the relationship of deficit to handicap.

The literature provides some evidence concerning the relationships among nature of deficit, type of stimuli, and environmental conditions. Throughout the course of the discussion that follows, evidence will bear on these questions: (1) What are the effects of the nature of deficit and environmental conditions on deficit-handicap relationships? (2) What are the specific effects of stimulus input on deficit-handicap relationships?

When Pauls and Hardy (1948) discussed factors that enter into the treatment of communicative disorders they noted that persons with sensorineural losses have more difficulty in learning to use amplification than do those with conductive losses. Even with a good hearing aid some clients with sensorineural losses never get clear reproduction of speech with amplification. In the case of conductive losses these problems are usually not so severe, although, if there is a long-term loss the client may have to relearn to ignore noise and distractions from the environment. Pestalozza and Lazzaroni (1954) stated that normal-hearing subjects and subjects with conductive losses may have reduced discrimination scores in the presence of noise, but with increased signal intensity, discrimination scores can approximate 100 percent. In contrast, in perceptive deafness, the effects of noise are to decrease the discrimination score and this cannot be overcome by increases in intensity of the stimulus material.

Tillman and Carhart (1963) demonstrated this phenomenon in an investigation of discrimination performance with a hearing aid (aided) and without a hearing aid (unaided). Subjects included groups of monaural listeners, presbycusics, and listeners with conductive and sensorineural losses. Subjects were tested for discrimination both in quiet and with competing sentences from a second loudspeaker. The signal-noise relation was as follows: The primary message was presented at 30 dB Sensation Level (SL) and the competing sentences were presented at 12 dB SL and at 24 dB SL. Under these conditions all groups showed poorer discrimination in the presence of a competing message, and this deterioration was accentuated under the aided condition. However, both young adults with sensorineural losses and presbycusics were much more affected by the presence of the competing speech than other subjects under aided conditions. Carhart and Tillman (1970) employed the same listening task in a later experiment. Four groups of six subjects had normal hearing, conductive losses, sensorineural losses with good discrimination, or sensorineural losses with poor discrimination. Subjects listened individually to monosyllabic word lists with a competing message. Two different conditions applied: (1) in a direct condition, words were presented on the side of the test ear and competing sentences were directed toward the nontest ear, and (2) in the indirect condition, words were presented toward the nontest ear and competing sentences toward the test ear. To effect these conditions loudspeakers were located at 45-degree angles to either side of front center. Effective primary to secondary signal ratios for the direct condition were 18.4, 12.4, 6.4, and 0.4 dB. For the indirect test conditions ratios were 5.6, –0.4, –6.4, and –12.4 dB. Normal-hearing subjects and subjects with conductive losses had almost identical articulation functions as a function of primary to secondary ratio. Articulation functions of the sensorineural group with good discrimination were displaced about 12 dB for both direct and indirect listening tasks. Sensorineural subjects with poorer discrimination were differentially affected by the direct and indirect listening tasks. Under the direct condition a consistent displacement of 15 dB was found as primary/secondary ratio decreased. For the indirect case the shift was greater and the slope of the articulation function decreased with decreasing P/S ratio. Thus we see that the influence on discrimination of the direction of the incoming speech and noise varies with the type of deficit.

Giolas and Ward (1967) described the reaction of subjects with unilateral hearing losses to the problem of directional input. They used a Critical Incidence Technique to determine the precise conditions under which their subjects experienced the most communicative difficulty. In the unilateral case it appeared that the most difficulty occurred with noise and in localizing sound sources. In addition, the subjects found it common to have a negative feeling in a difficult listening situation when the listener was a stranger and they had to explain their hearing loss to him. The method of overcoming some difficulties was to position the good ear toward the message source and to make use of visual cues.

Watson's (1965) investigation of partially hearing children who were experienced aid users found a relationship between type of deficit and speech discrimination similar to that reported by Tillman and Carhart. Watson questioned whether discrimination measurement under quiet conditions in the clinic would be representative of the performance of children in a classroom. Test material for this experiment was recorded in a sound-insulated room and also in an ordinary classroom with thirty pupils and an ambient noise level of 55–60 dB. Children with sloping audiograms of more than 10 dB drop per octave were more affected by the change from quiet to noise than those with flatter audiograms. The drop in discrimination scores for the group as a whole was on the order of 30 percent. For the subgroup with sloping high frequency loss the reduction was approximately 60 percent.

These studies exemplify the interaction of the variables that go into making up handicap. Although the primary variable here was type of deficit, it was not possible to evaluate the influence of the different types without considering additional factors such as presence of noise and communicative setting. The major agreement in these studies was that individuals with sensorineural losses are most adversely affected by introduction of competing signals.

Undoubtedly, there is other evidence of handicap-deficit asymmetry in the literature. For example, one can argue that if lipreading ability is not strongly correlated with extent of hearing deficit an asymmetry exists. Given the same degree of loss, a good lip reader is less handicapped than a poor lip reader. Few experiments have focused directly on the asymmetry concept. Systematic research would be valuable in further detailing the nature of the handicap that frequently accompanies hearing deficit.

Summary

A review of the literature reveals that a great deal of scientific research has been accomplished in the area of auditory deficit, and as a result there are scientifically based tests available for the measurement of auditory function. Procedures for determination of air-conducted and bone-conducted thresholds are described. On the basis of research, the Hughson-Westlake procedure for testing air conduction has been endorsed by the Committee on Conservation of Hearing of the American Academy of Ophthalmology and Otolaryngology. In testing speech-hearing, speech reception threshold and speech discrimination are the primary standardized measures. Most practicing clinicians employ the CID Auditory Test W-1 for SRT and the CID W-22 lists for discrimination testing. There also are special tests for determining the site of lesion in the auditory pathway. The SISI test and loudness balance tests for recruitment are ones that provide relevant information to the audiologist.

For children, pure tone tests based on operant procedures often are recommended at the younger age range. Procedures derived from the peep-show technique, play audiometry, and tangible reinforcement procedures are considered as examples of operant conditioning. Among objective procedures, impedance measures show increasing usefulness and evoked response audiometry finds application as a special test. Several speech reception threshold tests are available for children although little is known about the relation between SRT and pure tone thresholds. Comparisons among speech discrimination tests find the WIPI recommended for very young children and the PBK-50 for children 5½ years and older if the child has normal speech and language.

Typologies of hearing loss are frequently based on site of lesion although some are diagnostic for differentiating auditory impairment from other disorders in children.

Auditory handicap is discussed in relation to cognitive and perceptual processes. Upon comparing normal-hearing and acoustically handicapped children, the literature reveals no difference in intelligence when performance tests are employed. It is noted that deaf children perform less successfully than hearing children on many abstract tasks; however, there is disagreement on the proper interpretation of these findings. The literature also suggests that children sustaining auditory handicaps function less well on a number of visual memory tasks and in some aspects of visual perception.

Serious disruption of speech and language development is characteristic of children with hearing deficits. If children have severe congenital hearing losses, speech intelligibility is severely affected. Several researchers report that their most intelligible speech sounds and those that are most frequently produced are also the sounds with the greatest visibility. Less severe articulatory errors emerge in acquired hearing loss. Several voicing problems also are described.

Oral language production of deaf children is less well developed than that of hearing children. Experimenters characterize the sentences of deaf children as simple and stereotyped. Knowledge of syntax and usage of function words are not well developed. Misuse of main verbs contributes substantially to errors of production. The rate of improvement in language production with age is much slower than for normal-hearing children and there is greater variability within age levels. Performance of hard-of-hearing children appears to be superior to that of deaf children and more similar to hearing children. Written language production exhibits similar developmental delays. One experiment on the comprehension and production of passive sentences finds performance of deaf children equivalent to 6-year-old hearing children. Although we speak of delays in development it is not clear that deaf children follow the same stages of development as normal-hearing children. Some tests of language development are discussed, and difficulties related to test construction for hearing-handicapped children are noted.

Review of research on measurement of handicap indicates that available measures correlate highly with pure tone sensitivity but not with speech discrimination of words or sentences. An instrument sensitive to handicap associated with hearing loss is still needed.

It is apparent that an asymmetry can exist between deficit and handicap as a function of the individual involved. That is to say that not all persons with the same type and degree of hearing loss will be affected by it in the same way, for the utility of hearing is largely dependent upon the daily demands made upon an individual.

RECOMMENDATIONS

The following recommendations emerge from a review and evaluation of the literature dealing with the measurement and evaluation of hearing deficit and handicap. It is recommended that research be directed toward—

1. refinement and standardization of objective procedures for measuring auditory deficit of young children for pure tones and for speech
2. standardization of presently developed auditory tests not yet accepted for routine clinical testing, for example, the Synthetic Sentence Identification Test, Aural Overload, Critical Off-Time, and others
3. determination of the intelligibility of speech of the acoustically handicapped
4. delineating further the language problems of the preschool deaf child
5. determination of the relative importance of the contribution that can be made to language development of the acoustically handicapped child by using sensory pathways in addition to the auditory
6. acquiring normative measures of language proficiency among hearing handicapped
7. defining the norms for voice quality of speakers so as to have a frame of reference for the acoustically handicapped
8. determination of optimal levels of expressive communicative performance
9. development of a valid and reliable instrument for measuring handicap associated with hearing loss for children as well as adults
10. exploration of the memory encoding and decoding processes of the deaf
11. investigation of the interrelationships of lipreading skill, language development, visual perception, and cognition

12. scaling of the vocational situations in which hearing is very important, less important, and so on
13. development of an instrument that measures one's emotional reaction to his hearing impairment
14. the development of a classification or typology for auditory handicap
15. isolating and evaluating such factors as age, personality, educational level, vocational demands, and the like, that contribute toward the deficit-handicap asymmetry phenomenon
16. determining the extent of congruence between an individual's assessment of his hearing handicap and the assessment by those in his environment
17. construction of data-based formulas for predicting hearing handicap
18. determining whether or not family composition affects hearing deficit-handicap relationship
19. assessing the life-style of a family unit and its influence upon the deficit-handicap asymmetry
20. determining the relative contribution that message variables such as familiarity of the code, semantic content, and prosodic features of language make to the hearing deficit-handicap relationship
21. the measurement of the importance of skills in using other sensory channels that affect the hearing deficit-handicap relationship
22. determining the effects of extrafamily nonvocational social interactions on hearing deficit-handicap relationship
23. determining the effects of counseling upon the deficit-handicap relationship
24. development of scientifically derived procedures for placement of hearing-impaired individuals into educational and rehabilitative programs
25. measuring the effects of amplification upon the hearing deficit-handicap relationship

References

American National Standards Institute (1970). Specifications for audiometers S3.6–1969. New York: American National Standards Institute.

American Standards Association (1951). Audiometers for general diagnostic purposes. Z24.5–1951. American Standards Association, Inc., 70 East 45th Street, New York City.

Angelocci, A. A. (1962). Some observations on the speech of the deaf. *Volta Rev.,* 64, 403–405.

Angelocci, A. A., Kopp, G. A., and Holbrook, A. (1964). The vowel formants of deaf and normal-hearing eleven- to fourteen-year old boys. *J. Speech Hearing Dis.,* 29, 156–170.

Barker, J. O. (1960). A numerical measure of articulation. *J. Speech Hearing Dis.,* 25, 79–88.

Barker, J. O., and England, G. (1962). A numerical measure of articulation: Further developments. *J. Speech Hearing Dis.,* 27, 23–27.

Barr, B. (1955). Pure tone audiometry for preschool children. *Acta Oto-Laryng. Suppl.,* 121.

Berkowitz, A. O., and Hochberg, I. (1970). Self-assessment of hearing handicap in the aged. *Arch. Otolaryng.,* 92, 25–28.

Berlinsky, S. (1952). Measurement of the intelligence and personality of the deaf: A review of the literature. *J. Speech Hearing Dis.,* 17, 39–54.

Binnie, C., Elkind, D., and Stewart, J. (1966). A comparison of the visual perceptual ability of acoustically-impaired and hearing children. *Int. Audiol.,* 5, 238–241.

Blake, K. A., Ainsworth, S. H., and Williams, C. L. (1971). Paired associate rote learning in deaf and hearing subjects. *J. Speech Hearing Res.,* 14, 106–112.

Blumenfeld, V. G., Bergman, M., and Millner, E. (1969). Speech discrimination in an aging population. *J. Speech Hearing Res.,* 12, 210–217.

Bode, D. L., and Oyer, H. J. (1970). Auditory training and speech discrimination. *J. Speech Hearing Res.,* 13, 839–855.

Boone, D. R. (1966). Infant speech and language development. *Audecibel,* 15, 80–86, 88.

Bradley, W. H. (1959). Some relationships between pitch discrimination and speech development. *Laryngoscope,* 68, 422–437.

Brannon, Jr., J. B. (1968). Linguistic word classes in the spoken language of normal, hard-of-hearing, and deaf children. *J. Speech Hearing Res.,* 11, 279–287.

Brannon, Jr., J. B., and Murray, T. (1966). The spoken syntax of normal, hard-of-hearing, and deaf children. *J. Speech Hearing Res.,* 9, 604–610.

Calvert, D. R. (1962a). Speech duration and surd-sonant error, *Volta Rev.,* 64, 401–402.

Calvert, D. R. (1962b). Deaf-voice: A preliminary investigation. *Volta Rev.,* 64, 402–403.

Calvert, D. R. (1964). An approach to the study of deaf speech. Report of the Proceedings of the International Congress on Education of the Deaf. Gallaudet College, June 22–28, 1963. Washington, D.C.: U.S. Government Printing Office.

Carhart, R. (1951). Basic principles of speech audiometry. *Acta Oto-Laryng., 40*, 62–71.

Carhart, R. (1968). Future horizons in audiologic diagnosis. *Ann. Otol. Rhinol. Laryng., 77*, 706–716.

Carhart, R., and Jerger, J. (1959). Preferred method for clinical determination of pure-tone thresholds. *J. Speech Hearing Dis., 24*, 330–345.

Carhart, R., and Porter, L. S. (1971). Audiometric configuration and prediction of threshold for spondees. *J. Speech Hearing Res., 14*, 486–495.

Carhart, R., and Tillman, T. W. (1970). Interaction of competing speech signals with hearing losses. *Arch. Otolaryng., 91*, 273–279.

Carlin, T. W. (1968). Spectrographic presentation of the vocal quality of partially hearing school children. *Int. Audiol., 7*, 96–101.

Carr, J. (1953). An investigation of the spontaneous speech sounds of five-year-old deaf-born children. *J. Speech Hearing Dis., 18*, 22–29.

Carter, N. L., and Kryter, K. D. (1962). Masking of pure tones and speech. *J. Aud. Res., 2*, 66–98.

Chovan, W. L., and McGettigan, J. F. (1971). The effects of vocal mediating responses on visual motor tasks with deaf and hearing children. *Except. Child., 37*, 435–440.

Cody, T. R., Griffing, T., and Taylor, W. F. (1968). Assessment of the newer tests of auditory function. *Ann Otol. Rhinol. Laryng., 77*, 686–705.

Colton, R. H., and Cooker, H. S. (1968). Perceived nasality in the speech of the deaf. *J. Speech Hearing Res., 11*, 553–559.

Conrad, R. (1971). The effect of vocalizing on comprehension in the profoundly deaf. *Brit. J. Psych., 62*, 147–150.

Conrad, R. (1973). Some correlates of speech coding in the short-term memory of the deaf. *J. Speech Hearing Res., 16*, 375–384.

Conrad, R., and Rush, M. L. (1965). On the nature of short-term memory encoding by the deaf. *J. Speech Hearing Dis., 30*, 336–343.

Craig, H. B. (1965). A sociometric investigation of the self-concept of the deaf child. *Amer. Ann. Deaf, 110*, 456–473.

Dahle, A. J., Hume, W. G., and Haspiel, G. S. (1968). Comparison of speech Bekesy tracings with selected clinical auditory measures. *J. Aud. Res., 8*, 125–128.

Davis, H. (1948). The articulation area and the Social Adequacy Index for Hearing. *Laryngoscope, 58*, 761–778.

Davis, H. (1962). A functional classification of auditory effects. *Ann. Otol. Rhinol. Laryng., 71*, 693–704.

Davis, H., and Goldstein, R. (1970). "Audiometry: Other Auditory Tests." In H. Davis and S. R. Silverman, *Hearing and Deafness*, New York: Holt, Rinehart and Winston, pp. 221–252.

Davis, H., Hirsh, S. K., Shelnutt, J., and Bowers, C. (1967). Further validation of Evoked Response Audiometry (ERA). *J. Speech Hearing Res.,* 10, 717–732.

Davis H., and Silverman, R. (1970). *Hearing and Deafness,* 3d ed. New York; Holt, Rinehart and Winston.

Dirks, D. (1964). Factors related to bone conduction reliability. *Arch. Otolaryng.,* 79, 551–558.

Dix, M. R., and Hallpike, C. S. (1947). The Peep Show: A new technique for pure tone audiometry in young children. *Brit. Med. J.,* 2, 719–723.

Doehring, D. C., and Rosenstein, J. (1969). Speed of visual perception in deaf children. *J. Speech Hearing Res.,* 12, 118–125.

Egan, J. P. (1948). Articulation testing method. *Laryngoscope,* 58, 955–991.

Espeseth, V. K. (1969). An investigation of visual-sequential memory in deaf children. *Amer. Ann. Deaf,* 114, 786–789.

Ewing, Sir, S. W. G. (1963). Linguistic development and mental growth in hearing impaired children. *Volta Rev.,* 65, 180–187.

Fairbanks, G. (1958). Test of phonemic differentiation: The Rhyme Test. *J. Acoust. Soc. Amer.,* 30, 596–600.

Farrant, R. H. (1964). The intellective abilities of deaf and hearing children compared by factor analysis. *Amer. Ann. Deaf,* 109, 306–325.

Feldman, A. S. (1961). Problems in the measurement of bone conduction. *J. Speech Hearing Dis.,* 26, 39–44.

Feldman, A. S. (1964). Acoustic impedance measurement as a clinical procedure. *Int. Audiol.,* 3, 156–166.

Fletcher, H. (1950a). A method of calculating hearing loss for speech from an audiogram. *J. Acoust. Soc. Amer.,* 22, 1–5.

Fletcher, H. (1950b). A method of calculating hearing loss for speech from an audiogram. *Acta Oto-Laryng. Suppl.,* 90, 26–37.

Frisina, R. (1967). Diagnostic evaluation and recommendations for placement. *Volta Rev.,* 69, 436–442.

Fulton, R. T., and Lloyd, L. L. (1969). *Audiometry for the Retarded with Implications for the Difficult to Test.* Baltimore: The Williams and Wilkins Company.

Furth, H. G. (1961). Visual paired-associates task with deaf and hearing children. *J. Speech Hearing Res.,* 4, 172–177.

Furth, H. G. (1966). Research with the deaf: Implications for language and cognition. *Volta Rev.,* 68, 34–56.

Gaeth, J. H. (1948). A study of phonemic regression associated with hearing loss. Unpublished Doctoral dissertation, Northwestern University.

Giolas, T. G. (1966). Effectiveness of the Social Adequacy Index. *Ann. Otol. Rhinol. Laryng.,* 75, 1111–1116.

Giolas, T. G. (1970). The measurement of hearing handicap: A point of view. Maico Hearing Instruments, *Audiological Library Series,* Vol. 8, Report 6.

Giolas, T. G., and Ward, D. J. (1967). Communication problems associated with unilateral hearing loss. *J. Speech Hearing Dis.,* 32, 336–343.

Goda, S. (1959). Language skills of profoundly deaf adolescent children. *J. Speech Hear. Res.,* 2, 369–376.

Goetzinger, C. P., and Huber, T. G. (1964). A study of immediate and delayed visual retention with deaf and hearing adolescents. *Amer. Ann. Deaf.* 109, 297–305.

Goetzinger, C. P., Proud, G. O., and Embrey, J. E. (1962). Masking in bone conduction. *Acta Oto-Laryng.,* 54, 287–291.

Goldstein, R. (1967). "Electrophysiologic Evaluation of Hearing." In *Deafness in Children,* McConnell, F., and Ward, P. H., eds. Nashville, Tenn.: Vanderbilt University Press.

Goldstein, R., Kendall, D. C., and Arick, B. E. (1963). Electroencephalic audiometry in young children. *J. Speech Hearing Dis.,* 28, 331–354.

Green, H. (1958). The Pup-Show: A simple, inexpensive modification of the Peep-Show. *J. Speech Hearing Dis.,* 23, 118–120.

Guilford, F. R., and Haug, C. O. (1952). Diagnosis of deafness in the very young child. *Arch. Otolaryng.,* 55, 101–106.

Guilford, F. R., and Haug, C. O. (1960). Hearing testing in the very young child. *Trans. Amer. Acad. Ophthal. Otolaryng.,* 4, 269–271.

Harbert, F., Young, I. M., and Menduke, R. (1966). Audiologic findings in presbycusis. *J. Aud. Res.,* 6, 297–312.

Hardick, E. J. (1964). The self-concept of hard-of-hearing adults as measured by the semantic differential technique. Unpublished Doctoral dissertation, Michigan State University.

Hardy, W. G., and Bordley, J. E. (1951). Special techniques in testing the hearing of children. *J. Speech Hearing Dis.,* 16, 122–131.

Hardy, W. G., Pauls, M. D., and Haskins, H. L. (1958). An analysis of language development in children with impaired hearing. *Acta Oto-Laryng. Suppl.,* 141.

Harris, J. D. (1965). Pure-tone acuity and the intelligibility of everyday speech. *J. Acoust. Soc. Amer.,* 37, 824–830.

Hart, B. O., and Rosenstein, J. (1964). Examining the language behavior of deaf children. *Volta Rev.,* 66, 679–682.

Hartman, J. S., and Elliot, L. L. (1965). Performance of deaf and hearing children on a short-term memory task. *Psychonom. Sci.,* 3, 573–574.

Haskins, H L. (1949). A phonetically balanced test of speech discrimination for children. Unpublished Master's thesis, Northwestern University.

Heider, F. K., and Heider, G. M. (1940a). A comparison of sentence structure of deaf and hearing children. *Psych. Monogr.,* 52, 42–103.

Heider, F. K., and Heider, G. M. (1940b). A study of the spontaneous vocalizations of young deaf children. *Psych. Monogr.,* 52, 104–123.

High, W. S., Fairbanks, G., and Glorig, A. (1964). Scale for self-assessment of hearing handicap. *J. Speech Hearing Dis.,* 29, 215–229.

Hirsh, I. J. (1950). Pathology in speech communication. *J. Acoust. Soc. Amer.,* 22, 717–719.

Hirsh, I. J., Davis, H., Silverman, S. R., Reynolds, E. G., Eldert, E., and Benson, R. W. (1952). Development of materials for speech audiometry. *J. Speech Hearing Dis.,* 17, 321–337.

Hood, J. D. (1957). The principles and practice of bone conduction audiometry: A review of the present position. *Proc. Roy. Soc. Med.,* 50, 689–697.

Hood, J. D. (1962). Bone conduction. *J. Acoust. Soc. Amer.,* 34, 1325–1332.

Hoops, R. A., and Curry, E. T. (1963). Certain factors affecting a study of bone-conduction thresholds. *Laryngoscope,* 73, 34–53.

Hughes, R. B. (1961). Verbal conceptualization in deaf and hearing children. *Except. Children,* 27, 517–522.

Hughson, W., and Westlake, H. (1944). Manual for program outline for rehabilitation of aural casualties both military and civilian. *Trans. Amer. Acad. Ophthal. Otolaryng. Suppl.,* 48.

Hunt, K. W. (1965). *Grammatical structures written at three grade levels.* NCTE Research Report No. 3. Champaign, Ill.: National Council of Teachers of English.

Hurley, R. M., and Berger, K. W. (1970). The relationship between vibrator placement and bone conduction measurements with monaurally deaf subjects. *J. Aud. Res.,* 10, 147–150.

Hutton, C., Curry, E. T., and Armstrong, M. B. (1959). Semi-Diagnostic Test materials for aural rehabilitation. *J. Speech Hearing˙ Dis.,* 24, 319–328.

Ives, L. A. (1967). Deafness and the development of intelligence *Brit. J. Dis. Comm.,* 2, 96–111.

Jerger, J. (1968). Review of diagnostic audiometry. *Ann. Otol. Rhinol. Laryng.,* 77, 1042–1052.

Jerger, J. (1970). Clinical experience with impedance audiometry. *Arch. Otolaryng.,* 92, 311–324.

Jerger, J., Shedd, J. L., and Harford, E. (1959). On the detection of extremely small changes in sound intensity. *Arch. Otolaryng.,* 69, 200–211.

Jerger, J., Speaks, C., and Trammell, J. L. (1968). A new approach to speech audiometry. *J. Speech Hearing Dis.,* 33, 318–328.

Jerger, J., and Tillman, T. (1960). A new method for the clinical determination of Sensorineural Acuity Level (SAL). *Arch. Otolaryng.,* 71, 948–955.

Johnson, W., Darley, F. L., and Spriestersbach, D. C. (1963). *Diagnostic Methods in Speech Pathology.* New York: Harper & Row.

Keaster, J. (1947). A quantitative method of testing the hearing of young children. *J. Speech Dis.,* 12, 159–160.

Kohl, H. R. (1967). *Language and the Education of the Deaf.* New York: Center for Urban Education.

König, E. (1963). The use of masking noise and its limitations in clinical audiometry. *Acta Oto-Laryng. Suppl.,* 180.

Kreul, J. E., Nixon, J. C., Kryter, K. D., Bell, D. W., Lang, J. S., and Schubert, E. D. (1968). A proposed clinical test of speech discrimination. *J. Speech Hearing Res.,* 11, 536–552.

Kryter, K. D. (1963). Hearing impairment for speech. *Arch. Otolaryng.,* 77, 598–602.

La Brant, L. L. (1933). A study of certain language developments of children in grades four to twelve, inclusive. *Genetic Psych. Monogr.,* 14, 387–491.

Lee, L. L. (1970). A screening test for syntax development. *J. Speech Hearing Dis.,* 35, 103–112.

Lee, L. L., and Canter, S. M. (1971). Developmental Sentence Scoring: A clinical procedure for estimating syntactic development in children's spontaneous speech. *J. Speech Hearing Dis.,* 36, 315–340.

Lerman, J., Ross, M., and McLaughlin, R. (1965). A picture identification test for hearing impaired children. *J. Aud. Res.,* 5, 273–279.

Levine, E. S. (1963). Studies in psychological evaluation of the deaf. *Volta Rev.,* 65, 496–512.

Liden, G., and Kankkunen, A. (1959). Visual reinforcement audiometry. *Arch. Otolaryng.,* 69, 200–211.

Lightfoot, C. (1960). The M-R Test of bone conduction hearing. *Laryngoscope,* 70, 1552–1559.

Lightfoot, C., Carhart, R., and Gaeth, J. H. (1956). Masking of impaired ears by noise. *J. Speech Hearing Dis.,* 21, 56–70.

Ling, A. H. (1971). Dichotic listening and hearing-impaired children. *J. Speech Hearing Res.,* 14, 793–803.

Lloyd, L. L., Spradlen, J. E., and Reid, M. J. (1968). An operant audiometric procedure for difficult-to-test patients. *J. Speech Hearing Dis.,* 33, 236–245.

Locke, J. L. (1969). Short-term memory, oral perception, and experimental sound learning. *J. Speech Hearing Res.,* 12, 185–192.

Lowell, E. L., and Metfessel, N. S. (1961). Experimental concept formation test for preschool deaf. *J. Speech Hearing Dis.,* 26, 225–229.

Lowell, E., Rushford, G., Holversten, G., and Stoner, M. (1956). Evaluation of pure tone audiometry with preschool age children. *J. Speech Hearing Dis.,* 292–302.

MacGinitie, W. H. (1964). Ability of deaf children to use different word classes. *J. Speech Hearing Res.,* 7, 141–150.

Marshall, W. J. A., and Quigley, S. P. (1970). Quantitative and qualitative analysis of syntactic structure in the written language of hearing-impaired students. Institute for Research on Exceptional Children, University of Illinois.

Martin, F. N., and Pennington, C. D. (1971). Current trends in audiometric practices. *Asha,* 13, 671–677.

Martin, F. N., and Wittich, W. W. (1966). A comparison of forehead and mastoid tactile bone-condition thresholds. *EENT Mo.,* 45, 72, 74.

McCarthy, J. J., and Kirk, S. A. (1961). *The Illinois Test of Psycholinguistic Abilities: Experimental Edition.* The Institute for Research on Exceptional Children, University of Illinois.

McConnell, F. (ed.), (1968). *Proceedings of the Conference on Current Practices in the Management of Deaf Infants (0–3 Years).* Sponsored by the Joint Committee on Audiology and Education of the Deaf, and The Bill Wilkerson Hearing and Speech Center, Vanderbilt University School of Medicine, Nashville, Tenn. June 21–22.

McNamee, J. (1960). An investigation of the use of the C.I.D. Auditory Test W-22 with children. Unpublished Master's thesis, Ohio State University.

Mecham, M. J. (1959). *Verbal Language Development Scale.* Minneapolis: Educational Test Bureau.

Mecham, M. J., Jex, J. L., and Jones, J. D. (1967). *Utah Test of Language Development (rev. ed.).* Salt Lake City: Communication Research Associates.

Meyerson, L. (1958). Hearing for speech in children: A Verbal Audiometric Test. *Acta Oto-Laryng. Suppl.,* 128.

Meyerson, L., and Michael, J. (1964). Assessment of hearing by operant conditioning procedures. Report of the Proceedings of the International Congress on Education of the Deaf. Gallaudet College, June 22–28, 1963. Washington, D.C.: U.S. Government Printing Office, 236–242.

Myatt, B., and Landes, B. (1963). Assessing discrimination loss in children: A new approach toward a picture test. *Arch. Otolaryn.,* 77, 359–362.

Myklebust, H. R. (1963). Psychological and psychiatric implications of deafness. *Arch. Otolaryng.,* 78, 790–793.

Myklebust, H. R. (1964). Differential diagnosis for the deaf. Report of the Proceedings of the International Congress on Education of the Deaf. Gallaudet College, June 22–28, 1963. Washington, D.C.: U.S. Government Printing Office.

Newby, H. A., and Molyneaux, D. M. (1951). An analysis of 500 cases of hearing disability. *J. Speech Hearing Dis.,* 16, 213–217.

Nielson, K. (1961). Speech sound discrimination of preschool children as measured by the CID Auditory Test W-22. Unpublished Master's thesis, Michigan State University.

Niswander, P. S. (1968). Nonspeech sound discrimination in subjects with impaired hearing. Unpublished Doctoral dissertation, Michigan State University.

Nober, E. H. (1967). Articulation of the deaf. *Except. Children,* 33, 611–621.

Odom, P. B., Blanton, R. L., and McIntyre, C. K. (1970). Coding medium and word recall by deaf and hearing subjects. *J. Speech Hearing Res.,* 13, 54–58.

Odom, P. B., Blanton, R. L., and Nunnally, J. C. (1967). Some cloze technique studies of language capability in the deaf. *J. Speech Hearing Res.,* 10, 816–827.

Olson, J. (1961). Differential diagnosis: Deaf and sensory aphasic children. *Except. Children,* 27, 422–424.

O'Neill, J. J., Oyer, H. J., and Hillis, J. (1961). Audiometric procedures used with children. *J. Speech Hearing Dis.,* 26, 61–66.

Palva, T., and Palva, A. (1962). Masking in audiometry. *Acta Oto-Laryng.,* 54, 521–531.

Pauls, M. D., and Hardy, W. G. (1948). Fundamentals in the treatment of communicative disorders caused by hearing disability, Part II. *J. Speech Hearing Dis.,* 13, 97–105.

Penn, J. P. (1955). Voice and speech patterns of the hard-of-hearing. *Acta Oto-Laryng. Suppl.,* 124.

Pennington, C. D., and Martin, F. N. (1972). Current trends in audiometric practices: Part II. Auditory tests for site of lesion. *Asha,* 14, 199–203.

Pestalozza, G., and Lazzaroni, A. (1954). Noise effect on speech perception in clinical and experimental types of deafness. *Acta Oto-Laryng.,* 44, 350–358.

Pestalozza, G., and Shore, I. (1955). Clinical evaluation of presbycusis on the basis of different tests of auditory function. *Laryngoscope,* 65, 1136–1163.

Power, D. J., and Quigley, S. P. (1973). Deaf children's acquisition of the passive voice. *J. Speech Hearing Res.,* 16, 5–11.

Presnell, L. M. (1973). Hearing impaired children's comprehension and production of syntax in oral language. *J. Speech Hearing Res.,* 16, 12–21.

Price, L., and Goldstein, R. (1966). Averaged evoked responses for measuring auditory sensitivity in children. *J. Speech Hearing Dis.,* 31, 248–256.

Putnam, V., Iscoe, I., and Young, R. K. (1962). Verbal learning in the deaf. *J. Comp. Physiol. Psych.,* 55, 843–846.

Quiggle, R. R., Glorig, A., Delk, J. H., and Summerfield, A. B. (1957). Predicting hearing loss for speech from pure tone audiograms. *Laryngoscope,* 67, 1–15.

Quist-Hanssen, S. (1966). Subjective appraisal and objective assessment of the hearing of speech amongst a group of adults with impaired hearing. *Acta Oto-Laryng. Suppl.*, 224, 177–185.

Rainville, M. J. (1959). New Method of masking for the determination of bone conduction curves. *Translations of the Beltone Institute for Hearing Research*, No. 11, July.

Rapin, I., and Costa, L. D. (1969). Test-retest reliability of serial pure-tone audiograms in children at a school for the deaf. *J. Speech Hearing Res.*, 12, 402–412.

Rapin, I., and Steinberg, P. (1970). Reaction time for pediatric audiometry. *J. Speech Hearing Res.*, 13, 203–217.

Reichstein, J., and Rosenstein, J. (1964). Differential diagnosis of auditory deficits: A review of the literature. *Except. Children*, 31, 73–82.

Rintelmann, W. F. (1973). Five experiments on speech discrimination utilizing CNC monosyllabic words, Report SHSLR 1–73, Department of Audiology and Speech Sciences, Michigan State University.

Ross, M., and Lerman, J. (1970). A picture identification test for hearing-impaired children. *J. Speech Hearing Res.*, 13, 44–53.

Rutledge, L. (1954). Aspiration levels of deaf children as compared with those of hearing children. *J. Speech Hearing Dis.*, 19, 375–380.

Sanders, J. W., and Rintelmann, W. F. (1964). Masking in audiometry. *Arch. Otolaryng.*, 80, 541–556.

Sanderson, M. E. (1972). The articulation functions and test-retest performance of normal hearing children on three speech discrimination tests. Unpublished Doctoral dissertation, Michigan State University.

Schmitt, P. (1968). Deaf children's comprehension and production of sentence transformations and verb tenses. Doctoral dissertation, University of Illinois.

Schoenkerman, B. L. (1965). An empirical evaluation of Social Adequacy Index for Hearing. Unpublished Master's thesis, Michigan State University.

Siegel, G. M., Winitz, H., and Conkey, H. (1963). The influence of testing instrument on articulatory responses of children. *J. Speech Hearing Dis.*, 28, 67–76.

Siegenthaler, B. M., and Haspiel, G. (1966). Development of two standardized measures of hearing for speech by children. Pennsylvania State University.

Siegenthaler, B. M., and Kaplan, H. (1958). A comparison of picture response and hand raising techniques for pure-tone audiometry with young children. *Laryngoscope*, 68, 548–558.

Siegenthaler, B. M., Pearson, J., and Lysak, R. (1954). A speech reception threshold test for children. *J. Speech Hearing Dis.*, 19, 360–366.

Silverman, T. R. (1967). Categorization behavior and achievement in deaf and hearing children. *Except. Children*, 34, 241–250.

Simmons, A. A. (1962). A comparison of the Type-Token Ratio of spoken and written language of deaf and hearing children. *Volta Rev., 64,* 417–421.

Speaks, C. Jerger, J., and Trammell, J. (1970). Measurement of hearing handicap. *J. Speech Hearing Res.,* 13, 768–776.

Stevens, K. N., and House, A. S. (1955). Development of a quantitative description of vowel articulation. *J. Acoust. Soc. Amer., 27,* 484–493.

Studebaker, G. A. (1962). Placement of vibrator in bone-conduction testing. *J. Speech Hearing Res.,* 5, 321–331.

Studebaker, G. A. (1964). Clinical masking of air- and bone-conducted stimuli. *J. Speech Hearing Dis.,* 29, 23–35.

Studebaker, G. A. (1967). Clinical masking of the nontest ear. *J. Speech Hearing Dis.,* 32, 360–371.

Templin, M. C. (1966). Vocabulary problems of the deaf child. *Int. Audiol.,* 5, 349–354.

Tillman, T. (1963). Clinical applications of the SAL test. *Arch. Otolaryng.,* 78, 20–32.

Tillman, T. W., and Carhart, R. (1963). Effects of competing speech on aided discrimination of monosyllabic words. *J. Acoust. Soc. Amer.,* 35, 1900.

Troncynska, J. (1964). Comparative studies of audiometric bone conduction. *Acta Oto-Laryng.,* 58, 510–513.

United States Department of Health, Education, and Welfare (1965). Methodological aspects of a hearing ability survey. Washington, D.C.: Public Health Service Publication, Series 2, Number 12.

Vargo, S. W. (1968). Speech intelligibility of deaf adolescents. *Int. Audiol.,* 7, 360–367.

Vernon, M. (1969). Sociological and psychological factors associated with hearing loss. *J. Speech Hearing Res.,* 12, 541–563.

Vernon, M., and Brown, D. W. (1964). A guide to psychological tests and testing procedures in the evaluation of deaf and hard of hearing children. *J. Speech Hearing Dis.,* 29, 414–423.

Walter, J. (1959). Some further observations on the written sentence construction of profoundly deaf children. *Amer. Ann. Deaf,* 104, 282–285.

Watson T. J. (1965). Speech audiometry in varied acoustic conditions. *Int. Audiol.,* 4, 102–104.

Webster, J. C. (1964). Important frequencies in noise-masked speech. *Arch. Otolaryng.,* 80, 494–504.

Withrow, F. D. (1968). Immediate memory span of deaf and normally hearing children. *Except. Children,* 35, 33–41.

Zwislocki, J. (1963). An acoustic method for clinical examination of the ear. *J. Speech Hearing Res.,* 6, 303–314.

7
Rehabilitative Sessions

Once the assessment of hearing deficit and related handicap(s) has been made, the next steps to consider in the rehabilitation process are those dealing specifically with the means by which deficit or handicap(s) can be reduced. The focus of this chapter is on handicap reduction through rehabilitative sessions that utilize auditory, visual, and tactile input channels. Consideration is given to frequency, content, duration, and progression of the rehabilitative sessions. Numerous questions are posed, and where data are available the answers, or partial answers, to the questions are presented. At the outset, however, it is only fair to say that there is a dearth of scientific data available, relative to the handicaps associated with hearing loss, upon which scientific methods and procedures can be established. The methods and procedures utilized in the main are a form of clinical art derived by those who have worked with the hearing impaired in classrooms and clinics.

In general, the examining clinician gets information that serves to suggest what should be the broad goal of rehabilitative sessions. If, for example, he detects through testing that the hearing-impaired individual is in need of amplification, this can be provided. If the tests of auditory discrimination show that there are confusions among sounds of the language, the clinician will incorporate discrimination training into the program of rehabilitation. Tests of lipreading and other observations might show that utilization of visual cues is deficient; if this is the case, the program will probably incorporate training in the visual area. The speech might be fractionated as a result of the hearing impairment, with articulation and/or voice problems present. Certainly if this condition shows up during examination, the clinician will probaby incorporate speech therapy into the program. Likewise, if language deficiency is discovered by virtue of the examination, a program of language habilitation would become a part of the clinical sessions. However, even though there are indications from diagnostic test results in various areas concerning the ingredients that should be built into a program of rehabilitation, there are no scientifically derived guidelines, let alone formulas, to be followed when setting up specific programs of aural rehabilitation. If guidelines were to be set up, they would have to take into account such variables as age, age at onset of hearing loss, school or vocational demands, self- and social adjustment of the individual, communication effectiveness both at receptive and expressive levels, nature and severity of the hearing loss, and so on. Until such guidelines are available, it cannot be said that aural rehabilitation sessions are proceeding on a scientifically derived prescriptive basis.

Clinical Methods

The first construct, namely, clinical methods, is broad and it encompasses the subconstructs of visual, auditory, and tactile modalities. The visual aspect includes lipreading, nonverbal visual cues, and manual language. The auditory aspect includes auditory verbal and noverbal cues. Tactile cues refer to verbal as well as nonverbal messages transmitted through the skin. In each instance the source of the stimulus, the code or message, the transmission link, the receiver, and training methods will be considered relative to scientific data available in the literature and their importance in rehabilitation.

Lipreading

Although there is no evidence concerning the importance of factors affecting success in lipreading sessions in ongoing programs of aural rehabilitation, there are studies of the importance of particular variables in isolated and independent research investigations.

Reviews. O'Neill and Oyer (1961) have written a comprehensive review of the history of lipreading and included descriptions of lipreading tests, techniques and materials for teaching lipreading, and a summary of the research findings related to lipreading. They have categorized the experimental literature in terms of speaker variables, variables of the code, transmission link or environmental variables, and receiver variables. Oyer (1964) later suggested this approach as a means of specifying the variables that are important in the lipreading process. Morkovin (1947) was also concerned with a broad view of lipreading when he suggested the importance of considering the entire communicative setting and cautioned that training in speechreading should include sensitivity to all sensory speech cues including the environmental surrounding in which the lips are perceived.

The research in lipreading has been directed almost exclusively toward identifying significant variables that influence lipreading performance rather than toward methods of training. These studies may be thought of as providing a basis for the development of training methods in that the information they provide will allow training to concentrate on important features and ignore less important features of the lipreading process. The following discussion deals with findings related to the (1) speaker, (2) code, (3) transmission link, and (4) receiver.

Speaker variables. Facial expression and lip movement as variables have been studied by several investigators, and findings indicate that normal mouth movements are preferable to either exaggerated movements (Vos, 1965) or tight lip movements (Stone, 1957). The deleterious effects of tight and limited mouth movements may be the more serious, for Hartman reported (Quigley, 1966) that for deaf subjects lipreading was superior when the speaker overemphasized his facial expressions rather than when the speaker concentrated his expression around the mouth and lower jaw.

A rigorous comparison of *overexaggeration, natural,* and *constricted mouth movements* needs to be made before any conclusion can be reached regarding the effects on lipreading by hard-of-hearing and deaf subjects. The overall effects of the speaker have been reported by O'Neill (1951), who found that the person who was most visually intelligible as a speaker was also the most intelligible under nonvisual conditions. Pesonen (1968) also supported this with a similar finding in a study comparing speaker differences. Taken together, these findings strongly suggest that a natural speaking style facilitates lipreading.

Amount of facial exposure is still another speaker variable that is of importance. Two experiments dealing with amount of facial exposure have found that there is some benefit from greater exposure. Stone (1957) found that under some conditions sentences were more intelligible when there was greater facial exposure. Greenberg and Bode (1968) later compared the effects of full-face exposure and lips-only exposure on lip-reading success. They found that consonant discrimination was more accurate when the subject viewed the talker's entire face. This result is in agreement with the earlier findings.

The effects of *sex of the speaker* have been examined by several investigators with the thought of determining whether males or females were more lipreadable. Aylesworth (1964) found no significant differences among lipreading scores as a function of different sex of the speakers. Sahlstrom (1967) used a mercury-rubber strain gauge to measure facial movements of selected facial areas. Male speakers were found to produce greater intensity of facial movement over the total duration of a word than females. Leonard (1968) also measured sex differences related to three aspects of facial movements produced when common expressions and sentences were voiced and then whispered. Measurements of facial movements also were obtained by attachment of a mercury-strain gauge at six different loci on the speaker's face. He found no significant main effects due to sex or manner of production, voiced or whispered production, and there was no interaction due to sex and manner of production.

These experiments indicate that there is no firm evidence now available that favors either sex in terms of lipreadability. The data related to differences in facial movement between male and female speakers are inconsistent, and it seems that any differences that do occur are small and a complex function of the unit of speech. This is true also of differences in facial movement associated with voiced and whispered speech.

The natural tendency is to speak more slowly to hearing-handicapped persons in the hope that the visible aspect of the code can be more easily lip-read. However, slowing the *rate at which speech is produced* has not been found to influence lipreading performance. Byers and Liberman (1959) studied the effect of the rate of the speaker on lipreading performance, as did Black et al. (1963). Neither investigation found rates to have a significant effect on lipreading performance.

The question arises as to the amount of the visible aspect of the code that is necessary for effective lipreading. To answer this question Subar (1963) investigated the effects of incomplete visual information on lipreading scores. She blocked out random frames of filmed test words to deprive the viewer of specified amounts of visual stimuli. The test required subjects to lip-read filmed words under conditions of 15 percent, 30 percent, and 45 percent deletion. None of these levels of visual deprivation significantly affected lipreading performance.

The subtle *affective relationship* that exists between speaker and lip-reader has been thought to influence the success with which a speaker is lip-read. In order to test the hypothesis that a positive affective tone between interpreter and communicator leads to better lipreading than does a negative feeling, Lott and Levy (1960) completed two experiments. Some evidence was found that the "most preferred" members were lip-read more easily than the "least preferred" members among a group of college students. A second experiment contrived a situation such that two communicators assumed different roles as group discussion leaders, one "aggressive" and the other "moderate." A rating procedure in which subjects evaluated this role playing confirmed that the "moderate" leader attracted more favorable comments. Having thus manipulated the attitudes of the subjects, the "aggressive" and "moderate" leaders were used as communicators along with another control speaker in a lipreading test. The main hypothesis was not supported in that speaker differences were not significant.

Neither slowing the rate of speaking nor deleting frames from filmed visual messages had significant effects on lipreading performance. The experiment on affective factors and lipreading suggests that these two variables might be related, but more research is needed to clarify the nature of the possible relationship.

Code. The intelligibility of the visible aspect of a wide variety of speech signals has been investigated. Ease of recognition of vowels, consonants, monosyllabic words, and sentences has come under experimental investigation as well as the influence on lipreading of such variables as size of response set and number of repetitions of the stimulus word.

A systematic program of research at the John Tracy Clinic, University of Southern California, evaluated the *visual perceptibility of English speech* (Woodward, 1957; Woodward and Barber, 1960; and Woodward and Lowell, 1964). On the basis of a number of lipreading tests that they developed they were able to categorize the consonants into four major contrastive groups: bilabial, rounded labial, labiodental, and nonlabial. After analysis of their subjects' responses to all possible pairings of the various consonant sounds, these investigators concluded that in order to differentiate further among consonants within a homophenous group additional information is needed. This may come from grammar, phonemic content, or vocabulary. In related research Fisher (1968) studied homophenous sounds using consonants in a multiple-choice intellgibility test procedure. His results supported the listings of Woodward and Barber (1960) for the most part. He concluded that further research should aim at studying ability to recognize consonants as a function of redundancy rather than trying to categorize them into fixed groups.

The literature on lipreading has pointed out for years that certain sounds look the same as other sounds to the lip-reader. However this is really an overstatement, for *homophenous sounds* may not be entirely indistinguishable when they are in the context of meaningful words. This was demonstrated to be true by Roback (1961), who tested the ability of college students to identify homophenous words through the use of visual cues alone as presented on a silent film. Results of her multiple-choice test procedure indicated that homophenous words are not produced exactly alike on the lips since subjects were able to respond correctly more frequently than would be expected by chance alone. Visible differences in mouth opening among homophenous words most frequently identified in the Roback study were reported by Joergenson (1962), who made physical measurements of the forty-eight homophenous words used by Roback. Size and shape of mouth opening may have been the cues that allowed Roback's subjects to perform at better than chance level.

Two experiments have dealt specifically with *discrimination of consonants*. Franks and Oyer (1967) investigated the influence of the stem of monosyllabic words on the identification of the initial consonants by lipreading. It was hypothesized that the same consonant, united with different vowel-consonant word stems, would be identified with different degrees of accuracy. Results showed that the influence of the stem on the identification of the initial consonant was so prominent that the acceptance of the hypothesis was affirmed. Errors of identification were related to the number of possible alternatives. The more frequent errors associated with increasing the number of alternatives are consistent with an earlier finding by Sumby and Pollack (1954), who noted that speech intelligibility decreased with increasing size of the response set up to sixty-four items.

Position of consonants within words seems to relate to their lipreadability. Greenberg and Bode (1968) found initial consonants to be more easily identified than final consonants. Modified Rhyme Lists were used as stimuli because of the consonant-vowel structure of the monosyllabic words, which allowed the testing of both initial and final positions. The multiple-choice nature of the test permitted the limited response set of six items. Subjects attained higher scores for consonant identification when they were in the initial word position.

Although consonants appear to have been studied more thoroughly than vowels, the vowels have not been entirely neglected; Pesonen (1968), who studied the lipreadability of Finnish phonemes, suggested that the main reason for confusion in visual discrimination of vowels is the similarity in size and shape of the lip openings. He regarded the place of articulation as of minimal importance with respect to vowel confusion. He observed that consonants, on the other hand, were somewhat more visually discriminated according to place of articulation.

Two researchers have given attention to the visual *intelligibility of larger units of speech*. Brannon and Kodman (1959) compared the performance of skilled lip-readers and unskilled lip-readers in the visual identification of monosyllabic words and sentences. Subjects were found to differ when the stimulus material was sentences from the Utley Test of Lipreading, given in a face-to-face situation, but not to differ in lipreading scores for isolated words. The skilled lip-readers showed superior ability with the longer speech segments. The authors related the identification of words to the place of articulation and noted that lip sounds were more easily discriminated than sounds produced at the back of the mouth.

The relationship between sentence *familiarity* and sentence lipreading difficulty was investigated by Lloyd (1964) and Lloyd and Price (1971). In the earlier experiment, after subjects had rated the sentences on a five-point scale of familiarity, the ratings were compared to earlier data of Taaffe and Wong (1957), who had ordered the same sentences according to difficulty of lipreading. A correlation of $r = 0.31$ was found between the difficulty and familiarity of each sentence. This was interpreted as a significant but weak relationship. The second experiment included two groups of hearing-impaired subjects who rated the same sentences on a one-to-five scale of familiarity. Rating reliability was high, yielding a correlation of 0.93. For these hearing-impaired subjects a correlation of $r = 0.34$ was found between familiarity and difficulty, a value very similar to that found with normal-hearing subjects. When the familiarity ratings of the Lloyd (1964) normal-hearing subjects and the hearing-impaired subjects (Lloyd and Price, 1971) were compared, the observed correlation was $r = 0.71$, indicating significant agreement between the two types of subjects.

The ability of lip-readers to identify the *accented syllable* in three-syllable words was investigated by Greene (1964), who found that viewer subjects were able to determine correctly the accented syllable 70 percent of the time, well above chance level.

It is not uncommon for the instructor to repeat several times the words that are not lip-read on the first try by lip-readers. Does this help? Nielsen (1966) investigated the effects of *word repetition* on success of lipreading. She varied the usual testing procedure by having speakers read lists of frequently used words under several conditions: each word was uttered once on one list, twice successively on a second list, and so on through five successive utterances of each word. Subjects who viewed her filmed presentations of the stimuli were *not* assisted by the successive repetition of words. This finding suggests that repetition of the stimulus is not an important factor since a difficult word will not be identified even with additional exposures.

Because a variety of test materials have been employed in lipreading research, Brannon (1961) planned an evaluation of the *relative difficulty of several commonly used stimuli:* the Utley Test, spondee words, and phonetically balanced words. The most difficulty was found with PB words that had no consonant clearly visible or one consonant visible and one not visible. Words in these categories were correctly identified less than 20 percent of the time. Similarly, spondee words with fewer visible elements were identified less easily.

Grammatical form has been identified as an influential variable in sentence intelligibility (Schwartz and Black, 1967). Six kernel sentences, each containing a noun phrase and a verb phrase, were subjected to seven grammatical transformations such as the negative, query, passive, and various combinations of these. Normal-hearing subjects were allowed to see key words prior to lipreading each kernel sentence and its seven transformations. During the test phase, subjects identified the kernel sentences most easily. The negative form tended to have low intelligibility; the effect of the query transformation was dependent upon the particular sentence. Averaging over sentences, the correct identification scores ranged from 86.8 percent for the kernel to 62.0 percent for the negative-query transformation.

Upon summarizing the results of studies discussed above, we can come to some conclusions. It is clear that there are groups of consonants that are mutually contrastive, but that are indistinguishable visually within groups. The visibility of the consonant is influenced by the vowel-consonant stem with which it occurs. If the stem is known, there is a tendency for fewer errors. Initial consonants have been found to be more easily identified than final consonants in monosyllabic words. Identification of consonants seems to depend on place of articulation to a greater extent than identification of vowels, which are distinguished more by size and shape of lip opening. Homophenous words have been identified correctly more often than can be accounted for by chance. Monosyllabic words tend to be most intelligible visually when several consonants are visible, and least intelligible when there are no visible consonants or one highly visible consonant combined with one that is not visible. As a general rule, the more visible the elements, the more easily identified is the word, both for monosyllables and for spondees. Sentences have a higher correct identification in terms of percentage of words correct than do lists of isolated words, indicating the effect of context. There is some correlation between ratings of familiarity of sentences and difficulty of lipreading. Grammatical form can determine, in part, the intelligibility of a sentence.

Except for the grouping of consonants into mutually contrastive sets, there has been little generalization of these results to a variety of situations. For example, the finding that initial consonants are relatively more visible has been reported only for monosyllabic words and normal-hearing subjects. The research to date has been valuable as a start in identifying effective variables of the code and their interrelationships, but much more information is needed to complete our understanding of how the message or code influences the lip-reader.

Transmission link. Just as the speaker and code are important variables in the study of lipreading so is the transmission link or channel through which the message passes on its way to the receiver. Films, television, and face-to-face communication situations have differential effects on lipreading performance. Questions concerning the transmission media focus on comparisons of channels, conditions of lighting, physical distractions, distance and angle between speaker and receiver, and other environmental factors.

With regard to channels, Oyer (1961) demonstrated that gains in lipreading can occur through the *medium of television*. Ten weeks of lipreading training was given to a group of normal-hearing college students. Errors on a monosyllabic word test were substantially reduced following the training.

One study was made concerning *lighting* and its effect on lipreading performance. Thomas (1962) found that lipreading efficiency decreased negligibly as the intensity of room illumination decreased from 30 to 0.5 foot candles. She concluded that lip-readers who are well motivated and highly familiar with the message content can lip-read quite satisfactorily even under adverse lighting conditions.

With reference to physical *distractions* in the environment there have been several studies that give evidence suggesting that *auditory distractions* have more deleterious effects upon lipreading than visual ones. Leonard (1962) compared the effects of selected auditory distractions on the lipreading performance of twelve normal hearing college students. Four test conditions were employed: (1) quiet (ambient noise of 55 dB SPL), (2) white noise at 80 dB SPL, (3) running speech at 80 dB SPL, and (4) background music at 80 dB SPL. All of the auditory distractions led to significant deterioration of lipreading performance when compared to the quiet condition. Ciliax (1973) also examined the effects of auditory distraction on lipreading performance; however, he pretrained all but one group of his subjects in noise. Test results indicated that subjects trained in various sound backgrounds perform comparably irrespective of the particular noise background in which they received training. Auditory distraction should be further investigated as a function of receiver characteristics such as type and degree of hearing loss.

Visual distractions have not been found to influence lipreading performance. Miller (1965) analyzed the effects of selected visual distractions (a flashing light, a spinning disk, and nonpurposeful hand movements) upon lipreading performance. No significant differences were found between a control condition of no distraction and the three experimental conditions. Keil (1968) in a comprehensive study explored the effects of various peripheral visual stimuli on lipreading performance. She also found that the peripheral visual stimuli she employed as distractors had no significant effect on lipreading performance.

The question of *optimal distance and angle* between speaker and receiver has received some attention. Results of these experiments vary. Mulligan (1954) found that the distance between subjects and the filmed speaker did not significantly affect test results. However, Erber

(1971c) showed that distance was an effective variable when the speaker's face was brightly illuminated at mouth level. Correct word recognition decreased linearly from 5 feet to 100 feet, falling from approximately 75 percent correct to 11 percent. Consonants were more affected by distance than vowels. Both place of articulation and vowel context had significant effects on visibility of consonants. Quigley (1966) has reviewed the literature from other countries regarding speaker orientation and lipreading success and cites the results of Nakano of Japan, who suggested that the best lipreading occurred at the 45-degree angle. Unfavorable angles were compensated for by decreasing distance between speaker and receiver. Wurtemberger, in another study summarized by Quigley, found a decrease in performance from frontal to lateral views of the face. Neely (1956) also reported his research findings on viewing angle. His experimental arrangements allowed for aural as well as visual reception of the test stimuli. Average intelligibility was 61 percent when the speaker was visible but only 40 percent for the conditions where the receiver did not view the speaker. Distance values of 3, 6, and 9 feet did not have a differential influence on lipreading performance. Intelligibility scores decreased as the angle increased from a face-to-face situation to 90 degrees, or right-angle viewing.

The weight of the evidence indicates that the frontal viewing position, and the region between 0 and 45 degrees, provide the most favorable conditions. When the oral cavity is illuminated, distance becomes an effective variable.

Receiver. Efforts to identify factors that discriminate between successful and unsuccessful lipreading performance have been disappointing. The hypothesized effect of variables that intuitively seem important for visual reception of speech generally have not been confirmed in the laboratory. Some attention has been directed toward psychological variables as related to success or failure in the lipreading task. O'Neill and Davidson (1956) employed thirty normal-hearing subjects to determine whether visual perception, concept formation, level of aspiration, reading comprehension, and intelligence are related to lipreading skill. They found that concept formation scores based on the Hanfmann-Kasanin Concept Formation Test were the only ones significantly correlated with lipreading scores. The superior lip-readers were also found to complete the conceptual task of sorting twenty-two blocks into four categories based on shape in less time than poor lip-readers.

Several years later Simmons (1959) employed hard-of-hearing subjects to test many of the same variables and found some conflicting evidence. Her data showed no relationship between lipreading and concept formation even though she used the same tests as O'Neill and Davidson.

Simmons did find that an object span test of visual memory was significantly related to lipreading, although a digit span test was not predictive. Tiffany and Kates (1962) investigated concept attainment ability in yet another subject group, twenty-four students, 14 to 18 years old, from the Clarke School for the Deaf. Scores of lipreading performance obtained from the Clarke School Speech Perception Test served to separate subjects into groups of good and poor lip-readers. Poor lip-readers were not able to identify concepts as quickly, but both good and poor lip-readers followed the same strategy.

Comparisons among these studies concerning the relationship between concept formation and lipreading performance are difficult because of the differences in subjects and in methods of testing lipreading and concept formation. Certainly more research along these lines is desirable. The difference in results found with object and digit span measures is worth following up with a greater variety of stimulus material and a replication of tasks. One of the continuing problems in this and other areas of research on lipreading is the lack of well-accepted, valid criterion measures of lipreading. Simmons, for example, found that judges' face-to-face ratings of lipreading ability were different from film test results.

Goda (1959) suggested that there is an *interrelationship between various language skills,* so that an individual superior in one skill would tend to be superior in the other skills also. He found this to be the case with a group of adolescent deaf residential students who were tested informally for lipreading ability. However O'Neill and Davidson (1956) found no relationship between reading comprehension and lipreading with a group of normal-hearing subjects. Simmons (1959) found that sentence meaning and key word identification were related to performance on film tests of lipreading but not to the interview rating scales.

Several investigators have been attracted by the argument that the ability to *synthesize* and *analyze* stimuli might be related to success in lipreading. Tatoul and Davidson (1961) asked whether relatively good lip-readers, measured by scores on a film test of lipreading, would be better than poor lip-readers with respect to synthesis ability measured by performance on a letter prediction test but found no significant differences between groups. Kitchen (1968) explored nine facets of visual perception suggested as examples of visual synthesis: recognition speed for geometric forms, speed of organizing geometric form patterns, recognition speed of common words, speed of organizing words from scattered letters, speed of organizing sentences from scattered words, providing missing cues in sentences containing deleted letters, speed of perceiving letters and digits from their dotted outlines, supplying missing cues in nonverbal context (object recognition), and deriving wholes on the basis of partial cues (picture arrangement). The test stimuli (except for picture arrangement) were presented tachisto-scopically to thirty-two normal hearing university students who served as subjects. Recognizing letters and digits from their dotted outlines, and speed of forming words from scattered letters, were significantly related to lipreading scores from the Utley subtests for words and stories, and for total lipreading score. The total synthesis score for each subect, over all synthesis subtests, was also positively related to lipreading. Bode, Nerbonne, and Sahlstrom (1970) found a weak correlation between lipreading abilities of normal-hearing college students and their skill at filling in missing letters in sentences. Three additional tests (a visual closure speed test, the Disemvowelled Word Test, and a Sentence Completion Test) employed by Sanders and Coscarelli (1970) showed moderate correlations with the lipreading scores of normal-hearing and hard-of-hearing subjects. They found also that there was no relationship between lipreading scores and duration of hearing loss or amount of lipreading training. There does not seem to be any ready explanation for the positive results in the case of some variables and negative results in others. We must conclude that more research is needed.

Brainerd (1969) examined the influence of *analytical perception* to determine whether the ability to identify parts of the overall visual environment might not be related to success in lipreading. Twenty normal-hearing male university students served as her subjects. Analytic ability, measured by the Hidden Figures Test, showed a moderate positive correlation with lipreading ability based on the Utley Test, Form A.

The evidence is still fragmentary, but it suggests that some forms of synthesis and analysis as measured by the tests cited are related to the visual perception of speech. Confirmation of the existing relationships and extension of these findings to hearing-impaired persons are necessary.

Visual acuity is still another factor that has been studied rather extensively without consensus. Goetzinger (1964) found that depth perception and minor variations in acuity and in the phorias did not have an effect on lipreading ability. Neither was he able to demonstrate any superiority of binocular over monocular viewing. Lovering (1969) manipulated the visual acuity of his subjects through the use of optical lenses, providing visual distortions. The experimenter developed five experimental lipreading films made up of twenty sentences that differed in level of blurring. Minor deviations in acuity were not important, but more severe blurring had a deleterious effect. After intensive study of several factors, Hardick, Oyer, and Irion (1970) concluded that minor impairment in acuity does have an adverse effect on lipreading. Sixteen normal-hearing college students were selected from a group of fifty-three subjects on the basis of their performance on the Utley Test, Form A. Half had the top eight scores and half had the lowest scores. Subjects within the normal-vision group obtained significantly higher lipreading peformance scores on the sentence subtest of the Utley Test, and on the total score. However, since Goetzinger (1964) and Lovering (1969) failed to find mildly impaired visual acuity an effective variable, the question of its relationship to lipreading remains to be resolved.

Despite these experimental efforts to identify important characteristics of "good" lip-readers, the problem has stubbornly resisted attempts at solution. There has been contradictory evidence on the role of concept formation, visual memory span, and visual acuity. The ability to synthesize or analyze the visual environment must be studied in more detail before any relationship can be defined. A closer look at the relationship among the various language skills, including lipreading, needs attention.

The lack of agreement among the experiments investigating similar variables may arise from several sources. First, there may be no relationship between the variables studied, even though one experiment finds significant results. Second, the method of measuring lipreading might not be valid. That is, lipreading ability outside of the test situation might not be related to the results of the film tests commonly used. Finally, the performance variable that is thought to be related to lipreading might not give evidence of a relationship with the subjects selected for the experiment. For instance, normal-hearing subjects might not exhibit the same relationships as hearing-impaired subjects who have had to rely more on visual cues. The recent interest in lipreading research is heartening, but the results have been suggestive of further needs rather than providing conclusive answers at this time.

Training methods. The development of programmed instruction for the improvement of lipreading was described by Brehman (1965). This programmed material uses principles of discrimination learning to train the visual discrimination of phonemes. A special type of motion picture projector has variable speeds of presentation as well as tachistoscopic, frame-by-frame projection. Speeds range from one to twelve frames per second in slow motion and twenty-four frames per seecond in the normal motion mode. In practical application, a student can practice for visual phonemic discrimination. Brehman suggests a program in which a speaker utters two words with a slight pause between them, and the student then tries to discriminate which of the two words contains the target phoneme. The student can go from a two-word response set to eight alternative phonemes, depending upon his acquired skill. If he makes an incorrect choice with an increased number in the response set, he can go back and view a smaller set. Avery (1966) mentioned Brehman's paper as the only evidence of research activity in programmed instruction at that time, a reflection of the neglect of studies of lipreading in general. More recently, McDearmon (1967) proposed a programmed learning technique that begins with the contrast of two short, common phrases. Additional phrases are added and as progress is made, word groupings are longer, there is less review, speed of presentation increases, and the situation is made more difficult by unfavorable viewing conditions and distractions. Systematic evaluation of programmed instruction must be carried out before any judgment can be made about the effectiveness of this technique.

Filmed and televised instructions have also been attempted. Oyer (1961) reported that ten weeks of televised lipreading training resulted in improved lipreading scores for a group of normal-hearing college students trained on 100 monosyllabic words and travelogue materials. A rather large project involving television teaching of lipreading was carried out by Kosh (1963) of American University. Results showed that lipreading skills can be improved by using the television as a medium. An approach to filmed lipreading training through self-instruction was reported by Black et al. (1963). The investigators concluded that training led to improved lipreading responses to a given speaker and that the benefit transferred to a different speaker as well. Quigley (1966) reported Japanese studies by Ojima and Nakano, who demonstrated that normal-hearing subjects were able to improve lipreading scores for two-syllable words after practice, and that the lipreading scores of deaf children were related to length of training, r = 0.54.

The absence of systematic research that compares and evaluates alternative methods of lipreading training points this area out as one that requires experimental attention. Evaluation of training also must be extended to settings outside the clinical training environment. Since lipreading is a principal component of rehabilitative programs for hearing-impaired people, the need for answers to basic questions concerning training is immediate.

Lipreading tests. The need for a valid and reliable lipreading test, a tool for use in the measurement of handicap, has been of concern to some audiologists and teachers of the deaf. A valid instrument capable of quantifying the ability of a hearing-handicapped person to use lipreading as a channel for everyday communication is still not available. The purposes that an effective test of lipreading performance should serve have been enumerated by O'Neill and Oyer (1961) as follows: (1) to measure the basic lipreading performance of an individual, (2) to measure the results of lipreading practice or training, (3) to aid the proper placement of hearing-handicapped persons within a training program, (4) to determine efficacy of a particular rehabilitative measure with respect to pre- and post-training lipreading performance scores, and (5) to provide a valid and reliable test of lipreading performance for research purposes.

For discussion purposes the authors have divided this section into two parts: examples of some lipreading tests that are now available, and comparisons and evaluations of lipreading tests.

Examples of tests available. Some of the earliest filmed tests of lipreading, described in a 1940 monograph by Heider and Heider, were used to assess the lipreading ability of students at the Clarke School for the Deaf. Test stimuli included meaningless phonetic units, unrelated nouns, animal names, unrelated sentences and stories. To illustrate, the third test film contained 30 nouns, 30 sentences, and 2 stories of approximately 150 words.

The Mason filmed test (1943), designed for children, had two forms consisting of nouns selected on the basis of several criteria. When the test was administered, the child was instructed to draw an X through the picture of the word stimulus. Each test item included a picture of the test word and four foils. Test results of 138 deaf children yielded a correlation of 0.95 for the two forms.

One of the most widely used tests of lipreading performance is *How Well Can You Read Lips?* (Forms A and B), developed by Utley (1946). The test has three parts: Part I is made up of phrases and short sentences encountered in day-to-day communication. Part II consists of thirty-six words, and Part III consists of six stories about which five questions are asked after each is seen. Over 700 deaf and hard-of-hearing subjects viewed the film and provided data for evaluating the reliability of the test and establishing percentile scores. Utley found that the two forms, A and B, were highly correlated. Correlations were higher for the parts of the test that were more similar. That is, word scores were more similar to sentence scores than to story scores, and so forth. Teachers' ratings of ability were not strongly related to test scores, but such ratings have not themselves been found valid in other similar situations.

Reid (1947) offered some preliminary results of a test with three forms that included vowels and diphthongs, consonants, unrelated sentences, related sentences, and a story. Upon evaluation of the tests with ninety-nine girls from schools of the deaf she found that, although correlations between the three forms of the test were high, there was no significant relationship between test scores and receiver variables such as length of training in lipreading, mental age, IQ, and grade status. During the same year, Morkovin (1947) described the development of ten training films that have subsequently been used as tests of lipreading ability. The content of the filmed stories evolves around everyday experiences of the hearing-handicapped person.

From the John Tracy Clinic the *Film Test of Lipreading,* consisting of short unrelated sentences, was reported by Lowell and Taaffe (1957). Evaluation of the two forms of the test showed that there was no significant difference between the mean test scores. Recently this film was modified to produce a multiple-choice test of lipreading (Donnelly and Marshall, 1967). The aim of this test is to assess an individual's needs and his proper placement in therapy by the addition of sound to one form of the test, to serve as a comparison with the other form, which had only visual cues. The experimenters found satisfactory reliability for the two forms.

Others who have developed tests include Postove (1962), Nielsen (1970), and Myklebust and Neyhus (1970). However, these tests do not appear to be widely used for research purposes.

Comparison and evaluation. DiCarlo and Kataja (1951) analyzed the performance of forty-four normal-hearing and fifty-seven hearing-impaired subjects on the Utley lipreading test, *How Well Can You Read Lips?* Differences in performance between the hearing-handicapped group and the normal hearers were not significant. Within each group of subjects the test did allow discrimination of the good and poor lip-readers

O'Neill and Stephens (1959) evaluated the relationships among three filmed lipreading tests (Mason, Utley, and Morkovin) by comparing the performance of a sample of hard-of-hearing subjects on the three tests. They obtained correlations between the various tests ranging from 0.49 to 0.56, all of which are significant ($p \leqslant .05$). No relationship was found between the Utley Test, Part Three (stories) and the Morkovin Test. Further analyses were made of the relation between instructor ratings and test scores. In most cases, teachers' ratings did not correlate significantly with the obtained measures of lipreading performance. Simmons (1959) compared performance on the same Mason and Utley tests with similar results.

Research on lipreading tests identifies several problems. Perhaps the most important is the development of a valid lipreading test based on appropriate outside criteria. Comparisons of one filmed test with one or more other filmed tests cannot demonstrate the validity of the tests, only that they are measuring the same ability to a greater or lesser extent. Low correlations of test results with teachers' ratings and with judges' ratings suggest that some of the cues available in ordinary conversation may not be represented in existing tests.

Visual—Nonverbal

There is probably no clinician who would deny the important effect of nonverbal visual clues on success in the lipreading situation. Elevation of the eyebrows, a frown, a head movement, and so forth can contribute greatly in terms of extramessage content. Yet the literature does not reveal any research data that specify how useful these clues are to those who are hearing handicapped. To be sure, there are those who have studied the elements of nonverbal communication as a silent language, but not as directed toward supplementation of communication that has been fragmented by hearing loss.

A few examples of research with normal-hearing subjects will illustrate the type of experiment that might be replicated with hearing-impaired subjects. Ellsworth and Carlsmith (1968) studied, quite apart from the area of hearing handicap, the interaction of eye contact and verbal content of an interview as they affect the subject's reaction to the situation and the interviewer. They found that subjects liked the interview better if the content was favorable and eye contact frequent; if the content was unfavorable, eye contact made the situation seem more negative. One can conclude then that eye contact does provide a communication channel. An experiment by Mehrabian (1968) provides another example of recent research on nonverbal visual cues. He found that distance from the addressee, eye contact, backward lean, and shoulder orientation were all significantly related to degree of positive or negative attitude toward the addressee.

As research continues to uncover the communicative meanings of nonverbal visual cues, there has been an accompanying growth of interest; for example, a book of essays by Birdwhistell (1970), a psychological interpretation of gestures in everyday life (Feldman, 1959), and an analysis of nonverbal interaction in interpersonal communication (Barnlund, 1968). Barnlund mentions several sources of cues including architecture, furniture placement, choice of seat location, and personal apparel as well as the more familiar facial expression and gestural pattern. His reference list of 133 sources indicates the volume of research in this area. Although none of these authors has been concerned with the ability of hearing-handicapped persons to interpret nonverbal visual cues, this seems a useful area of study.

Manual Language

There has been a continuous controversy between those who propose the manual approach and those who advocate use of the oral approach with the hearing handicapped, and even more lately those who advocate total communication. Even though manual language has been used for hundreds of years, there has been only little research directed toward measuring the comparative efficiency of oral versus manual approaches.

Moser et al. (1960) presented a discussion of the historical aspects of manual communication for the deaf. The authors point out that hand alphabets have been in existence for at least 1000 years, although their use in the formal education of the deaf is of more recent origin. In the constellation of manual signs in current use by the deaf, it was speculated that many had possible origins in religious orders practicing vows of silence.

It is obvious from a review of the literature that there has been minimal research effort directed toward developing a system of optimal manual signs. Equally meager is the information on (1) how to teach effectively a system of signs, (2) the communicative limitations due to signing, and (3) the assets of signing systems. The preponderance of research is devoted to examining the value of manual communication as part of the total communication setting. This topic will be considered later under multisensory methods.

One study directly bearing on manual communication, by Moser et al. (1961), was concerned with the feasibility of using finger spelling for communication under various conditions of distance between sender and receiver. Meaningless triplets of letters provided the messages, which were transmitted under various indoor and outdoor conditions at distances ranging from 20 feet to 400 feet. The authors concluded that distance was an important factor in success of receiving words by finger spelling. Correct reception tended to fall off slightly up to 175 feet and then more rapidly for distances up to 400 feet. Performance outdoors was superior to that indoors.

Only one descriptive article was found that spoke directly to the training of manual communication skills. Fant (1961) described a programmed learning approach to teaching sign language to deaf students. Each lesson of the program is built around a single hand shape.

There apparently are no research data that relate manual language skill to sender, code, or receiver characteristics. The very limited research makes it difficult to evaluate the effectiveness of manual communication. For the same reason the development of training methods has been hampered. Since many profoundly deaf people use manual communication as a primary mode of communication, more experimentation is needed.

Auditory Training

The aim of auditory training is to help the hearing-impaired person use his residual hearing to the best advantage. The responsiveness of the individual to training can be considered to depend upon speaker variables, variables of the code, the transmission link, and receiver variables and training methods.

Speaker. The role of the speaker in auditory training has not attracted much attention. The single study directly concerned with speaker differences was carried out by Palmer (1955). Adult hard-of-hearing subjects with sensorineural or conductive losses, and normal-hearing subjects, listened to nine speakers who presented phonetically balanced word lists. Three speakers were adult males, three adult females, and three were 12-year-old girls. Articulation functions based on three intensity levels were obtained for each subject with each speaker. No differences were found in the 50 percent correct identification value as a function of speaker.

This result is reassuring for the clinical rehabilitation program in that the sex of the speaker and other speaker variables were not found to have a differential effect. However, the differences between an auditory training program and the presentation of PB word lists make generalization difficult.

There remains a need for research on the effects of speaker variables in *training,* the transfer of effects from one speaker to another, the possible interaction of speaker and training material, and the interaction effects of speakers with various receivers.

Code. Watson (1961a) has provided an excellent review of classical studies in the acoustics of speech and related these findings to the aural rehabilitation process. Information about the physical characteristics of the stimuli that make up the training material is relevant for auditory training programs. The frequency and intensity characteristics of speech sounds have been related to the position of the speech organs when vowel sounds are produced and to the analysis of differences between voices. There has been research on the characteristics of consonants, the influence of one speech sound on another, and the temporal characteristics of speech. The pattern of errors and correct responses of the hearing-impaired person to such well-defined stimuli can lead to an understanding of the cues that allow him to discriminate speech sounds and to the development of appropriate materials for a training program.

The following studies, all of which concern different aspects of the code, proceed from a more molecular approach—with interest in the individual speech sounds—to the molar variables such as the context in which a word unit appears.

Consonant and vowel discrimination. Miller and Nicely (1955), in an often quoted article, reported an analysis of confusion errors among consonants that were presented to subjects in noise and with high- and low-pass filtering. As each of sixteen consonants was presented, the subject was required to guess which one he heard. Confusion errors showed consistent patterns for conditions of noise and low-pass filtering. An articulatory analysis of the consonants yielded five dimensions that characterized the consonants: (1) voicing, (2) nasality, (3) affrication, (4) duration, and (5) place of articulation. Noise and low-pass filtering had little effect on voicing and nasality, but severely affected place of articulation. The authors presented the dimensions as relatively independent in the perceptual process.

The identification of one category of consonants, voiceless fricatives, by subjects with high-frequency loss, was studied by Lawrence and Byers (1969). Five subjects were instructed to identify sixteen different consonant-vowel syllables. Errors of identification resulted from confusions within the pair /s/ and /ʃ/ and the pair /f/ and /ϴ/. The authors postulated that low-frequency energy, intensity, and duration of the fricative sounds, and formant transitions of vowels served as possible cues.

Martin and Pickett (1970) investigated the ability of listeners with sensorineural hearing losses to discriminate the $F2$ transition in synthetic sounds. The measure of interest was the smallest amount of transition the subject could hear. Transitions had a terminal frequency of 1500 Hz. When the $F2$ transition was presented alone, discrimination was as good as in normal-hearing subjects, but when $F1$ was added, discrimination was poorer and more variable. In related research Pickett and Martony (1970) studied the difference limen for frequency using synthetic vowel sounds with low-frequency formants as stimuli. The four reference formant frequencies were 205, 275, 400, and 825 Hz. Subjects were asked to decide which one of three serially presented stimuli had a higher frequency than the other two in the triad. Subjects with severe-to-profound sensorineural hearing losses were as accurate as normal-hearing controls at the two lower frequencies. At the higher reference frequencies discrimination was not as good. Similar results at several sensation levels indicated that intensity was not a factor.

A study of discrimination of vowels by hearing-impaired subjects was reported by Owens et al. (1968). They concluded that vowel sounds lacked efficiency for discrimination testing purposes because of the low number of errors that occurred.

The intelligibility of vowels and consonants may be influenced, in part, by coarticulation effects of adjacent speech sounds. Gay (1970) studied the influence of vowel environment on consonant identification under different conditions of filtering. Normal-hearing subjects listened to consonant-vowel syllables filtered through five low-pass cutoff conditions, either at 800, 1000, 1200, 1400, or 1600 Hz. Vowels were highly intelligible under almost all conditions. Consonant-vowel combinations, on the other hand, showed a great deal of variability in their resistance to filtering effects. Gay related his results to the use of small sample, phonetically balanced word lists such as the W-22. He suggested that a more useful procedure would be to make up a test containing consonant-vowel combinations that occur frequently and also are influenced adversely by filtering.

The influence of coarticulation effects on hearing-impaired listeners apparently has not been studied. These data are needed so that similarities and differences between filtering effects and the effects of hearing impairment can be identified. Gay (1970) pointed out that filtering does not reproduce the same conditions as sensorineural loss, a fact that has been empirically demonstrated by Rhodes (1966). Rhodes used low-pass filters to modify CNC (consonant-nucleus-consonant) words so that the frequency composition would reflect the same configuration as the stimuli received by the hypacusic subjects (subjects with high-frequency hearing losses). Two filter cutoffs were employed, 1000 Hz and 2000 Hz, to match the two types of audiometric configuration presented by the hearing-loss subjects. Theoretically both the normal hearers and the hypacusic subjects had identical acoustic cues available to them. There was a significant difference in discrimination performance in favor of the hypacusic subjects when the cutoff was at 1000 Hz but no difference was found at the 2000 Hz cutoff. The author speculated that the hearing-loss group, with a slope beginning at 1000 Hz, could discriminate acoustically altered speech better than the normal hearers as the result of learned behavior, a compensation for the high-frequency loss. Analyzing the phoneme errors made in the Rhodes experiment, Egolf, Rhodes, and Curry (1970) identified critical vowels and consonants, those that produced the greatest discrepancies between normal-hearing and hearing-impaired listeners. Vowels with high-frequency second formants were among those most commonly confused by normal hearers. Consonant errors showed no clear-cut pattern of differences for the two types of listeners. Rhodes and Corbett (1970) used the same filter cutoffs to modify CNC words and CID sentences that were presented to young subjects between 9 and 19 years old who had sensorineural hearing losses. These young subjects did not show the same superiority in speech discrimination with the 1000 Hz cutoff exhibited by the older subjects in Rhodes' earlier experiment. These experiments indicate that low-pass filtering cannot replicate the effects of hearing impairment. Systematic research is needed to fill in the gaps in our knowledge about perception of speech sounds by both normal-hearing and hearing-impaired individuals.

Word intelligibility. Oyer and Doudna (1959) analyzed the discrimination performance of hard-of-hearing subjects who listened to two repetitions of CID W-22 Lists (phonetically balanced words). The majority of the subjects had mild hearing losses so that the overall correct response rate was close to 90 percent on the initial presentation of the lists. Error responses were primarily ones of substitution rather than omission, especially in the final position. An extension of this research by Oyer and Doudna (1960) concerned the effects of word familiarity on substitution and omission errors. When the words were categorized according to Thorndike-Lorge familiarity categories, 68.5 percent were most familiar, with rating AA, 14.5 percent had an A rating, and 17 percent were less than A. Substitution errors tended to increase slightly, and omission errors showed a concomitant relative decrease as word familiarity decreased. Substitution errors were usually words from the most familiar group regardless of the rating of the stimulus word. A relatively small number of the total set of stimulus words, 38 of 200, were found to account for one half of the response errors.

Two studies, based on normal-hearing subjects, give evidence that meaningfulness and length of word are effective variables. Hirsh et al. (1954) presented subjects with words and nonsense syllables under conditions of noise and high- and low-pass filtering. Words were almost always more intelligible than nonsense syllables, with the exception of the condition where all frequencies above or below 1600 Hz were eliminated. Although words with spondaic stress were highly intelligible under a variety of conditions, in general correct identification was directly related to the number of syllables contained in the word. Black (1952) found a positive relationship between intelligibility and familiarity of the words, which is consistent with the difference between nonsense and meaningful words. Words of two syllables were somewhat more intelligible than one-syllable words, and within each group intelligibility values generally increased with increasing number of speech sounds. Words accented on the second syllable were slightly more intelligible than those accented on the first syllable.

Intraword factors that have been found to influence intelligibility include phonemic content, position of phoneme in words, meaningfulness of words, syllabic structure, and the number of speech sounds in the word. Procedural differences make comparisons between experiments difficult, and in a number of cases the results must be confirmed for the hard-of-hearing population. The research summarized above suggests that within words the final sounds are more subject to error than initial sounds, substitution errors are more common than omissions, meaningful and familiar words tend to be relatively more discriminable than other types of words, and words with several syllables have high intelligibility.

Effects of word context. Rubenstein and Pickett (1957) had normal-hearing subjects listen to pairs of complete declarative sentences. Each sentence of a pair had the same test noun, but the noun position was in either the initial, medial, or final position. The speech signal was compressed so that all words would have the same intensity. Under these conditions, the initial sentence position had highest intelligibility.

O'Neill (1957) compared the intelligibility scores of words presented in sentences with those presented out of context as a list of single words. He found that words in context were recognized more easily. The difference between context and isolation conditions ranged from

19 percent to 26 percent for S/N ratios of −6 dB, 0 dB, 6 dB, and 12 dB. Traul and Black (1965) investigated context effects in more detail by comparing, in five contexts, words of low intelligibility, each of which had a high probability error response. The context conditions were (1) a word in isolation, (2) a word repeated twice in succession, (3) a word said with a message warning the listener to avoid the most common error response, (4) a word placed in the middle of a group of seven second-order approximation words, and (5) a word midway in a third-order approximation phrase. Two measures were derived from the data. The intelligibility of each word was measured as the percent agreement between the stimulus and the response, averaged over the group of subjects. Disparity among responses was measured in bits of information, a measure directly related to the number of different responses to the same stimulus. As contextual cues increased from condition 1 to condition 5, word intelligibility increased. The amount of information decreased with increasing context, indicating that there was more agreement among responses to the stimuli. Both measures confirm the importance of context in aiding auditory discrimination.

The position of a word in a sentence, the type of context, and the presence or absence of context all have an effect on intelligibility. It appears now that the more closely the context resembles a sentence, the greater the intelligibility; and, within the sentence, relative intelligibility increases from the beginning to the end, at least for nouns that are an important key to sentence intelligibility. These results are consistent with the fact that as the sentence progresses there tends to be less and less uncertainty as to the remaining words because of the predictable nature of word sequences in the English language.

It seems reasonable that these findings would apply to the hard of hearing as well to the normal hearing if the hearing-impaired person has developed language normally. Congenital or early impairment may prohibit normal development so that contextual cues would have little or no effect on intelligibility.

Transmission link. The limited experimental evidence on which to base auditory training procedures points up the need for an expanded effort to understand the role of the transmission link in the rehabilitation process. In the classroom, group auditory training units are frequently available as part of the daily educational program. The following summary covers comparisons among auditory training equipment.

Boyd and Jamroz (1963) compared three group hearing aid systems. The first system delivered the sound signal to both ears but had a single microphone, one amplifier, and one attenuator controlling the sound level. The second system differed from the first by having separate attenuator controls for each ear. The third system had individual microphone, amplifier, and attenuator controls for each ear—a completely binaural system. Young adult subjects with binaural average hearing levels between 75 dB and 89 dB listened to five lists of ten monosyllabic words each. After two repetitions of a practice list, the subjects were each tested for discrimination under the three amplifying systems. Test scores failed to show any advantage of the binaural system over the other two systems.

Calvert (1964) studied three amplifying systems typically found in classrooms in the United States. The three types were conventional group auditory trainers, individual hearing aids, and loop induction systems. Each system has certain advantages and weaknesses. Auditory trainers have the benefit of an output over the entire frequency range, but a disadvantage is their relative lack of flexibility. Additionally, children must change to individual amplification systems outside the classroom. Individual aids avoid this problem, but their effectiveness in the classroom is often limited by ambient noise and varying distances from the speaker. Loop induction systems offer some of the same advantages as the group amplifiers and individual aids since, in the loop system, individual aids are used in conjunction with a centrally located transmission system. Problems arise from cross talk if there are loop systems in adjacent rooms, and the loop induction system may be difficult to repair. Evidence on the relative merits of the three types of amplification was obtained from a questionnaire sent to teachers of the deaf in California. They were instructed to rank order their preferences on the basis of eleven factors related to classroom teaching. Responses returned by 69 teachers representing 595 children showed that individual hearing aids were ranked highest and group amplifiers were the lowest. The largest number used conventional group amplifiers, 69 percent, while only 4 percent used loop induction systems. A substantial number of teachers used a combination of conventional group amplification and individual aids. Those teachers who had used the loop system ranked it higher overall than those without prior experience with it.

In order to extend these preliminary findings, more objective measures of the effects of training are needed to determine if teacher preference is associated with superior performance of children trained under the various systems. Calvert's data suggest that perhaps the teachers are not favorably impressed with the group amplifiers that they now have, and therefore assume that some other system would be better. If the teachers have not experienced the systems under evaluation, these ratings must be influenced by unknown factors to some extent.

Hudgins (1953), using deaf students at a residential school, investigated the effectiveness of auditory training through a group hearing aid. The performance of two groups of students with an experimental group aid and a conventional group aid was followed over a two-year period. Initial and periodic follow-up test batteries measured speech perception, speech intelligibility, speech production, and educational achievement. The experimental group hearing aid, developed at Central Institute for the Deaf, could amplify sound sources up to 140 dB and deliver the signal to as many as thirty-six pairs of earphones. The aid also incorporated compression limitation and attentuation of frequencies less than 500 cycles prior to the compressor action. The experimental group spent the day in a sound-absorbent room with the new group aid while the control group was in a regular room with the older group aid that amplified the sound source by 45 to 50 dB before serious distortion occurred. Both groups had the same training but with aids that differed in quality. The emphasis of the report was on the benefits of auditory training for profoundly deaf children rather than a precisely controlled comparison of the conventional and experimental group aids. This was, in part, due to the lack of strict control over usage occasioned by the replacement of older units with the new type of amplification during the course of the experiment. Measures of lipreading and speech discrimination were based on responses to monosyllabic word lists and a lipreading film. Both groups improved in lipreading in response to monosyllabic words, especially in the first year, but the gain was not apparent in the film test. Speech discrimination through the auditory channel improved from 17 percent to 35 percent in the experimental group during the first year and remained essentially unchanged in the control group at a correct response level under 15 percent. No significant additional gain was observed in the second year of the experiment. Speech intelligibility of the two groups changed only slightly, both for words and for sentences, as measured by a percentage of correct understanding by a group of listeners. Measures of speech rhythm and fluency also showed slight gains. Hudgins, hypothesizing that younger children might exhibit more improvement in speech intelligibility, studied a group of profoundly deaf children who started training at the third-grade level. In this case speech intelligibility increased 15 percent for words and 27 percent for sentences for the experimental children. At the same time a control group showed no change. The effect of the experimental training program on educational achievement was not entirely clear. In the first experiment, the gain in grade level over the two-year period was 2.2 grades for the experimental subjects and 1.4 for the control subjects. With the younger children of the second experiment, the control group showed slightly more gain than the experimental group. However Hudgins' research has demonstrated that profoundly deaf school-age children can benefit in speech intelligibility from auditory training, and that the younger the child, the greater is the effectiveness of training.

Clearly the many variables that are relevant for group auditory training with amplification still need to be investigated. Questions of content of the program, duration of training, sequencing of auditory skills, and methods of evaluating the results of training are some that require attention.

Receiver. Central to effective planning for auditory rehabilitation is the determination of those who can benefit from such training. In order to adapt the program to the individual, the professional must select appropriate stimulus materials, methods of presentation, and schedules of training. The amount of deficit, type of loss, duration of loss, and age are some of the variables that one would expect to influence these decisions. Several of these variables have been investigated and reported in the research literature.

Siegenthaler (1949) examined the relationship between type of hearing loss and ability to perceive differences in voicing, pressure pattern, and influence of consonants on vowels. Three types of subjects were studied, those with moderate flat loss, those with high-frequency losses, and normal-hearing subjects. During the test sessions, pairs of words that differed in one of the characteristics were shown to the subjects. When one of the words was presented auditorily, the subject was to select which of the pair he heard. The words were also presented unpaired as a list to which the subject responded by writing the word he heard. Normal-hearing subjects were able to detect differences in all characteristics better than either group with hearing losses. Both experimental groups had equal success in detecting voicing differences, but subjects with flat losses were more successful in detecting differences in pressure pattern and influence. The subjects with high-frequency losses were less like the normal-hearing group and their discrimination scores for the list of words were much lower than scores for the other two groups. These data indicate that the high-frequency loss condition presents greater difficulties in word discrimination.

Oyer and Doudna (1959) compared the errors made by conductive and nonconductive sensorineural and mixed-hearing-loss subjects in response to CID W-22 Word Lists. The nonconductive subjects made approximately twice as many vowel and consonant confusions as subjects with conductive losses. Within the subject groups error patterns were similar, but subjects with conductive losses had relatively less trouble with blends and more trouble with nasals than the nonconductive subjects.

Wedenberg (1954) investigated the effectiveness of training for young preschool children who exhibited a variety of audiometric configurations. He reported the results of auditory training administered to children having the following types of loss: poor high-frequency response and good low-frequency response, high-frequency loss and poor response at low frequencies, flat loss in the formant areas, severe flat loss across all frequencies, and reponse to vibration only. Training began with emphasis on relatively high intensity vowels and consonants, which the child would be likely to hear. Lipreading was not introduced until the child had learned to attend to sound stimuli, and hearing aids were introduced only after the child had developed a vocabulary of a few words with the auditory techniques. Preliminary results indicated that children with good low-frequency response and high-frequency loss and those with moderate flat losses were helped most by training. Children with profound flat losses were not able to utilize the training and were referred to a school for the deaf. In terms of using a hearing aid, the flat loss cases responded best to this in training, the group with ability to detect vibration only responded to some extent, and the high-frequency loss subjects showed little benefit.

Lichtenberg (1966) compared the speech discrimination of hard-of-hearing children with that of normal-hearing-and-speaking children and speech-defective children. A paired sentence format was used for a pre- and post-test of vowel and consonant discrimination. Each item consisted of a pair of sentences that differed only in the test word. During eighty training sessions after the initial test, twelve hard-of-hearing subjects were given intensive drill work in auditory discrimination. Eight hard-of-hearing subjects, who had only thirty sessions, served as a control. The sentence test was again administered three to four months later. There were very few errors in vowel discrimination either before or after training. Consonant errors were more numerous. Normal-hearing-and-speaking subjects had fewest errors, speech defective subjects were intermediate, and the-hard-of hearing subjects had the most errors. On the second testing the normal-speaking-and-hearing group showed significant improvement, even without training. The hard-of-hearing group who had intensive training also improved from an initial 11.0 mean number of errors to a post-training average of 6.67. The control group had no significant reduction in errors, nor did the speech defective subjects show a change over the three- to four-month interval.

Research that related receiver characteristics to auditory response has described some of the differences in speech discrimination that arise from different types of hearing loss. High-frequency loss contributes more to discrimination errors than conductive loss or flat sensorineural loss. It has been demonstrated that auditory training provides the most benefit to children when good low-frequency response is coupled with high-frequency loss or moderate flat losses.

Ross and Newby (1965) proposed a multiple distortion hypothesis to explain the poor speech discrimination associated with sensorineural loss. They suggested that persons with sensorineural hearing loss have sources of endogenous distortion, and the more distortion there is, the more an added exogenous noise would adversely affect discrimination ability. They attempted to identify independent factors that influence speech discrimination to determine if the interaction of these internal distortions *with noise* would produce a greater decrement than a simple summation of individual effects. As it turned out, they were unable to test the hypothesis since most of the variables they examined did not show a relationship with speech discrimination. This difficulty eliminated from consideration difference limen for frequency, difference limen for intensity, and size of linear range. The extent and configuration of hearing loss were the only variables related to the speech discrimination scores.

In connection with difference limen for frequency, Strizver (1958) related this variable to the speech discrimination ability of severely hard-of-hearing subjects. Twenty advanced students at the Clarke School for the Deaf were subjects. A pure tone difference limen was obtained at 500 Hz, 1000 Hz, and 2000 Hz, as well as threshold values at these frequencies. Strizver was forced to use an indirect measure of speech discrimination because with only auditory stimulation the scores were too low to detect differences among subjects. The measure he used was a combined lipreading and hearing score compared with lipreading alone. Any benefit from auditory cues could then be attributed to speech discrimination. He found somewhat mixed results in that there was a positive correlation between this measure of speech perception and the difference limen at 500 Hz but not at 1000 Hz and 2000 Hz. On the other hand, the speech perception measure correlated significantly with pure tone threshold at the two higher frequencies but not with the 500 Hz threshold value.

More clear-cut results were found by Bradley (1959) when he tested difference limens for three subject groups. Children aged 9 to 14 years represented three categories: normal hearing and speech, normal hearing and defective articulation, and impaired hearing and impaired articulation. The DL for frequency within each group increased with increasing frequency from 500 Hz to 1000 Hz to 2000 Hz. The defective articulation group had DLF's larger than the normal hearing group, but the children with impairment in both hearing and speech were markedly inferior to the others.

Still another approach to understanding the speech discrimination process of the hard of hearing was described by Watson (1961a). He reported the results of a preliminary study that required subjects to write what they heard when nonsense syllables were spoken at a level of approximately 85 dB close to the ear. Spectroanalyses of the sounds were plotted and compared to the subjects' audiograms. Predictions were made as to what sounds the subjects were likely to perceive correctly. If the words contained formants that fell within the hearing range of the subject, it was predicted that these words would be correctly identified. The predictions were found to be accurate 52 percent of the time for vowels and 60 percent of the time for consonants. In 24 percent of the cases the vowel was wrongly identified even though there appeared to be hearing for all three formants of that phoneme. In 19 percent of the cases consonants were not identified when there appeared to be hearing for all formants.

These results and the failure ·of low-pass filtering to simulate high-frequency loss accurately indicate that reduced acuity is not the only factor in determining speech discrimination. Attempts to identify these other factors have not been successful to date, and a model that accounts for the poor speech discrimination associated with high-frequency loss is still needed.

Training methods. Although auditory training is a component of most educational and rehabilitative programs, there is a scarcity of research comparing and evaluating the methods now in use. Summaries of the existing research are organized according to age of subjects.

Programs for young children. The assumption that early experience with auditory stimulation is an essential factor in the development of communication skills of the deaf and the severely hard-of-hearing child is generally accepted. The importance of such early training and the consequences of training have been reported by several investigators.

Hardy et al. (1958) argued for an emphasis on training that uses phrases and sentences to familiarize the subject with the relationships among sounds that occur in connected speech. Language, then, would be the important basis for training, not gross discrimination among sounds. Their position was based on a study comparing language development of hard-of-hearing and normal-hearing children. The approach that should be emphasized during training may depend upon the nature of the hearing impairment. For example, the child who has a congenital or prelanguage impairment may reflect his sensory deficit in delayed or disrupted language development. In this case the emphasis on language rather than speech, as advocated by Hardy et al., would be warranted.

McCroskey (1967) reported the effects of early *home auditory training* for young infants on speech production. Comparisons of production of the phoneme /a/, through sonographic evidence, indicated that children entering the nursery school who had been through a training program as infants had tracings that more closely resembled those of normal-hearing children than did the tracings of those without infant exposure to amplified sound.

Recently, some systematic research on infant and preschool management has been described by those associated with the McGill University Project for Deaf Children. The goals and the rationale of their total management approach are explored in two articles by Ling, Ling, and Jacobson (1968) and D. Ling (1971). Results of rehabilitative training have also been reported. Lach et al. (1970) compared the vocalizations of seven deaf children at the beginning of training with later vocalizations recorded periodically after training started. At least one parent and the child came for weekly sessions during training and then carried out the program at home. Before training, two of the children were marked deviant in voice quality and five were less deviant. After a year of training, during which each child was fitted with two hearing aids, there were no cases of markedly deviant voice and five were rated normal. Specific speech sound improvements were also noted. Six of the seven subjects produced more vowels and consonants, the ratio of consonants to vowels increased, plosives and semivowels increased, and glottal consonants decreased. At the end of training, one child was essentially normal in development and all children except one had produced at least one word. A. Ling (1971) reported the progress of ten infants, aged 11 to 33 months, whose parents underwent a parent counseling program. Parents were advised in the use of hearing aids and methods to improve speech communication skills including listening training, identification of environmental sounds, and encouragement in vocal play. For older children books, toys, and games were used. Progress was monitored by the Griffith Mental Development Scale, which assesses five aspects of behavior: locomotor, personal-social, hearing and speech, hand-eye coordination, and performance. Locomotor, hand-eye coordination, and performance measures were all normal at the beginning of training or after six months in the program. Personal-social development was slightly below the norm due to difficulty in verbal tasks. Speech and hearing showed significant improvement throughout training but still remained well below the norm. Progress in the speech and hearing area was not significantly related to degree of hearing loss, scores on other subscales, position in family, or age at beginning of training.

The increasing interest in training for the young child is evident in a report by McConnell (1968), who edited the proceedings of a Conference on Current Practices in the Management of Deaf Infants (0–3 years). This report includes the comments of teachers and administrators of home training programs and demonstration programs of various types throughout the United States. Participants described their admission procedures, the content of the parent training sessions, and the methods used to evaluate the programs. Evaluation was noted as the most critical need. The lack of objective measuring instruments makes it difficult to determine the value of alternative training procedures.

Programs for older children. A training program for discrimination of nonspeech sounds, developed by Saleh (1965), was given a preliminary field test with ten children. The stimulus materials consist of a set of six films about the farm, the city, home, a concert, a circus, and Christmas. At the end of the filmstrip there is a review of the twelve sounds that occur in the story. A ten-week training program with the films was evaluated subjectively with an estimate of 50 percent improvement in sound identification. One of Saleh's picture-sound sets about the farm was the basis for programmed training on sound recognition (Doehring, 1968). For each of twelve stimulus sounds there were three pictures that served as multiple-choice alternatives. During training, four sets of thirty-six trials were presented with each sound occurring three times per set. Normal-hearing children, 7 years or older, usually recognized all of the sounds correctly the first time. Among the deaf children, most were able to recognize at least a few, but there were large individual differences. Nineteen of the twenty-six deaf subjects reached the criterion of learning after training. The author concluded that most deaf children can learn to discriminate nonspeech sounds such as these with training. Further, programmed instruction seems to be an efficient way to accomplish this.

Other studies have been concerned with the training of frequency and vowel discrimination. A recent experiment by Gengel (1969) illustrates the effects of training on frequency discrimination, an ability that has been related to speech discrimination (Strizver, 1958; Bradley, 1959). Gengel provided three sessions of training for twenty-three deaf children and for twenty-one hard-of-hearing children. A control group of normal hearing subjects had either one or two sessions. Initially, the difference limen for frequency (DLF) was determined by the method of constant stimuli for two standard frequencies, 250 Hz and 500 Hz. During training, paired frequencies were presented to each child individually, with the difference between the standard and comparison stimuli decreasing over the test period. Training was found to have the most benefit for deaf children. They showed a decrease in DLF at both frequencies so that after the third session the median value was half of the initial value. Hard-of-hearing subjects showed gains at 500 Hz but not at 250 Hz. The amount of hearing loss was found to be correlated with the size of the DLF when both measures were based on the 500 Hz tone.

In a training program for children 5 to 11 years old, with severe to profound hearing losses, Doehring and Ling (1971) administered programmed instruction in vowel discrimination. Sets of monosyllabic words that differed only in the vowel sound served as stimuli. During a training series children showed more rapid learning of vowel discrimination in terms of the number of trials required to learn to the criterion; the number of trials decreased with successive training series. Retraining of vowel discrimination for each series also required fewer trials than original learning. Disappointing results were found in a transfer test. There was essentially no change from pre- to post-test scores, neither for words used in training nor for novel words. The authors speculated that the change in task from a three-item stimulus set to a thirteen-item set was too large a step.

When auditory training has been carried out there has been a consistent effect in the direction of better discrimination. It would be particularly useful to have more evidence on conditions of training that lead to transfer of training. Even though Doehring and Ling did not find positive transfer, their experiment points up the need for these measures.

Principles of operant conditioning have been applied in several instances to auditory discrimination behavior. Smith and Hodgson (1970) studied the effects of reinforcement on the speech discrimination performance of normal-hearing and hearing-impaired children aged 4 to 8 years. Each child responded to three PBK 50-word lists. For children in the experimental group correct responses were followed by a reinforcement on the second of three successive word lists. The control group received no reinforcement. Both normal-hearing and hearing-impaired children showed improvement with reinforcement, and facilitating effects carried over to the succeeding list to some extent. The authors attributed the positive effects to improved attention and interest associated with reinforcement.

Schultz and Kraat (1970) considered the therapy situation as an example of operant learning. Within this context they recommend the analysis of discrimination errors in terms of a confusion matrix where both hits and false alarms are considered. In this experiment, five children with moderate to severe hearing losses responded to consonant-vowel stimuli and the data were than analyzed. Confusion matrices provided insight into appropriate therapy goals, and a related measure attributed to Pollack and Norman (1964) evaluated pure auditory sensitivity disregarding the variable of the criterion that the subject used.

An ingenious method of measuring the listening responses of hearing-impaired children was decribed by Mira (1970). Children watched a movie that had separate controls for the video and audio portions of the display. In one condition both the audio and video decreased over time unless the child pressed corresponding switches at a predetermined rate. In the other condition only the audio needed to be maintained. Four of twelve subjects consistently maintained switch pushing to keep the audio signal and three additional children sometimes responded. Nonlisteners made no effort to keep the audio signal. Response patterns did not seem to be related to age or hearing level. Mira notes that the procedure can be used to evaluate the effects of rehabilitation and also that variations in the procedure can encourage listening.

These experiments illustrate that principles of operant conditioning can be applied successfully to auditory discrimination learning. If the operant paradigm is appropriate, we can expect that it will provide guidelines for other aspects of training as well, such as scheduling of reinforcement and sequencing of training.

In the literature several investigators have suggested a *unisensory auditory approach* in educational programs for hearing-impaired children. Stewart, Pollack, and Downs (1964) argue for a unisensory program on the grounds that each child has a potential for using his residual hearing and this potential will be realized to a fuller extent when the impaired auditory modality is emphasized. Neurophysiological studies are offered in support of their view. Reference is made also to a preschool program in which children who received language and speech training auditorily through natural play activities made more gains in communicative and academic skills than children in a structured multisensory control group (Stone, Fiedler, and Fine, 1961).

Imai and Hoshi (1966) also described such a training program for 5-year-old children. Training began with the discrimination of gross sounds. The second stage included discrimination of musical sounds and rhythmic variations and, in the final stages, discrimination of speech sounds. The areas of improvement were stated to be language understanding, vocabulary level, and voice production. Unfortunately, data were not presented to support the authors' conclusion that this auditory training was superior to an earlier multisensory approach.

The verbotonal method of Guberina (1964), primarily auditory in nature, has received attention in recent years. In this system stimuli are filtered through various octave bandwidths in order to find the most sensitive region of response for the individual. When the optimal field of hearing has been identified, training is initiated with material transmitted under the frequency and intensity conditions that allowed maximum understanding. Speech may be intelligible, under some conditions, with only small bands of frequency represented. Guberina states that frequencies previously near threshold may be heard more clearly when they are presented in combination with the optimal bandwidths. The method has its greatest success with hard-of-hearing people, but the deaf can also profit by using the whole body as a receiver. In this case, measurements of the response to vibrations are made at various parts of the body. A special device that transmits frequencies down to 1 Hz is used in training. Low-frequency components of speech sounds are transmitted before the high-frequency components to facilitate perception of the high frequencies. Exposure to this training initiates speech production. After two or three years of continuous practice, during which the child is exposed to everyday situations that provide a visual context, a foreign language may be introduced to correct voice and articulation. When speech and hearing have developed, education follows rapidly. Hearing aids are also delayed until this time.

Several research groups in the United States are applying the verbotonal method in laboratory controlled conditions. In one application of Guberina's verbotonal methods (Rea, 1968), both normal-hearing subjects and subjects with sensorineural hearing loss were tested with filtered pure tones and disyllables, for example, /sisi/, /lala/, and with unfiltered stimuli. For the sensorineural subjects, but not the normal subjects, detection thresholds for pure tones were related to disyllable thresholds, whether filtered or unfiltered. Factor analysis determined two factors, ". . . a facility for low-frequency acuity" and "A second factor termed a mid- to high-frequency acuity factor." Discrimination tests were administered using PB words to determine whether these stimuli would be more intelligible if they were band-passed according to the maximum sensitivity of the subject based on detection thresholds. Intelligibility was not greater for the band-passed material. The author recommended more research on the intelligibility of verbotonal stimuli and conventional speech stimuli using more limited bandwidths.

Adult discrimination training. Auditory training for the adult who has acquired a hearing loss and must relearn some of the cues necessary for speech discrimination is an important application of rehabilitation. At this time there is a surprising lack of data on which to base an effective program. Only one research effort yields data relative to the question. Bode and Oyer (1970) compared several procedures for improving the speech discrimination of hard-of-hearing adults. The major variables were the type of response required of subjects and the type of noise background in which the speech stimuli were embedded. Two types of responses were elicited; write-down and multiple-choice. The background noise, which was speech babble, remained at the same intensity or varied in intensity, becoming louder as the practice session progressed. Three hours of practice with monosyllabic words was found to improve scores for CID W-22 words and Rhyme Test words, but not the Semi-Diagnostic Test material. An interaction of effects was observed; the varied signal-to-noise (S/N) condition produced better results with the multiple-choice response, but either steady or varied noise yielded similar results with write-down responses.

Although there is a growing body of research on auditory training for infants and older children, no concurrent trend appears for training of adults who have acquired a hearing loss. Perhaps one reason is the strong emphasis on hearing aid selection and orientation found in rehabilitative programs for adults.

Hearing Aid Selection

Probably the most commonly recommended rehabilitative proce-dure for hearing-impaired clients is the selection and evaluation of a hearing aid. Certainly this aspect of rehabilitation has attracted an extra-ordinary amount of research.

Hirsh (1966) provided an overview of recent developments in hearing aid design and outlined some major trends. The most obvious ad-vance has been the development of the transistor with subsequent min-iaturization of hearing aid circuitry. The possibility of stereophonic hearing arrangements has been made more practical by this miniaturiza-tion. New developments in microphones and earphones have permitted a broader band of frequencies for transmission, more uniform gain and frequency characteristics, less distortion at high-gain levels, and a con-sequent increase in the variety of patients who can be helped with hearing aids. Lybarger (1966) also noted the substantial reduction in cubic volume of both body and ear-level hearing aids during the time period 1940 to 1970. In many instances the size reduction has been accomplished with no compromise in performance of the aids. Fre-quency response has not been affected, particularly in the body aid, but in ear-level aids there is a reduced low-frequency response capability. In the smaller aids there also is a need to eliminate harmonic distortion. Both Lybarger (1966) and Stutz (1969) reported similar frequency of purchase statistics that show behind-the-ear and in-the-ear models in-creasing in popularity.

The proceedings of a conference on hearing aid evaluation proce-dures sponsored by the American Speech and Hearing Association and edited by Castle (1967) portray the status of research and clinical prac-tice at that time. The purposes of the conference were (1) to evaluate portions of data collected on a questionnaire sent to various facilities, (2) to determine the needs for research on hearing aid evaluation pro-cedures, and (3) to evaluate and recommend revision of existing mini-mal requirements for hearing programs regarding hearing aid selection. Six panel groups served the conference, each with one of the general topics that follow: Tests and Measurements, Characteristics and Pro-curement of Hearing Aids, Testing of Children, Testing of Adults, Follow-up Procedures, and Professional Qualifications and Standards. This report includes an excellent discussion of hearing problems, possi-ble solutions, and guidelines and directions for research.

Response characteristics of hearing aids. Modern advances have allowed present-day hearing aids to become smaller, more powerful, and more flexible. Although these features offer convenience and cosmetic improvement, primary concern should be centered on increased efficiency in communication. Hearing aids must be developed that circumvent problems of individual tolerance for amplified sound and that enhance response characteristics such as reception of auditory stimuli, particularly speech, for a wide variety of hearing impairment. Frequency characteristics, represented by frequency response curves of hearing aids, have received considerable research attention and discussion. One aim has been to determine the frequency patterns that seem most appropriate for the majority of hearing aid users.

Watson (1961b) summarized two post-World War II studies undertaken by the Electroacoustics Committee of the British Medical Research Council and by the Psycho-Acoustic Laboratories (PAL) of Harvard University. The British study recommended a 12 dB gain per octave, from 250–750 Hz with a rather uniform response thereafter. The PAL report suggested a uniform response from 300–4000 Hz or a rise of 1 dB/octave coupled with a tone control allowing for adjustment up to 7 dB/octave.

Using a large number of hard-of-hearing individuals, Sheets and Hedgecock (1949) evaluated these proposed design objectives for hearing aids. Results showed no significant differences between selective amplification that mirrored the audiogram and flat amplification. An analysis of the subjective judgments by subjects found that approximately equal numbers chose the flat and moderate high-pass patterns, but very few chose the marked high-pass pattern. The authors concluded that there is little justification for the use of selective amplification in fitting most hard-of-hearing persons with electronic hearing aids. Supporting evidence was reported by Harris et al. (1961), who found sentence intelligibility was superior when aids had flat control, 50 dB gain, and 75 dB SPL input. Thompson and Lassman (1969), however, found a very slight benefit in speech discrimination from selective high-pass amplification over flat amplification for subjects with sensorineural hearing losses. Later, when Thompson and Lassman (1970) studied the subjects' reactions to the two types of amplification, preference for flat over selective amplification was approximately 80 percent.

Range of frequency response and distortion measures also have been investigated to determine their relative importance in hearing aid performance.

Jerger and Thelin (1968) analyzed twenty-one commercial hearing aids according to three characteristics. Frequency response was classified by an Index of Response Irregularity (IRI), a measure of the irregularity of the frequency response envelope. In addition to IRI there were measures of effective bandwidth and harmonic distortion. Using the Synthetic Sentence Identification (SSI) stimulus materials as an evaluation instrument, scores of normal-hearing subjects correlated well with IRI and with bandwidth below 1000 Hz but not with harmonic distortion. Olsen and Carhart (1967) determined that width of frequency response was relatively more important than harmonic distortion and intermodulation distortion in a study of speech discrimination in noise. The wider the frequency response the better was the discrimination. Confirming results were reported in an experiment by Witter and Goldstein (1971). They asked normal-hearing subjects to make quality judgments about speech material transduced through different hearing aids. Subjects listened to paired recordings from different aids, alternating between them until they made a choice. Preference judgments were most highly related to frequency range and transient response and, to a lesser degree, to harmonic distortion and high- and low-pass cutoff frequency. Intermodulation distortion was not a significant factor.

Since flatness and range of frequency response are predictions of hearing aid performance, the reliability of data reported by hearing aid manufacturers becomes important.

Kasten and Lotterman (1967), comparing the response curves drawn from sample instruments with curves provided by the manufacturers of the instruments, revealed that in some cases wide discrepancies existed with respect to both gain and output configuration. Because of the great amount of variation that emerged, the authors concluded that in clinical management of hearing aid evaluation it would be advisable to require follow-up visits after a hearing aid has been purchased.

Considering the effects of electroacoustic properties of hearing aids that have been experimentally determined, it appears that the most important are the flatness and smoothness of the frequency response, the width of the frequency response, and bandwidth under 1000 Hz. Distortion variables have not had a strong effect, perhaps because the hearing aids tested have met requirements for this characteristic.

Frequency transposition and modification. In recent years research studies have evaluated the effects of manipulating the frequency response characteristics of hearing aids to provide optimal selective amplification for specific types of audiometric configurations. The majority of the literature refers to a downward frequency transposition or an extended low-frequency range for the hearing aid, both attempting to gain maximum benefit for those persons who have residual hearing in the low-frequency range. An argument has been made for providing the hypacusic with information at frequencies where there is greatest auditory sensitivity, the low frequencies, rather than boosting the high frequencies. However, research has shown that downward frequency shifting has an adverse effect on intelligibility when the harmonic relations between the frequency components are not maintained.

Tiffany and Bennett (1961) suggested that hypacusics might benefit from transposed speech, despite an initial reaction of reduced discrimination, if training were provided. The hypothesis was tested by Bennett and Byers (1967). They employed a proportionate frequency shift procedure so that harmonic relations were maintained. Performance on the Fairbanks Rhyme Test was compared for word lists played at normal speed and at 90, 80, 70, and 60 percent of normal. At normal speed the fifteen hypacusic subjects averaged 76.3 percent correct, but they attained 79.2 percent and 84.1 percent correct at speeds of 90 and 80 percent of normal, respectively. The two slowest speeds reduced intelligibility below 67 percent. Although there is no portable miniaturized unit with slow-play capability, Bennett and Byers suggest that the method might be used for auditory training.

Frequency transposition units have provided an alternative to slow-play as a means of increasing the utilization of the low-frequency range. Oeken (1963) employed a unit that reduced frequencies by one half an octave to an octave. Sensorineural subjects with a steep drop in hearing level of 40 dB between 1000 Hz and 1500 Hz were tested in free field with monosyllabic words, phrases, and a short story. In almost every condition normal speech was more intelligible than transposed speech.

On the other hand, Johansson (1966) reported some success after training with a novel frequency transposition system where one channel of an amplifier imposed no modification on the normal speech frequency range, but a second amplifier channel separated the voiceless consonants by a high-pass filter and modulated them down to the low-frequency range. Case histories of some children illustrated the substantial gains in speech discrimination that were possible after a year of training; one child showed a shift from 0 to 40 percent in discrimination and another increased from 45 to 85 percent.

Ling and Doehring (1969) also experimented with a system that provided linear amplification to one ear and transposed speech to the other. Their vocoder coded the frequencies from 1000 Hz to 4000 Hz into ten lower-frequency channels spaced at 100 Hz intervals between 100 and 1000 Hz. Profoundly deaf children aged 7 to 11 were given picture-sound discrimination training. When a word was spoken the children selected one of two pictures. Training conditions included linear amplification to both ears, linear amplification to one ear and coded speech to the other, and coded speech to both ears. Over a series of training sets the trials to reach criterion of learning decreased but the training did not generalize to a set of test words. On both a pretest and a post-test, children with linear amplification in both ears obtained the highest scores.

Ling and Druz (1967) had found similar results when they provided daily training sessions for eight subjects from the Montreal Aural School. In this experiment, training on sound discrimination of vowels, different classes of consonants, and intonation patterns was carried out on two different instruments. One group training on a low-frequency speech training aid with a frequency response from 60 Hz to 6000 Hz. Others trained on a transposing instrument that transposes speech normally over the frequencies 70 Hz to 700 Hz, and transposed frequencies from 2000 Hz to 3000 Hz downward to the band 750 Hz to 1000 Hz. Final test scores were higher for both groups compared with initial test results, but the extended low-frequency aid produced higher final scores than did the tranposing instrument.

D. Ling (1964, 1969) in a series of comparisons between conventional and transposed speech in auditory training found that linear amplification was always at least as effective as any of the experimental systems.

Frequency transposition has *not* demonstrated consistent benefits over those provided by linear amplification. Slow-play speech at 80 percent or 90 percent of normal speed with proportionate frequency shifting has been found to facilitate discrimination in hypacusic subjects, but this feature is not available in the commercial hearing aid. According to Erber (1971d) a critical review of the literature finds little evidence of benefits from frequency transposition.

Frequency modification has been achieved through a variety of procedures other than transposition. An approach by Rice (1965) used a receiver that attenuated the input signal at a rate of 12 dB per octave for frequencies over 600 Hz. This resulted in a flat low-frequency response curve. All of the severely deaf children who were tested with the attentuated high frequencies preferred the modified hearing aid, but comparative data for speech intelligibility were not provided.

Other experiments have investigated the use of an extended low-frequency response for those with high-frequency hearing loss. D. Ling (1964) compared the effects of a conventional hearing aid and an experimental aid that introduced a 9-inch, 2-mm tube through a hole drilled in a standard mold. This tubing acted as a low-pass filter providing low-frequency components not transmitted by standard amplification. After intensive auditory training, profoundly hard-of-hearing children who had used the experimental aid showed superiority in certain areas of speech reception and production. Similar results were also reported in a later paper by Ling (1969).

The commercially available Vocalizer was designed as an extended range low-frequency hearing aid for persons with profound hearing impairment. Briskey and Sinclair (1966) evaluated this instrument through observations of the effects on speech development. Sonogram analyses suggested improved vocalization by infants, teen-agers, and young adults. Briskey et al. (1967) pursued this line of research, comparing the effects on voice characteristics of a low-frequency aid and a standard aid with a 300 Hz to 3500 Hz range. Children with the experimental aid showed more improvement in pitch, rhythm, patterning, duration, and intensity than did the children with the standard aid. Improved threshold levels for selected speech sounds were reported by Leckie and Ling (1968) when deaf children were tested with an experimental aid with a frequency response from 80 Hz to 3500 Hz.

Tentative conclusions concerning extended low-frequency amplification are possible. The presence of low-frequency sounds helps the severely and profoundly hard-of-hearing child in certain voice characteristics, threshold sensitivity for speech sounds, and speech reception.

For persons with a narrow dynamic range between threshold of audibility and the intensity where sounds become intolerably loud, incorporation of compression amplification into a hearing aid design has been one solution to the problem. Aside from providing a ceiling for sound intensity, compression amplification can eliminate the need for frequent adjustment of the gain control as the hearing aid user confronts rapidly changing environmental conditions. According to Lynn and Carhart (1963) there is little experimental evidence to support the assumption that these advantages are obtained without any sacrifice in intelligibility of speech. However, Burchfield (1971) later found some supporting data when he used a modified version of the instrument described by Lynn and Carhart in an experiment with subjects who exhibited loudness recruitment. Speech discrimination was better under conditions of compression amplification than it was with conventional amplification.

Thomas and Sparks (1971) described another type of signal modification in which they processed monosyllables through a high-pass filter with a cutoff at 1100 Hz and an attentuation slope of 12 dB per octave. Then the speech signal was infinitely amplitude peak clipped and presented to hearing-impaired listeners at three sensation levels. The majority of subjects, thirteen out of sixteen, performed better with modified speech than unmodified speech.

Among the techniques used to improve speech reception and production, only extended low-frequency response for severely and profoundly deaf subjects has shown a consistent positive effect. Frequency transposition still has not improved on linear amplification, and other forms of signal modification have not received systematic study.

Audiometric materials in hearing aid selection. The literature shows that a wide variety of stimulus materials and procedures are used in hearing aid selection and evaluation procedures. Speech detection thresholds, speech discrimination testing, speech reception thresholds, auditory distortion tests, and bands of filtered noise have all been employed to evaluate and select hearing aids for clients.

Little support can be found for the use of standard speech discrimination and SRT measures in hearing aid selection. Although McConnell, Silber, and McDonald (1960) reported high test-retest reliability coefficients for aided speech discrimination scores used in a hearing aid selection procedure, there is considerable evidence that speech discrimination is not a *valid* measure (Shore, Bilger, and Hirsh, 1960; Zerlin, 1962; Jerger, Malmquist, and Speaks, 1966; Nance and Causey, 1968; Thompson and Lassman, 1969). Zerlin recorded running speech and W-22 word lists after they were passed through six hearing aids and then obtained preference ratings using a paired-comparison procedure. Responses to the W-22 word lists failed to differentiate among the hearing aids. Nance and Causey found random selection of a hearing aid from a group of aids meeting VA standards was as successful as clinical selection based on aided discrimination scores in quiet and noise. At the end of a one-month trial period, there was no quantitative differences between discrimination scores for the clinically selected aids and the aids chosen arbitrarily. Shore, Bilger, and Hirsh, and Thompson and Lassman also concluded that speech discrimination in quiet and noise is not able to differentiate among hearing aids. It is possible that the hearing aids sampled by these studies were so similar that an adequate test of the audiometric material was not possible. However, Jerger, Malmquist, and Speaks introduced differences among aids by using three types: (1) flat response characteristic and minimum distortion; (2) less flat response and minimum distortion; and (3) flat response and considerable harmonic distortion. Significant differences among the aids were not demonstrated to any large degree by performance on W-22 lists, CNC words, or PAL PB word lists. The PAL Auditory Test 8, a multiple-choice test with a sentence imbedded in a competing message, did produce sharp differences that favored aids A, B, and C in order of superiority. When the hearing-impaired subjects were divided into categories according to type of loss, degree of loss, and slope of audiometric configuration, each subgroup ordered the aids consistently according to the sentence test scores. The authors concluded that responses to monosyllabic words *do not* reflect true hearing aid performance differences.

An article by Haug, Baccaro, and Guilford (1971) presents the counterview that PB word lists can be effective test stimuli. They frequently found at least a 20 percent difference between the best aid and the poorest aid tested. Nevertheless, the weight of the evidence indicates the need for alternative hearing aid selection materials.

Several alternatives can be found in the literature. Following their earlier research comparing sentences and monosyllabic words, Jerger and his associates sought other measures that would provide more appropriate criteria for hearing aid selection. Jerger, Speaks, and Malmquist (1966) tested two assumptions underlying conventional selection procedures. They asked first whether behavioral measures can reflect differences in hearing aids. Then, if the measures can, will people presenting a variety of audiometric configurations benefit from different hearing aids? The PAL Test 8 provided the stimulus material in both studies. The first experiment found that physical differences among three experimental hearing aid conditions were reflected in sentence identification test scores of both normal-hearing listeners and those with sensorineural hearing loss. Their second experiment found the rank ordering of aids was the same, however, regardless of audiometric configuration.

Special attention has been given to evaluation procedures for binaural hearing aids. Heffler and Schultz (1964) questioned the adequacy of routine procedures for deciding upon the selection of a monaural or a binaural hearing aid. They recommended that four test conditions be employed: (1) discrimination testing in the presence of competing sound, (2) low S/N ratio to allow the binaural system to show improvement, (3) elimination of localization, and (4) use of relatively long duration speech signals with credit given for partial discrimination.

Olsen and Carhart (1967) found that speech discrimination of monosyllabic words in a competing sentence background did vary systematically from hearing aid to hearing aid, especially at low S/N ratios. At S/N ratio of 6 dB, differences among hearing aids were large enough to be of practical importance.

Since research has shown that speech discrimination can be influenced by many parameters of the listening situation, hearing aid evaluation and selection procedures must reflect these findings. Stimulus material should include competing messages, and both monaural and binaural listening should be represented in a variety of S/N ratios. Isolated words apparently cannot differentiate among hearing aids. Several new electroacoustic and behavioral correlates of hearing aid performance are available. The Index of Response Irregularity, size of bandwidth under 1000 Hz, and overall width of the frequency response illustrate electroacoustic properties associated with aid performance. The Synthetic Sentence Identification Test, the Intermodulation Distortion Test, and monosyllabic words with a competing message at a low S/N ratio provide behavioral measures shown to be superior to standard discrimination and SRT tests.

A variety of other selection procedures that do not call for the use of speech material have been reported in the literature.

Shore and Kramer (1963) described a clinical procedure in which evaluations of specific hearing aids were completely eliminated and no particular hearing aid unit was recommended. Persons completing the hearing test battery were simply given a form with advice on shopping for a hearing aid. A questionnaire was administered later to adults tested by conventional hearing aid selection procedures and to adults under the experimental procedure. Under the conventional procedure somewhat less than 50 percent of those advised to buy a hearing aid followed through by buying the particular make that was recommended; 15 percent bought an entirely different aid and 15 percent bought no hearing aid at all. In the experimental group 70 percent followed the recommendation to buy a hearing aid and 30 percent did not.

Gillespie et al. (1965) considered the idea that a master hearing aid would save time and compare favorably with the traditional method of hearing aid selection. After comparison of the two approaches, they observed that both procedures were comparable in determining gain and maximum power outputs in hearing aid selection. The master hearing aid was not a time-saver, however, and was not more reliable than traditional methods.

An approach called "triplet audiometry" was described by Huizing et al. (1960). With the aim of fitting aids for various audiometric patterns, normal speech was processed through appropriate filters and divided into three frequency bands. For example, three frequency ranges might include one below 900 Hz, one between 900 Hz and 1800 Hz, and a third from 1800 Hz to 7500 Hz. Articulation functions determined for each band were used to select hearing aids with appropriate compensatory frequency characteristics.

Still another technique proposed by Miller (1968) used octave bands of filtered noise as stimuli in aided and unaided sensitivity determination. This type of stimulus was recommended for determining an appropriate amplification level for very young hearing-impaired children. In an experimental study of six profoundly deaf children, free field aided thresholds using the octave band-filtered noise were compared to unaided thresholds. Unaided thresholds for pure tone and filtered noise bands showed close agreement, and the unaided noise thresholds showed improvement over unaided levels.

Gengel, Pascoe, and Shore (1971) published a preliminary report on a similar procedure for children with severe and profound hearing losses in which narrow band noise centered at octave intervals from 250 to 4000 Hz served as stimuli for the measurement of three response characteristics: Maximum Linear Output, Maximum Gain, and Maximum Volume setting for Linear Output. In selecting a hearing aid, thresholds for pure tones and noise bands were considered in relation to the hearing aid characteristics so that the sensation level at which the child would receive speech could be estimated.

Markle and Zaner (1966) evaluated an experimental procedure for determining hearing aid gain requirements for persons demonstrating recruitment. The conventional approach of determining acoustic gain of hearing aids by approximating the amount of hearing loss for speech provided a comparison criterion. Twelve adults with bilateral sensori-neural hearing losses served as subjects. Each subject was tested under three conditions: (1) unaided, (2) aided, with the average acoustic gain preset to approximate the unaided SRT (conventional), and (3) aided, with the average acoustic gain preset to amplify the intensity of average speech to a value of 50 dB below the unaided Most Comfortable Loudness level (MCL). An evaluation of the data indicated that the conventional gain settings, where gain equals the Speech Reception Threshold, are greater than the experimental gain settings, where the gain equals the Most Comfortable Loudness level minus 50 dB. The conventional gain settings provide lower SRT values and MCL levels that fall below the intensity of speech. Experimental gain settings provide MCL levels that appear to cluster around the intensity of average speech.

Several audiologists have suggested that a formal or informal lipreading test should be incorporated as part of a hearing aid evaluation procedure (Dodds and Harford, 1968; Siegenthaler and Gruber, 1969). This technique makes possible a comparison of the patients' shifts in communicative efficiency aided and unaided. Data have been reported concerning the measures that result from such a procedure (Kahn, 1964). Semi-Diagnostic Test words were recorded on tape and a speaker was filmed for color motion-picture presentation. Discrimination scores were obtained for sixteen subjects with sensorineural loss under conditions of auditory, visual, and combined stimulation both with and without a hearing aid. Combined scores were better than auditory only scores in both aided and unaided testing. Although aided combined scores were not significantly better than unaided combined scores, Kahn concluded that inclusion of the auditory, visual, and combined methods of presentation would add information in clinical hearing aid evaluation.

Apparently there is a lack of satisfaction with hearing aid selection procedures based on the traditional measures of SRT and speech discrimination.

Nevertheless Burney (1972), in a survey of accredited audiology clinics across the country, found that clinics were evaluating several aids with each client as was the case at the inception of hearing aid evaluation by clinics in the mid 1940s. Tests to determine speech discrimination, speech-reception threshold, tolerance, and pure tone sensitivity were still being used.

It has been contended that we should not work toward hearing aid selection for the client but rather toward hearing aid elimination. If through our hearing aid evaluation we eliminate those aids that are definitely not to be considered further, there will remain several aids, any one of which would benefit the client.

Effects of earmold coupling on frequency response. Lybarger (1967) presented a thorough discussion of variables associated with earmold coupling. Factors that most affect low-frequency response are the stiffness of the diaphragm, the venting arrangement, and the size of the outer ear cavity up to the eardrum. He has determined that the primary peak region of the freqeuncy response curve is influenced most by tube length and diameter, diaphragm constants, and the damping plug.

Empirical comparison between vented, open, and unvented earmolds have been reported. McClellan (1967) found that a vented earmold allowed better speech discrimination than a conventional unvented earmold when subjects with sensorineural losses were tested in noise. Hodgson and Murdock (1971) also reported data favoring the vented acoustic coupler. When Dodds and Harford (1968) tested sensorineural subjects, an open earmold was significantly superior to a conventional closed coupler and slightly better than a vented earmold in terms of speech discrimination. In a later report of questionnaire data (Dodds and Harford, 1970), respondents were more often full-time users if they had open molds. Jetty and Rintelmann (1970) used a CROS hearing aid (see discussion on page 159) to compare the effects of four acoustic couplers on SRT scores and speech discrimination of conductive subjects and subjects with steeply falling and gradually sloping sensorineural hearing losses. In addition to the conventional, vented, and open earmolds they tested a crimped polyethylene tube bent at approximately 90-degree angle. Coupler effects on SRT's, which are small, tended to favor the conventional and open earmolds. Larger differences in speech discrimination were found for both types of sensorineural subject; the three modified earmolds were superior to the conventional earmold and produced similar scores. Conductive subjects were not affected by type of coupler. The superiority of the vented or open earmold has not always been demonstrated experimentally. Revoile (1968) found no differences in speech discrimination related to conventional and vented earmolds, nor did Northern and Hattler (1970).

We find that in all cases of sensorineural loss the vented or open earmold has been at least as effective as the conventional type, and sometimes significantly better. When subjective attitudes are considered, vented models are generally preferred.

Binaural hearing aids. Considerable research during the past two decades has been addressed to the supposition that binaural hearing is superior to monaural hearing. Hirsh (1950) summarized the assets of binaural hearing in terms of threshold measures, levels of masking, localization, and intelligibility. The binaural threshold for hearing has been found on the order of 3 dB lower than the monaural threshold, a phenomenon referred to as binaural summation. Since there is relatively little information on the effects of binaural reception on speech perception, its application to hearing aid selection is not fully understood. It is known that under noise conditions, no binaural summation takes place, but rather the reverse has been observed; namely, interaural inhibition occurs with certain interaural phase relationships between the noise and the signal. There is some evidence that localization ability improves under the binaural condition. In order to utilize binaural hearing for improved localization with amplification, the hearing aid must be designed with two complete microphone pickups, one at the location of each ear. Relative performance of binaural and monaural hearing aids in quiet and in noise was critically reviewed by Berger (1964). He noted that every study has found that binaurally aided discrimination was superior when speech signals and competing noise were introduced through different source locations. There was a tendency for the discrepancy in discrimination favoring the binaural hearing aid to increase as the S/N ratio became more unfavorable.

There are many comparisons of speech reception thresholds and speech discrimination measures for binaural and monaural aided conditions in the literature. In a number of experiments in which subjects were tested in quiet conditions, there was only a small difference in favor of the binaural mode, but in noise binaural amplification showed increasing superiority (Hedgecock and Sheets, 1958; Markle and Aber, 1958; Belzile and Markle, 1959; Wright and Carhart, 1960). However, conflicting results were found in several instances. When Jerger and Dirks (1961) replicated the procedures of Belzile and Markle they found a similar pattern of effects for subjects with conductive losses, but results were divergent in both amount and pattern of improvement for subjects with sensorineural losses. One change in procedure might account for some of the differences. Jerger and Dirks placed the monaural aid on the subject's head whereas Belzile and Markle placed it on the body where head movement would not alter the relative positions of the microphone and sound sources.

In a comparison study of binaural, pseudo-binaural, and monaural amplification systems DiCarlo and Brown (1960) failed to find better speech discrimination in quiet or in noise, although Wright and Carhart (1960) have reported that a binaural system was superior to monaural and diotic systems in both quiet and noise.

Jerger, Carhart, and Dirks (1961) tested subjective reports by users of binaural aids that claim improved ability to understand speech in difficult listening situations. Intelligibility measures for words presented with competing sentences and for sentences with competing continuous discourse did not demonstrate the marked superiority that one would expect from subjective reports. They concluded that binaural amplification produces little or no objective improvement in ability to understand speech either in quiet or with competing stimuli.

After examining responses to a questionnaire on attitudes of hearing aid users, Dirks and Carhart (1962) suggested that there is some conviction on the part of respondents that two aids are better than one even though performance differences have not been demonstrated by research. This agrees with a survey of the attitudes of fifty successful binaural hearing aid users by Kodman (1969), who found that thirty individuals had switched from a monaural aid to binaural amplification.

Harris (1965) reviewed many of the studies heretofore mentioned, and presented an interpretation of the contradictory results by reference to the geometry of the listening situation and the possible operation of the sound shadow effect of the head in the presence of a masking noise. An experiment comparing various conditions of monaural, diotic, and dichotic listening supported the principle of improved signal-to-noise level with binaural hearing mode. Harris concluded that an improvement of 20 percent is the lower limit for the benefit to be expected from binaural hearing aid fitting.

CROS hearing aids. The development of miniaturized hearing aids has not only allowed binaural amplification for bilateral hearing losses, but it has also provided an extended application to cases of unilateral hearing loss. CROS amplification refers to the *contralateral routing of signals*. In this application of binaural hearing, signals coming to the poor ear are picked up by a hearing aid microphone, amplified, and routed electrically across the head to an earphone mounted near the good ear. A plastic tube then carries the acoustic signals from the earphone into the open ear canal of the good ear. A popular application of this concept can be realized by utilizing eyeglass frames for the routing of the electrical wiring.

The BICROS, used in cases of bilateral hearing loss with one unaidable ear, is another special application of binaural amplification. This arrangement assumes that one ear is "aidable" even though there is a bilateral hearing loss. A microphone is located near each ear. Each microphone picks up signals and routes them to a mixer where they are amplified and routed to an earphone or receiver, which in turn delivers the amplified signals from both sides of the head into the one and only usable ear. Conventional eyeglass ear-level hearing aids can be converted to the BICROS arrangement with little effort. Persons with bilateral hearing losses, demonstrating good hearing through 500 or 750 Hz and then markedly depressed hearing at the higher frequencies, have enjoyed some success with the CROS amplification arrangement. Apparently the problem of acoustic feedback can be circumvented, since the ear canal of the aided ear is left unoccluded as much as possible. This results in an attentuation of low-frequency sound where residual hearing is relatively good and at the same time permits receiving the sounds that the person would not ordinarily hear.

Most of the literature related to the special application of binaural hearing describes client satisfaction and improved localization ability. Harford and Musket (1964), Harford and Barry (1965), Harford and Dodds (1966), Rintelmann, Harford, and Burchfield (1970), and Lotterman and Kasten (1971), all discuss the benefits of CROS or BICROS hearing aid arrangements.

Localization

Normal-hearing persons are able to locate the source of auditory stimulation with a high degree of accuracy in many situations that pose problems for the hard of hearing. The research literature provides information on the effects of intensity of the sound source, the difficulties produced by monaural hearing loss, and the possibility of training localization ability.

Signal intensity. In several localization experiments, Bergman et al. (1965) screened a large population of blind adults for hearing impairment and then tested a group with confirmed hearing losses. Lateralization and fusion of test sounds were studied at two intensity levels under monaural, binaural, and unaided listening conditions. Greatest success was found with binaural amplification at the higher intensity level.

The effect of signal intensities from 10 dB to 45 dB SL was studied by Butler and Naunton (1967). Nine normal-hearing subjects fitted with a muff on one ear to simulate a monaural hearing loss listened to bursts of broad-band noise, located at one of nine positions covering the area from front center to 90 degrees left and right of the listener. When the signal was presented on the side of the muffed ear, accuracy of localization improved as the sensation level of the signal increased. In a control condition, with both ears uncovered, maximum errors occurred with the weakest intensity and the source at 80 degrees. Confirmation of these trends was obtained from one subject with otitis media who had a 31 dB unilateral loss and from two subjects with a 10 dB interaural threshold difference. The authors attributed the greater accuracy at higher intensity levels to interaural time difference cues for location rather than interaural intensity differences.

The relative importance of different cues for localization, under a variety of conditions, was reported by Wright (1967). His findings seem to imply that if the signal is intense enough persons with unilateral or bilateral high-frequency hearing losses should be able to use low-frequency time differences to improve their localization ability.

Types of hearing loss. The special problems of unilateral hearing loss have been treated in several papers. Viehweg and Campbell (1960) compared localization ability in normal-hearing and monaurally impaired listeners for a sound source presented at eight locations. The number and size of errors were measured in noise and quiet. Localization became increasingly difficult for the monaural listeners as the stimulus was shifted from the front toward the back, especially in terms of the error size. Accuracy of localization also decreased with greater impairment, supporting the critical importance of binaural cues. The authors attributed the lack of relationship between duration of loss and localization ability to mean that the difficulty is permanent. Bergman et al. (1965) also found that the elderly subjects of their experiment, who were impaired monaurally, had severe problems in lateralization in the unaided or monaurally aided conditions despite the long-term nature of their hearing problem.

Hochberg (1963) examined the case of poor localization that is sometimes found with normal-hearing persons. He hypothesized that subjects presumed to have normal hearing would tend to have some interaural discrepancy if their localization ability was less accurate than is typical of the normal hearing. Seventy subjects were grouped according to their interaural threshold differences into categories 0–5 dB, 6–10 dB, 11–20 dB, and over 21 dB. Subjects with interaural differences greater than 21 dB were found to have poorer localization ability.

Harris and Sergeant (1971) carried out an experiment comparing monaural and binaural minimum audible angles in which three experienced listeners were asked to state whether a moving pure tone and noise signals had moved to the right or to the left of a starting point that had two locations, 0 degrees or 60 degrees azimuth. Under certain conditions monaural listening was as good as binaural: when noise bursts were the source and with an 800 Hz signal at 0 degrees azimuth. Accuracy was poorer at higher frequencies but even under the worst conditions there was usable monaural directional hearing.

Two studies relating sound localization accuracy and type of hearing loss have reported some areas of agreement and occasional disagreement. Jongkees and Veer (1957) included a wide variety of hearing problems in their subject sample of over sixty persons. They categorized subjects into the following types: chronic otitis media, atresia of the meatus, sensorineural and mixed loss, otosclerosis, fenestrated otosclerosis, tympanoplasty, and unilateral total deafness with both normal hearing in the good ear and with a hearing loss in the good ear. They found that neither a conductive hearing loss nor a unilateral loss necessarily resulted in pathological localization. Although some subjects in every diagnostic subset had localization difficulty, patients from the perceptive loss group often had problems with directional hearing.

Nordlund (1964) supported the finding that conductive hearing loss was not associated with severe problems in directional hearing, but he also found very little disruption among subjects with cochlear pathology.

Localization training. Viehweg and Campbell (1960), Rees (1965), and Hochberg (1963) have presented data that suggest no automatic or spontaneous benefit is derived from everyday experience with sound localization. There are three experiments, however, that have shown improvement is possible with normal-hearing subjects who have simulated unilateral losses.

Bauer et al. (1966) plugged one ear of normal-hearing subjects for three days. Broad-band noise sources were then perceived as if they had been shifted toward the unplugged ear at the beginning of the period, but the subjects compensated for the difference between ears during the period without training. When training was provided, the orientation time was reduced to less than half.

Perrott and Elfner (1968) also found that training can improve localization accuracy. In the first of two experiments, six normal-hearing subjects listened to signals presented from one of two speakers mounted 45 degrees to the left and right of center, 24 inches from the subject. Performance was compared under three conditions: (1) normal binaural listening, (2) monaural listening with the other ear plugged, and (3) monaurally with the signals matched for sensation level. The number of errors increased from condition 1 to condition 3, from almost perfect accuracy to performance at chance level. A second experiment studied the influence of training on localization, again under three conditions: (1) one ear plugged, (2) one ear plugged and equal sensation levels, and (3) one ear plugged and intensity differences reversed for the two ears. After training, subjects were found to localize as well monaurally as the binaural listeners of the first experiment if the difference in intensity was maintained.

Elfner et al. (1970) later found that with training, normal-hearing subjects with simulated monaural hearing losses can achieve an 80 percent correct response rate.

Since hearing-impaired individuals have not yet been shown to improve their localization ability with training, this must be demonstrated before the results of research with normal-hearing subjects can be applied. Identification of intensity, time differences, and spectral composition as cues for localization should provide the needed bases for training.

Side Effects of Amplification

There is some evidence in the literature that the application of powerful hearing aids can further reduce auditory sensitivity. In other words, a noise-induced hearing loss can be demonstrated.

Macrae and Farrant (1965) compared the effects of two hearing aids on eighty-seven children, all exhibiting bilateral sensorineural hearing losses. One hearing aid had high gain and the other had average gain. The investigators concluded that the use of high-powered hearing aids can cause deterioration of hearing in an aided ear. The extent of the deterioration depends upon the power of the hearing aid, the number of hours of usage, the gain of the hearing aid (to a limited extent), and the degree of hearing loss in the aided ear at the outset of use.

Ross and Lerman (1967) included some of these variables in their study and found a multiple correlation of 0.80 when average relative shift in hearing was correlated with average hearing loss, when the aid was first worn, and the hours per week an aid was used. They concluded that deterioration of hearing can be caused by hearing aids, and recommended that clinicians limit the maximum power output of aids to about 130 dB SPL and provide frequent audiological follow-up for children.

Macrae (1968a) reported on temporary threshold shifts (TTS) after use of a powerful hearing aid in four deaf children. Substantial amounts of TTS were found over a wide range of frequencies. In three of the children the recovery time for TTS appeared to be at a slower rate than that obtained for recovery from the same level of TTS in normal-hearing subjects. However, in a follow-up study Macrae (1968b) found recovery from TTS at a rate of about 3 to 4 dB, very close to the rate of 4 to 5 dB found for recovery from high values of TTS in normal-hearing subjects reported by Ward (1960).

In a third report Macrae (1968c) presented the effects on residual hearing of four different hearing aids varying in gain. Basically, the results of this research substantiate the previous findings by Macrae and Farrant (1965). An average of 5.2 dB of deterioration was found with moderately high-gain instruments, and a 7.0 dB deterioration was found for high-gain instruments.

A case study described by Roberts (1970) suggested that children with progressive hereditary hearing losses may be susceptible to damage from hearing aid use.

The evidence demonstrates that amplification can indeed lead to a deterioration in residual hearing. Recognition of this risk has led to changes in hearing aid design, reducing the maximum gain available.

Hearing Aid Orientation

Despite the familiar complaint of hearing clinics that hearing aid users fail to return for orientation programs (Castle, 1967), there is little information on the reasons for the low rate of return. An exception is the detailed report of Rassi and Harford (1968) who investigated, by means of a questionnaire distributed to former clients, the reasons for continuation or noncontinuation in hearing aid selection and orientation programs. Approximately 70 percent of the 201 returns reported that an aid was purchased, and 61 percent had bought the aid recommended by the clinic. Three fourths of the people who purchased hearing aids did not return for the recheck session. Reasons given were, in order of most frequent response, (1) not knowing a recheck was recommended, (2) hearing aid performing satisfactorily, and (3) putting off the appointment—procrastination. The poor attendance at the recheck sessions was consistent with low enrollment in lipreading classes that were suggested for one fourth of the people. Of the 20 who enrolled, only 12 reported that the training was helpful.

Additional information concerning reasons underlying the failure to make use of aural rehabilitation sessions is contained in a unpublished report by Oyer et al. A number of facilities cooperated in interviewing thirty-three clients who had not followed recommendations made at the time of their audiometric evaluation. Although no one from this sample had returned to the clinic for additional rehabilitation, twenty-two had followed the recommendation of the audiologist for or against purchase of a hearing aid, six had ignored the recommendation, and the remaining five provided no information. Lack of motivation was the reason most often given. Many of these subjects felt that they did not need help or that they would not get help. Among the other reasons, scheduling difficulties were mentioned by ten people, five mentioned illness or old age, and one claimed that the cost was too great.

Northern et al. (1969) surveyed attitudes of military patients toward aural rehabilitation and found a generally positive attitude toward programs of aural rehabilitation in which respondents had participated. There was widespread support for the continuation of the program.

The variables that influence clients to return for orientation and training sessions after hearing aid fitting really have not been identified. Some clinics report favorable results while others have poor success. Systematic follow-up of clients from a sample of clinics is needed so that significant aspects of the orientation program can be discovered.

Tactile Input

Aside from routine use of the auditory and visual sensory modalities, there have been several attempts to incorporate the tactile modality in aiding the deaf and profoundly hard of hearing in the understanding of speech. At this time, it is generally understood that tactile reception of spoken language cannot provide a substitute for hearing. Rather, the currently held position asserts that the tactile modality can provide a reasonable supplement to visual speech cues or to residual hearing function. This was not always believed to be true. Early researchers assumed that the deaf could be taught through the skin. Later work by VonBekesy (1957a, 1957b, 1959), and Geldard (1940, 1954, 1957, 1960, 1961), compared the two modalities relative to receiving spoken language and described the similarities as well as the many differences. Of significance is the limited capability of the skin to receive the frequencies within the critical speech range. The literature describes a number of stimulus transmission systems that transduce acoustic energy for direct reception by the cutaneous sensory receptors. Both mechanical vibrations and electrical impulses have been employed as sources of stimulation in these efforts.

Source. Gault (1924 and 1926a) described two of the earliest types of transduction. The first consisted of a long speaking tube positioned through several walls. Subjects sat at one end of the tube and were required to make gross discriminations between various tuning fork vibrations and speech sounds. The second system used a disk-shaped receiver similar to the earpiece of a telephone receiver. Subjects received amplified messages on the fingertips.

Later, Gault and Crane (1928) in conjunction with the Bell Telephone Laboratories designed and constructed a Teletactor. Speech energy was divided into five frequency bands, amplified, and introduced to each of the five fingers of one hand by simple vibrators. According to Pickett (1963) the primary difficulty with the system was that it employed frequencies that were out of the range of sensitivity by the cutaneous sensory receptors. For practical purposes, 75 to 800 Hz is the optimal frequency range for tactile stimulation.

To overcome the sensitivity problem, transmission systems have been developed that transpose frequencies downward to a lower range (Keidel, 1958; Pickett and Pickett, 1963). However, interfering effects of multiple vibrators were still evident.

Code. As can be seen, the majority of the research has involved the utilization of tactile stimulus transmission systems incorporating multiple vibrators. The concept of frequency transposition has had foremost attention. The rationale was that transposition would provide information to the cutaneous sensory receptors from high-frequency sound composition that otherwise would be out of the frequency range of the cutaneous receptors. Geldard (1954, 1957, 1960), Geldard and Sherrick (1965), and Gilson (1968) have described some problems inherent to this approach. The use of multiple simultaneous stimulation causes significant threshold elevations due to the masking effects caused by competing stimuli. When six to eight vibrators were used simultaneously, nearly 50 percent of the values tested had threshold elevations of over 19 dB, the highest being 32.5 dB. Alluisi, Morgan, and Hawkes (1965) found similar results.

Due to the many limitations of the cutaneous sensory receptors, the limited frequency response capabilities, and the masking effects of multiple vibrators applied to the fingers, Geldard (1957, 1960) advocates recoding verbal stimuli. Using the dimensions of loci, duration, and intensity, verbal or written information is transposed to patterns over ten loci in the human integument. *Speech sounds are not used* in this transposition. Rather, each letter of the alphabet is coded into a pattern of stimulation. A 60 Hz sinusoidal signal of varying intensities and durations provides the basic stimulus. Geldard refers to this procedure as "vibratese language."

Most of the early studies employing speech stimuli for tactile reception utilized Gault's Teletactor. Gault (1924) submitted a 28-year-old deaf female to 200 hours of practice with the Teletactor. The subject learned to distinguish about 50 percent of a list of 1972 monosyllabic words.

In another study, Gault (1926b) had a subject participate in twenty-eight half-hour training sessions. Subsequent to the training the subject was able to discriminate ten sentences with about 75 percent accuracy. A change of speakers or reduced rate of speaking significantly altered these results, however.

The Teletactor was used by Cloud (1933) in a study of eight deaf subjects who completed one year of training. They exhibited improvement in several aspects of speech production. Dean (1934) also found success in speech training of young deaf students.

In an experiment using transposed frequencies, Pickett and Pickett (1963) evaluated the potential of a ten-channel tactile vocoder for discrimination of vowels and consonants. They concluded that the employment of ten vibrators presents two basic problems. First, the masking effect, alluded to earlier, obscures certain discriminations. The /i/, /I/, /e/ sounds were particularly difficult. A second problem concerned immobilizing all fingers of both hands, at best a cumbersome procedure. The Picketts suggest three or four discreet loci may be the maximum number that can be used profitably in simultaneous stimulation.

Tactile thresholds for spoken phonemes have been studied by Haas (1970) using an improved tactile transducer, the Clevite Bimorph (PST-5B). Thresholds were determined for all phonemes except the /s/ and /ꞱΘ/, those with the lowest relative power. Vowels had lower thresholds than consonants; the range of threshold values for consonants was wide. These measures were highly reliable and intersubject agreement was excellent. At suprathreshold levels subjects consistently were able to describe the tactile stimuli on the three dimensions—intensity, duration, and pattern.

Two studies extended the findings of Haas. Higgins (1971) compared threshold values obtained with four different voices: adult female, adult male, boy, and girl. The general pattern of threshold values was similar, but not identical, to those values found by Haas. Goldstein (1972) trained subjects to discriminate consonant-vowel syllables using two transducers, the Clevite Bimorph and a bone-conduction vibrator. The bone vibrator was found to be superior to the Bimorph. Research findings to date have shown that tactile discrimination of phonemes and larger speech units is possible with a variety of transmission systems when a closed set of stimuli is presented. Taction is potentially a useful supplement to vision and audition; however, at this time no transmission system has been developed to the point of practical application.

Receiver. The role of individual differences in response to tactile stimulation has received little attention. One article by Gray (1964) studied the relative sensitivity of adults and adolescents for various pure tone frequencies. A transducer was placed on the palm of the subject's hand while frequencies ranging from 10 to 2000 Hz were presented. For the adults, sensitivity was greatest in the range 51–100 Hz. Adolescents had a wider range of response, including the bands 1–50 Hz and 51–100 Hz.

Multisensory Approach

Audiologists and educators of the deaf have commented many times upon the advisability of utilizing several input channels simultaneously for rehabilitative purposes. The thought is, of course, that there is reinforcement of the stimuli that are presented simultaneously in different modes. There are some data that support this general notion.

Communication methods. Geldard (1960) discussed the particular merits of the auditory, visual, and tactile channels in communication. Audition is particularly appropriate for temporal discrimination and the interpretation of successive stimuli. The visual modality performs best when stimuli are presented simultaneously and in other instances where spatial orientation is important. The tactual modality uses cues of locus, intensity, duration, and frequency. Geldard cautioned that the tactual channel cannot replace the auditory or visual channels, but it can serve as an avenue for supplementary information.

Describing the Russian viewpoint concerning compensatory mechanisms and hearing loss, Morkovin (1961) argued that alternative behavior can develop to replace the impaired response mode when the particular stimulus situation is encountered repeatedly. Since language is considered to be the key to development of memory and of concept formation, it assumes a critical role. Morkovin mentions the need for a combination of language and sensory training. Through cortical analysis and synthesis, the information from several channels can aid the hearing-impaired person. For example, visual, kinesthetic, and tactual cues can be useful in lipreading.

A system based on visual and tactile components was found to be effective in speech training programs described by Zaliouk (1954). In his program dynamic speech sounds are received by lipreading and by finger and hand movements in contact with the speaker's articulatory organs. Finger movement allows the subject to discriminate vibrations and airstream cues that distinguish among the phonemes. Static sounds are differentiated by the different speech organs that are involved in articulating the phonemes. Movement of the hand and fingers aids proper phrasing, syllabic accent, and natural voice production. This method of symbolizing the phonemes is the core of the training program, with auditory training and amplification playing a subsidiary role.

Multisensory programs predominate in educational settings, combining hearing aids and auditory training with instruction in speech reading; in some programs manual communication also is included. Quigley (n.d.) has described several of the most common methods of communication used in teaching the deaf. The Oral Method calls for input through auditory and visual channels and no manual communication. The Simultaneous Method uses the auditory and visual channels for speech reception simultaneously with finger spelling and signs. In pure form, information is always presented in correct word order, although in practice, Quigley reports, some word classes are often omitted. The Rochester Method is similar to the Simultaneous Method in that it uses speech, speechreading, writing, reading, and finger spelling; but it does not use signs. In a combined system, often found in residential schools, children are first exposed to the Oral Method and later shifted to manual training if they fail to show progress in oral communication.

Garretson (1960) presented some of the advantages and the aims of the Simultaneous Method in suggesting that this method attempts to convey ideas and information meaningfully and fluently by means that can be used both in and out of the classroom. By using hearing aids for cues from residual hearing and, at the same time, lip movement cues and finger spelling and signs, the deaf student is expected to attain receptive skills and good comprehension of material.

Details of the Rochester Method, which emphasizes language acquisition, are described in a paper by Scouten (1967). English words and syntax are made visible through speech, writing, and finger spelling. Scouten points out that speechreading is more useful for key words than for development of correct syntax. Since concepts are developed through syntax rather than vocabulary alone, it is important to teach proper usage. Finger spelling provides a supplement to speechreading and facilitates the learning of correct word order and syntactical rules. The early use of visible English, syntax, and vocabulary training promotes a state of speech readiness that is required for oral articulation. In this connection, Scouten states that intelligible speech, not normal speech, should be the aim, since "normal" speech is impossible.

Cornett (1967) maintains that the normal communication of the deaf should be English as it is used by the hearing population. He describes a system he devised referred to as "cued speech." Cued speech combines speechreading with a system of manual cues that discriminate between similar visual configurations. Twelve cues are available that enable the viewer to identify phonemes if they are used in conjunction with speechreading. Four hand positions are associated with four groups of visually contrastive vowels. A set of eight hand configurations identifies the consonants. The two types of cues, associated with vowels and consonants, can be combined for more rapid communication than is possible with finger spelling. Cornett feels that the utility of this method for young children in the classroom will be confirmed by research with cued speech.

There are, however, some individuals who believe that a multisensory approach to rehabilitation of the aurally handicapped is less effective than a unisensory approach.

Stewart et al. (1964) describe theoretical bases that underlie the use of a unisensory auditory approach with the limited-hearing child. They advocate that lipreading cues be kept minimal throughout the program as they might limit the usefulness of the auditory training.

Imai and Hoshi (1966) also advocate the unisensory auditory system. Their approach is based on the notion that early development of the auditory sensory modality is of primary importance even in profoundly hard-of-hearing subjects. Therefore, the authors experimented with the exclusion of lipreading and other visual clues in an early training program for 5-year-old children. Basically, there are three parts to their program. The first consists of exposure to and discrimination of gross sounds. The second part concerns exposure to and discrimination of musical sounds and the rhythms of music. The third phase emphasizes speech sounds and "slowing" speech. Although no statistical data are given, the authors concluded that this approach was significantly superior to a program they had used in the past in which a multisensory approach was used. They based their statement on the fact that measures of language understanding, vocabulary level, and voice production were significantly superior for the subjects trained by the acoustic method only.

Methods including manual communication. Morkovin (1960) presented research by Morozova and Korsunskaia, who trained a group of children combining oral and finger-spelling techniques. Measures of the children's independent active vocabulary and their speechreading vocabulary at 5 to 6 years of age were definitely superior to those of a control group using only oral training. It is somewhat difficult to interpret the Russian figures, however, since the details of how the vocabulary was determined are not available. Quigley (1966) felt that the counts were estimates made by teachers of how many words the children had learned. The striking disparity between the 2000 word count for the experimental group and only 90 for the control group should be verified.

In 1964 Hester studied the influence of finger spelling on achievement scores of deaf children at the New Mexico School for the Deaf. His results supported the facilitating effects of finger-spelling methods upon reading level and total grade equivalent, both measured by the Stanford Achievement Test. The beneficial effects of finger-spelling training on lipreading ability were more pronounced when training was introduced early. A group of 10-, 11-, and 12-year-olds who had been trained in finger spelling were superior to a group of 14-, 15-, and 16-year-olds. The results always suggested the superiority of the method that included finger spelling whenever a difference existed.

Stuckless and Birch (1966) investigated the influence of manual training in infancy and early childhood upon later speech intelligibility, reading ability, written language skill, and psychosocial adjustment. When compared to a control group without manual experience, children exposed to early manual training were superior in speechreading, reading comprehension, and written expression. Little or no differences were found in speech intelligibility and psychosocial adjustment.

Although there has been some concern about the deleterious effects of manual skills on oral skills, Montgomery (1966) found that manual and oral skills are not incompatible. Fifty-five profoundly deaf children, mean age 15 years, 10 months, were assessed for lipreading ability, voice production (intelligibility), and fluency in manual communication using signs and finger spelling. There was no negative correlation between lipreading and manual ability, but rather a positive correlation between the Donaldson Lipreading Test scores and the manual score. Favoring the inclusion of manual training was the finding that although 71 percent of the children were fluent in finger spelling, only 25 percent could lip-read well, and a very limited 7 percent had intelligible speech. Such poor speech intelligibility would make the opportunity for lipreading among deaf persons very rare.

Quigley (n.d.) reported an extensive five-year experiment that included a survey comparison of the Rochester Method and the Combined System as alternatives in developing language and communication in deaf children. The survey results indicated that the Rochester Method yielded generally superior scores in educational achievement and in reading and written language ability. Analysis of individual schools found that differences in favor of the experimental approach were stronger for the younger children. The absolute difference in grade-level average was not greater than one grade, but it was fairly consistent. A second part of Quigley's report summarized an experiment that compared the effects of the Rochester Method and the Oral Method of communication. Sixteen deaf children, aged 3.5 to 4.5, were studied in a controlled communication environment under each of the two methods for the duration of the four-year program. The group of youngsters trained with the Rochester Method had significantly better scores on the finger-spelling test and on most measures of reading ability and written language. They were even superior to the oral group on measures of speechreading. Quigley concluded that, although the absolute differences were not large, even small gains can mean a lot when the overall level of achievement in deaf children is low. When good oral techniques are combined with finger spelling, the latter can benefit the child and there is no deleterious effect on oral skills. The younger the child, the more effective is the introduction of finger spelling.

All studies reviewed tend to support the inclusion of manual methods in communication systems adopted for deaf children. Furthermore, it seems that the earlier training is started the greater the benefit that can be expected. Finger spelling, as a supplement, appears to facilitate the development of oral skills. No research has investigated individual differences in relation to methods of communicating, however, and group differences tend to be small when they have been reported. Much more evidence is needed before the controversy over manual communication can be settled.

Auditory and visual modalities. A number of studies have reported the effects of adding visual information to the auditory stimuli traditionally used in threshold measurement, discrimination testing, and loudness balance judgments. The generally improved performance levels that obtain with bisensory stimulation compared with single modality conditions illustrate the facilatory interaction of the auditory and visual channels.

The contribution of visual cues to the perception of speech has attracted considerable attention. Extensive data concerning the intelligibility of vowels, consonants, words, and phrases was reported by O'Neill (1954).

Thirty-two normal-hearing subjects listened to each type of material under four S/N ratios. Listening conditions were varied by allowing the speaker to be viewed or not viewed producing auditory-visual and auditory-only conditions. The facilitating effect of visual cues was reflected in two performance measures. In one case, mean percent correct response to the four types of speech material was computed for the auditory-visual and the auditory-only conditions, averaging over the four signal-to-noise ratios. The visual-only scores were based on performance at the −20 dB S/N ratio. Percentage correct data are shown below.

	Vowel	Consonant	Word	Phrase
Auditory-visual	66.0	76.0	78.0	68.0
Auditory only	50.0	49.0	59.0	49.0
Visual only (−20 dB)	44.5	72.0	64.1	25.4

Scores achieved with the combined sensory information were consistently higher than either the auditory-only or the visual-only scores. Another view of the data was obtained by determining the percentage increment in correct response that occurred as the S/N ratio increased from −20 to +10 dB. By taking the difference between the auditory-only and auditory-visual at S/N ratios −20 and at +10, it was found that the visual contribution was greatest for consonants, and then, in order, for words, vowels, and phrases. The visual information was increasingly important as the S/N ratio decreased, as the data indicate:

PERCENT DIFFERENCE (VISUAL-AUDITORY)—(AUDITORY-ONLY)
AT S/N RATIOS OF −20 dB AND +10 dB

	Vowels	Consonants	Words	Phrases
S/N −20 dB	29.0	57.0	43.0	17.0
S/N +10 dB	5.0	17.0	5.0	2.0

The same general effect, an increasing dependence upon visual cues at decreasing S/N ratios, has since been observed by other investigators (Sumby and Pollack, 1954; Sedge, 1965; Erber, 1969; Sanders and Goodrich, 1971).

Erber (1969) determined in greater detail the precise relationship between visual and auditory speech reception in an effort to specify the minimum S/N ratio at which auditory cues can benefit the normal-hearing person. Using words of spondaic stress for stimuli, Erber found that at S/N ratios below −18 dB, auditory response was at chance level, but auditory-visual recognition rose above its base level at about −24 dB. This implies that minimal auditory cues must have contributed even at the −24 dB S/N to produce the improved scores. Erber (1971a) followed up with an experiment that measured the auditory detection threshold for spondaic words in noise. He hypothesized that this might be the point where auditory-visual discrimination improves beyond the auditory-only discrimination. For normal-hearing subjects the value at which detection began to increase above the chance level corresponded to the value in the earlier experiment where auditory-visual presentation showed improvement. In a third experiment Erber (1971b) investigated the auditory reception threshold, auditory recognition, and audiovisual recognition of words by normal-hearing, severely hard-of-hearing, and deaf children. If auditory cues are above detection threshold then they can improve word recognition above the lipreading level for all groups. The greatest improvement was shown by normal-hearing children; severely impaired children were intermediate, and deaf children showed the least benefit from added auditory information.

A University of Oklahoma Research Institute Report (n.d.) presented results on the use of speech discrimination tests to study the effects of bisensory presentation on the understanding of speech in normal- and hard-of-hearing subjects. Articulation functions for bisensory stimulation were similar for all subjects and exceeded substantially the corresponding functions from either vision or audition separately. The group with a sloping audiometric configuration showed relatively greater improvement than the group with flat type. Gains in discrimination scores tended to be greatest at the lower sensation levels. Siegenthaler and Gruber (1969) found that discrimination scores with bisensory testing usually exceeded the sum of scores for hearing and lipreading separately.

Withrow (1965) has recommended that audiovisual material using motion pictures should be employed to improve the short-term memory processes of the deaf. Since lipreading depends upon the synthesis of sequentially presented visual cues, he argues that this training would be useful.

These studies are unanimous in finding that the availability of both auditory and visual cues facilitates receptive speech intelligibility. Visual cues tend to have greater influence when the listening situation is more difficult at low intensities and in noise.

Has there been systematic evaluation of how auditory and visual systems interact? The answer is *yes* because Brown and Hopkins (1967) studied separate visual and auditory threshold functions and a bisensory threshold function to measure precisely the interaction of the two sensory modalities. A theoretical threshold curve for the bisensory condition was based on the hypothesis of probabilistic adding of the responses to the separate unisensory stimulus levels. The observed bisensory function was in good agreement with that predicted.

Individual experiments have examined bisensory effects on loudness balance judgments and paired-associate learning. In a study by Karlovich (1968) eight young adult subjects with normal-hearing sensitivity performed ABLB matches for a 1000 Hz tone by adjusting the intensity of a comparison stimulus. Each subject made four balances at 20 dB and 50 dB sensation levels during the first experimental session. The second and third sessions introduced a visual stimulus which, in one case, was synchronized with the onset of the standard auditory stimulus and, in the other case, with the onset of a comparison stimulus. Visual stimulation was found to have a positive effect on the perception of loudness, an effect that was more pronounced at the higher intensity level of the auditory stimulus. The author concluded that there can be interaction between different sensory modalities.

Gaeth (1963, 1967) reported the results of a series of experiments with normal-hearing and deaf children in a paired-associate learning situation. Stimulus material varied in meaningfulness and sensory mode of presentation. Comparisons were made for visual, auditory, and auditory-visual presentations of the paired stimuli. Initial testing with familiar words as stimuli revealed that normal-hearing and hard-of-hearing children with mild to moderate hearing losses learned as well under the visual procedure as they did with a combined auditory-visual presentation. When hearing loss was between 61 and 75 dB the visual procedure was significantly more effective than the combined procedure. In subsequent experiments the test items included nonsense syllables, nonmeaningful symbols, noises, and simple words. The combined mode of presentation was never superior to single mode presentation. Learning curves for the audiovisual procedure either coincided with the curves for the better unisensory procedure or fell between the two unisensory learning curves.

Costello and Purcell (1968) studied the effects of incomplete auditory and visual stimuli on paired-associate learning. Film presentations of paired words and alphabet letters were filtered to provide the defective stimulus patterns. Subjects with normal hearing and vision had ten learning trials under three unisensory conditions, normal auditory, defective auditory, and defective visual. Two additional conditions combined normal-auditory with defective-visual and defective-auditory and defective-visual stimuli during training. Adding defective-visual information to normal-auditory stimulation did not improve learning. However, when both channels of information were defective, the bisensory condition was superior. Apparently some cues from both modalities were used when both were defective.

Details of a discrimination training program using both auditory and visual methods were described in some detail by Hutton (1960). After eighteen hours of training, the average improvement in combined auditory and visual discrimination was 8.3 percent. Those clients who showed a lopsided gain for either audition or vision alone had less benefit from combined stimulation than did those who showed more equal gain in the separate modalities. Those under 50 years of age improved more than those over 50 years.

When experimental tasks have called for recognition of speech material it has been found that audiovisual stimulation surpasses either auditory or visual presentation alone. This has been demonstrated for both normal-hearing and hearing-impaired subjects and for adults and children. In tasks that involve paired-associate learning the superiority of the bisensory stimulation has not been found unless both auditory and visual cues were defective. The paired-associate paradigm calls for rote learning of arbitrarily related stimuli, a feature that distinguishes this task from learning in educational settings.

Tactile and visual modalities. Two experiments have been reported on the use of tactile cues to supplement visual lipreading cues. Pickett (1963) tested sixteen deaf Swedish children for discrimination of phonemes and words. Subjects placed their fingers on ten vibrators, associated with different frequency.

Johnson (1963) investigated bisensory perception of monosyllabic words on spondees after subjects were trained on a tactual system. Four 2-inch speakers placed on the forearm were used to provide vibratory cues. Spaced training sessions provided a total of five hours of practice in the direct perception of monosyllabic words and spondees through cutaneous stimulation. Lipreading scores were improved over pretraining levels when cutaneous stimulation was provided with the visual cues after training.

There has been no practically useful application of tactual communication systems combined with visual communication. Recent advances have been made with tactile devices for the blind and this avenue remains an attractive possibility for aiding hearing-impaired persons. As yet, however, no easily learned coding system has been discovered nor has the direct reception of tactile stimuli been very successful.

Auditory, visual, and tactual-kinesthetic modalities. In Finland, Pesonen (1968) carried out an extensive series of observations and experiments dealing with the speech reception and speech production of deaf children. The relationship between speech reception and speech production was studied with stimuli presented through single sensory channels using visual, auditory, or tactual-kinesthetic cues, and by combined channels. A variety of measures showed a strong relationship between reception and production. The conclusion was drawn that speech production errors are due to faulty reception rather than to disturbance of the feedback system. Among the single channels, reception and production were most similar for visual stimulation. Therefore, the production of phonemes was considered to be controlled by memory traces of visual stimuli. Factors affecting visual intelligibility of vowels and consonants were discussed. Reception of phonemes was better when all sensory channels were used than when any single channel was used. Suggestions for training deaf children were offered. An analytic approach is recommended employing both multisensory and single-sensory training and phoneme reception. A multiple-choice procedure differentiates distinct clusters of phonemes first, and then the more difficult differentiation of phonemes within clusters follows. After receptive differentiation is learned, production can be improved. Pesonen is an advocate of a multisensory analytic approach to oral communication.

Training Instruments

Instruments have been developed that allow the acoustically handicapped to visualize their voices and the voices of normal-hearing speakers for comparison. Anderson (1960) described a Pitch Indicator that displays a continuous graph of vocal frequency as a function of time. The subject can watch the display change as he varies the frequency of his vocal output. Gray et al. (1961) recommended the use of cinefluorography as an aid in correcting defective articulation. This procedure allows a continuing motion-picture view of the tongue, lip, and jaw movements that take place when the subject speaks. As a supplement to other training methods, cinefluorography can make correct articulatory movements visible. Pronovost (1967) has described the development of several devices that produce visual displays of speech.

Since the early work of Steinberg and French (1946) and Potter, Kopp, and Green (1947), there has been continuing interest in devices designed to aid the deaf in attaining normal speech. The report of a conference on speech analyzing aids appears in the March 1968 issue of the *American Annals of the Deaf,* including the research papers and the discussion that followed. Stark et al. (1968) described a new modified version of the original Visible Speech Translator (VST), developed at the Bell Telephone Laboratories. The VST displays spectral and amplitude contours on a storage oscilloscope screen. Pilot work with eight deaf adults showed that it is possible to modify pitch, duration of utterance, nasalization, and segmental structure. Other investigators who offered speech aids that were appropriate for pitch modification include Pickett (1968), Martony (1968), and Borrild (1968). Phillips et al. (1968) were concerned with discovering the most effective training method for maximal improvement in pitch and intonation. They found that training with pattern matching of stimuli presented on a storage oscilloscope led to successful modification. Aside from pitch and intonation, there were aids designed to improve timing, articulation, spectral distribution, loudness, and even concept development.

Receptive communication was also the subject of research by participants. Practice in direct speechreading from spectrographic patterns was investigated (House et al., 1968) but was not found successful, in part because subjects were not able to use high-frequency cues. Upton (1968) reported an eyeglass speech reader that uses an acoustic analyzer to program the lighting sequence of a circle of dots imbedded in the center of the eyeglass lens. When the subject views the speaker, light movement from one position in the circle to another is superimposed on the lip movements, giving cues as to the acoustic composition of the sound. As a supplement to lipreading it would allow homophenous words to be discriminated; in practice the device has not been able to serve in its present form because of the rapidity of ongoing speech. Kringlebotn (1968) found that a vibrotactile aid with five small bone conductors at the fingertips was useful as a supplement to lipreading. Deaf children were able to achieve 100 percent recognition after training when the response set was limited.

Bridges and Huckabee (1970) trained three subjects, using a visual speech display that traced energy peaks of signals on an oscilloscope. Subjects had severe high-frequency hearing losses and showed difficulty producing unvoiced fricatives and plosive consonants. During training, the subject spoke a word, then the experimenter spoke the same word and traced the pattern that appeared on the oscilloscope with an ink marker. On successive trials the subject tried to match the pattern.

Thomas and Snell (1970) advocated a plot that shows first and second formant frequencies on a grid of lights making up a 12×12 matrix. The formant $F2$ is on the vertical axis and $F1$ is on the horizontal axis. When a word is spoken the changing array of lights presents a pattern that can be traced on the plastic surface of the display. Five subjects participated in an experimental test of the display. Recognition of twenty words, selected on the basis of vowel and glide, was the task. During training, each word was repeated four times while the subject listened and also watched the display. Subjects could play the training tape as often as they wished. During the test, words were presented for identification in a random order. A 97 percent recognition level was achieved. Next, three deaf subjects underwent articulation training with the device. The subjects were instructed to match the pattern produced by the experimenter in a demonstration. After two or three hours of training, subjects read again a list of words that they had produced before training. Analysis of improvement in articulation showed that changes in glide patterns were primarily responsible.

Tactile feedback as an aid in pitch modification and control has recently been reported by Willemain and Lee (1970). The output from a throat microphone is channeled according to eight pitch frequency bands and transduced tactually through solenoids that poke the speaker's fingers. Frequency bands can be grouped into three categories, such as "high," "low," or "ok" bands for tactile representation, or, more simply, into the two bands "high" and "low." Deaf school-age children were able to improve and control their pitch with the help of the tactile feedback.

Crane and Evans (1962) described a modified Language Master used to teach speech to the congenitally deaf. The instrument is multisensory, using auditory, visual, and tactile cues. Auditory stimulation is provided by a playback tape recorder. The message is also spelled out through lettering to utilize the visual channel, and a vibratory reproduction of the input stimulus can be applied to the larynx.

Apparently there are many successful instruments for improving particular aspects of voice and articulation. Most of the instruments, however, have not gone beyond the demonstration stage. Reliability and validity studies are needed and also investigation of individual differences with respect to effects of training.

Speech and Language Training

There has been a fairly large body of research devoted to identification of problems encountered by the deaf and hard of hearing in voice quality, articulation, and language development. Considerably fewer research results are available in the area of training methods to overcome these deficiencies.

Speech training. Boone (1966) reviewed some of his research findings on the modification of voice qualities and suggested training methods that might prove beneficial. He found that the fundamental frequency of deaf boys' voices tended to be too high when they reached the age of 17 to 18 years. The suggested method of correction includes instructing the child on the nature of the problem and providing feedback so that he knows when he is using a low pitch and when a high pitch. In order to correct abnormal resonance, which was found in deaf children regardless of age, Boone recommended speech drills that provide an awareness of different patterns of contact of the tongue with areas of the mouth. The deaf need to carry the tongue in a higher, more forward position. Awareness and correction of articulation and timing of speech sounds were considered to require training also.

A case study of correction of falsetto voice in a 20-year-old deaf woman was reported by Engelberg (1962). Following an explanation of the physiological and phonatory factors, training was provided using tactile and kinesthetic cues to compare high- and low-pitch patterns. Techniques included phonating (1) with the head extended backward, (2) in a lower pitch on request, and (3) in her highest pitch and dropping abruptly to her lowest pitch. Engelberg states that after eleven sessions the woman had achieved a normal pitch pattern.

Quigley (1966), in his review of foreign research, covered a number of experiments on oral training. One by Masyunin described a method of improving phrasing and intonation. Deaf students were shown Russian sentences, one at a time, and were told to pronounce them. The sentences were written so that a marker indicated the location of pauses. The experimenter first repeated the sentence as the subject had said it, with pauses after each word. Then he spoke the sentence correctly in a loud voice. The student repeatedly pronounced the sentence, first with the written copy and then imitating the experimenter, who said it with correct stress and intonation. Children with even a small amount of residual hearing showed improved phrasing.

Another study covered in Quigley's review, by Tato and Arcella, concerned a training program designed to increase the rate of speaking of deaf subjects. The mean duration per syllable after a month of training was reduced from 0.47 seconds to 0.28 seconds. This compares fairly well with the 0.2 per second average of normal-hearing children. However, the intelligibility of the speech when it was more rapid did not show consistent improvement; 27 percent had improved substantially, 36 percent were about the same, and 37 percent showed marked deterioration in intelligibility.

More recently two experiments in the United States have described methods of modifying pitch and intensity in speech of deaf students, with moderate success. Holbrook and Crawford (1970) described a monitoring system that allows the subject to see when he is in the right frequency and intensity range. When the frequency is correct a white light remains on and a timer is activated. When intensity is too loud a red light shows up and a white light goes off. Subjects were asked to keep the white light on as they read aloud and to keep the red light off. A shaping procedure with successive approximations to correct frequency was employed. Of four subjects who participated, two maintained their conditioned pitch level three months after training; two had shifted back toward the pretraining level.

Millen (1971), reporting the results of a case study, found increased rate of production with distinct pauses between words after five hour-long sessions and home practice. Further practice showed improvement in producing unvoiced sounds. Similar results were claimed for other subjects.

Bel'tyukov and Masyunin (1968) described an auditory training technique to improve pronunciation of deaf children with various amounts of residual hearing. They trained students first to discriminate vowels and consonants, and then to correct their pronunciation. Although quantitative measures were not reported, they indicated that improvement was found, particularly in the vowels. Students with residual hearing up to 1024 Hz and 2048 Hz were able to benefit from this training. Subjects who perceived frequencies only up to 512 Hz were able to take advantage of training for syllabic stress and speech sound duration.

No generally accepted methods have been developed for the rehabilitation of speech production. Additional experiments were discussed in the previous section, on training instruments, but these too are at the exploratory stage of development.

Language training. Aside from problems of defective speech production, language comprehension and language production are also delayed as the result of hearing impairment. Interest in the language training of hearing-impaired children has been spurred by advances in psycholinguistics and recent knowledge about acquisition of language in normal-hearing children, although most of the programs summarized here do not directly utilize a linguistic approach.

Relatively few experiments have investigated methods of receptive language training. Among those who have studied the problem, programmed instruction has been the most widely used. Falconer (1960, 1961, 1962) designed and tested a device for teaching word recognition to young deaf children. Eight profoundly deaf children were taught fifteen nouns in ten training sessions. Children showed high accuracy in recognition after training and equally high retention after two weeks. Programmed instruction was successfully applied to remedial reading for deaf children (Beckmeyer, 1963). McGrady (1964) administered programmed instruction in concept formation to both deaf and normal-hearing subjects. Concept learning tasks were based on four classificatory nouns; two were rather specific, *birds* and *fish,* and two were more general, *insects* and *animals.* Deaf children showed considerable improvement after training. Before programmed instruction they made twice as many errors as the controls; on the post-test the two groups were very similar, with approximately 3 or 4 percent errors. There was a tendency for both groups to make errors on the more general terms, *insects* and *animals.*

Pfau (1970a) varied the stimulus mode, response mode, and type of reinforcement in a program designed to teach adolescent children the names of ten unfamiliar animals. Increasing the number of input modalities led to fewer errors during training. In this experiment extrinsic reinforcement had no effect.

After years of development, a system of programmed instruction for the development of functional receptive language has been introduced by Project LIFE (Wooden and Willard, 1965; Wooden, 1966, Pfau, 1969, 1970b, 1970c). Programmed training filmstrips emphasize structural meaning derived from syntax, function words, and morphology. Training begins with simple sentence structures and then progresses to more complex language throughout four levels of training films. Supplementary films are available for developing perceptual and thinking activities at the prereading level. Project LIFE is now being employed in a supplemental role for language training in a number of schools.

Bricker and Bricker (1970) described an ambitious oral language training program covering both receptive and expressive skills for various types of severely language-handicapped children. Training includes not only object naming and concept learning but also more advanced levels of language such as imitation and sentence production. The process leading up to sentence production is structured in sequential steps. Control of behavior at each step is achieved by application of operant techniques including differential reinforcement and successive approximations to the desired response.

Training methods in written language also have emphasized programmed instruction. Birch and Stuckless (1962, 1963) completed two experiments that support the feasibility of this approach. The first study compared the effects of programmed instruction with conventional teacher instruction. Twenty program units covered nouns, verbs, predicate adjectives, comparative adjectives, and predicate nominatives. Results were similar for the two types of instruction, but programmed training was more efficient, requiring less than half the time spent on standard teacher instruction. In their second experiment, the authors focused on an older group of adolescent deaf students to determine whether their errors in written language could be modified by programmed instruction. Preliminary analyses of compositions led to the selection of ten categories for programming, including several verb forms, articles, prepositions, conjunctions, and noun number. Each of the ten categories was developed into two parallel linear programs, one in a deductive format and the other in an inductive format. During training, one experimental group had a single presentation of each program while a second group had repeated presentations of each program. The major conclusions were that (1) repeated presentations of the programs had a positive effect on the subjects' usage of grammar but only one presentation did not have a significant effect, and (2) there was no difference between the deductive and inductive formats.

Rush (1966) emphasized improved visual memory as a basis for programmed instruction in written language of deaf adolescents. Subjects were trained to recall longer and longer units of correct grammatical sentences as visual cues were progressively decreased. A significant increase in post-test scores was found, and the benefits of training were still evident after ten weeks.

A less structured approach to modification of sentence writing was described recently by Eachus (1971). He used the Mediated Interaction Visual Response System, a technique in which subjects write responses on an overhead projector; this system allowed the experimenter to see and react to sentences as they were produced by a group of deaf fourth-grade students. A token reinforcement program was effective in controlling the rate and accuracy of sentence writing behavior. During the last training sessions, when reinforcement was contingent upon the production of compound and complex sentences, every subject attempted sentences of these types and achieved some correct productions before the experiment ended.

The increasing number of experiments and the broad scope of some recently developed language training programs reflect a growing recognition that language is the source of many educational and vocational problems faced by the hearing-handicapped population. As is the case with normal-hearing children, much more research is needed for greater understanding of the stages of development typically found in severely hard-of-hearing and deaf children and for methods of training children to an adequate level of language performance.

Gestural Training

There is a vast literature available on nonverbal communication. Only a few of these studies have been concerned directly with hearing-impaired people and their understanding and usage of gestures.

Hirsh (in Quigley, 1966) discussed the various types of gestures that people commonly use in conjunction with verbal symbols. Included were gestures of the hands, movement of the head, facial mimicry, expression of the eyes, and general body movements and positions. Hirsh believes that these gestures constitute a communication system that follows a set of laws different from those for both verbal language and the language of signs. A deaf person can communicate fully only when he has learned to use these accepted gestures appropriately. A plan is presented to establish such gestures, and an inventory is given of which ones should be learned.

Tervoort (1961) reported a long-term study in the development of esoteric symbolism in young deaf children and its relationship to the development of traditional communication forms.

He filmed out-of-class conversations of young deaf children in a number of schools for the deaf in Europe and the United States and applied linguistic analysis to the data. The results indicated that deaf children tend to develop a relatively primitive esoteric system of gestural communication on a purely visual basis with a relatively small vocabulary. This system differs from the formal language of signs and does not become such without training. According to the author, if training is not applied, the communication of the deaf child will not develop into normal communication. The basic conclusions were these:

1. The young deaf child usually develops a system of communication that deviates from the acoustical language of his environment in that it follows the structuring principles of a visual system and grows up to a completely different system of communication.
2. However, the young child is almost always also exposed to the teaching of the language of the surrounding cultural community. The teaching prevents the esoteric system mentioned above from fully developing. This preventive teaching can either prevent signing or coordinate it with the language taught. Prevention is only successful when started earlier than the preschool age and applied completely. Uncontrolled signing and too-late enforced speech are harmful.

There is a dearth of scientific data that describes the effects of gestural training upon the language development process. This is an area that should command substantial attention.

Patterning of Sessions

There are four essential elements associated with the patterning of sessions of aural rehabilitation. They are (1) content of the sessions, (2) the frequency with which sessions are held, (3) the duration of the individual sessions, and (4) the progression of content in the sessions.

As in some other areas of the aural rehabilitation process there has been some thought given to the patterning of sessions, followed by advocacy but little research.

Although not a research article, McDonald and Frick (1957) contend that whether or not a patient's problem is one of voice, articulation, hearing, or stuttering the frequency and duration of treatment sessions should not be dictated by clinical or institutional scheduling restrictions. They averred that the mastery of a new skill requires at least three stages of learning: (1) learning the basic abilities requisite to the development of skill, (2) development of the skill, and (3) habituation of the skill. The authors suggest that the frequency and duration of the treatment sessions should vary among these stages of therapy in an optimal situation. No research data are presented to support the authors' statements. However, case histories are presented that promote the logic of the discussion. For example, clinical experience has indicated that clients should be seen frequently during the first stages of the therapy routine.

No data are apparent that deal with the manner in which sessions in aural rehabilitation should progress relative to the skills that should be mastered, when they should be mastered, and the relationships that should exist in the teaching of the various skills related to language, lipreading, and speech.

Clinical Milieu

There are three significant aspects within the clinical milieu in which the acoustically handicapped individual is working. They are the act of counseling itself, the client characteristics, and the clinician-client interaction.

Counseling

Counseling is most appropriate at several stages in the aural rehabilitation process. This type of aid to the client is often required at the time of diagnosis and evaluation to explain the nature of the difficulty, to motivate the client to continue rehabilitative programs, and to help the client, after training, in family, social, vocational, and educational adjustments. Most of the literature discusses the problems encountered in counseling on the basis of practical projects undertaken.

Levine (1960) carried out a project that included, as one aim, the training of personnel to identify and overcome the adjustment problems that face the deaf. Certain areas of training required special emphasis: deaf language usage and communication methods; psychological, social, and educational effects of early deafness; counseling and psychological techniques as applied to the deaf.

Harrison (1967) made the point that effective rehabilitation of the client depends upon questioning the client about his reactions and counseling him during the clinical evaluation. Case histories were used to illustrate the necessity of taking into account the client's subjective feeling of satisfaction with, and motivation to continue, rehabilitative treatment.

An outpatient diagnostic-therapy program for children and their parents was described by Giolas, Webster, and Ward (1968). During a four- to six-week session the parents met together, while the children underwent audiological and psychological testing along with individual and group therapy. Parents were given information on types of hearing loss, the effects of hearing losses, uses and limitations of hearing aids, the care of hearing aids, and home training techniques designed to aid auditory and speechreading skills. A main goal of the diagnostic-therapy program was to indicate the subsequent training that would be appropriate for each child. Informed and understanding parents were considered a necessary part of the program.

McDaniel (1965) reviewed vocational rehabilitation services for the hearing impaired, programs that concentrated on counseling and job placement. He concluded that one immediate need is to determine the relationship between aural deficit and several variables: types of service required, methods of rehabilitation, and vocational goals. At this time the stereotyped image of the hearing-impaired individual is a serious problem. House (1969) put forth the view that a mild or moderate hearing loss might not affect the individual's ability to work. Arbitrary standards often prevent job placement and advancement. Case studies were presented that exemplified the problems encountered by the aurally handicapped person.

A research study by Neuhaus (1969) dealt with parent attitudes and the emotional adjustment of deaf children. His purpose was to determine parent attitudes in order to better understand the development of personality traits alleged to exist among deaf children. Subjects were eighty-four deaf children, twenty-eight of whom were in each of the three age ranges 3 to 7, 8 to 12, and 13 to 19 years. They all had met the following criteria; a score of at least 90 on an IQ scale appropriate for the age, no severe secondary problems, both parents living—with no language problem, and an educational level of at least eighth grade. Shoben's *University of Southern California Parent Attitude Survey* was used to measure parents' expressed attitudes toward children. In order to determine parents' attitude toward disability, the *Attitude Toward Disabled Persons Scale* by Yuker, Block, and Campbell (1960) was employed. The child's emotional adjustment was measured by the *Haggerty-Olson-Wickman Behavior Rating Schedules* (1930), and also by ratings by three staff members who had known the child at least six months. Findings on maternal and paternal attitudes indicated that the expressed maternal and paternal attitudes toward children significantly affected emotional adjustment of the child. There was a significant relationship between maternal attitudes and adjustments for all three age groups. Paternal attitudes affected those in the 8-year-old category and older. Parental attitudes toward disability did not show any significant relationship with emotional adjustment.

In testing the congruence of parental attitudes, that is, whether mother and father had positive attitudes, both negative, or one positive and the other negative, the following results were found: Congruent positive attitudes toward the child resulted in a better adjustment than congruent negative attitudes. If the mother had positive attitudes and the father negative, this showed better adjustment compared to mother negative and father positive. The author feels that the maternal attitudes are the more important. Parental attitudes toward children did not vary with the different age groups, but the parental attitudes toward disability showed a less accepting attitude as age increased.

Almost no research has been done in the area of counseling techniques and procedures with the acoustically handicapped. Evaluation of existing programs is also lacking. While most audiologists agree that counseling is an important if not a crucial part of the rehabilitation process, there are no experimental findings to guide such programs.

Client Characteristics

Although the hearing-loss and handicap pictures might be highly similar among a group of individuals, the success that a clinician will experience in working with individuals is in great part a function of the characteristics of the clients, or parents or those responsible for them. Attitudes toward the training procedures, motivation to do something about their handicaps, past experiences dealing with the problem, and so on, are all important if success in a program of rehabilitation is to be achieved.

The literature provides examples of work that has been accomplished in aural rehabilitation with different populations, such as the hearing-impaired blind by Bergman et al. (1965), postrubella deaf children by Vernon (1967), the geriatric group by Alpiner (1965) and Hudson (1960). These are all useful narrative accounts. However, there does not appear to be research directed toward determining the relative effects of specific characteristics on the trainability or retrainability of persons with hearing loss.

Clinician-Client Interaction

No information seems to be available concerning the interaction of the clinician and acoustically handicapped client in clinical settings.

Summary

In this chapter an attempt has been made to review and evaluate the literature dealing with rehabilitative sessions. Special effort has been made to highlight those studies that present data that are useful in terms of the conduct of aural rehabilitative sessions. However, other literature, nonexperimental in nature, that seemed valuable to the discussion was also included.

There has been considerable research on various aspects of the lip-reading process, but little that relates directly to rehabilitative sessions per se. In the main, the effort has been to develop instruments that measure lipreading performance, and also to study in some detail the variables associated with the speaker, code, transmission link, and the viewer or receiver.

It has been found that a *speaker* who is most intelligible visually will be most intelligible under nonvisual conditions, and that natural speaking style is best for lipreading. Full facial exposure has been found superior to restricted exposure of face or lips for lipreading purposes. The additional clues the receiver receives undoubtedly increase his performance scores. Sex of speaker seems to make little difference relative to intelligibility in lipreading, although male speakers have been found to produce more intense facial movements than females. It is not entirely clear whether or not a speaker's whispered utterance is visually different from his spoken utterance. The rate with which a speaker talks seems to have no significant effect upon his lipreadibility. Frontal viewing of a speaker and viewing in the region within 45 degrees to either side are generally superior to more extreme angles of regard.

Insofar as code is concerned, there has been a development of categories of sounds perceived visually, namely, bilabial, rounded labial, labiodental, and nonlabial. Words that look similar on the lips of the speaker are homophenous. Research results show that viewers can distinguish among many of these words, and this fact should be emphasized in rehabilitative sessions. As regards the influence of sound position on identification, it has been shown that sounds in the initial position are more readily identified than those in final positions. Determination of accent in three syllable words can be made by viewers well above chance level. The tendency is for the speaker to repeat words that are not lip-read correctly the first time. Research results reveal that repetition of words is not indicated if they are incorrectly identified, for up to five additional exposures to difficult words makes no significant difference in their identification. In the main, the more visible are the elements of a word, the greater is its visual intelligibility.

As regards the transmission of speech to be lip-read, research has shown that lipreading can be taught and that it can be learned via a two-dimensional medium. Television and films then can be used as media for rehabilitative sessions. There must be light in the environment for lipreading to take place; however, research has shown that light may be minimal for efficiency in lipreading if the viewer is highly familiar with the message elements. As regards distracting environmental elements, it has been shown quite clearly that auditory distractions significantly interfere with lipreading, whereas visual distractions do not interfere with lipreading proficiency.

More attention has been given to the study of the receiver in lipreading than perhaps any other factor. In summary, it can be said that the relationship between the receiver's concept formation ability and his success in lipreading tasks is not yet settled. Some research shows a relationship, whereas other research fails to do so. Visual memory is positively related to proficiency in lipreading whereas amount of hearing loss, age, reading comprehension, and speech discrimination ability do not appear to be related directly to lipreading proficiency. The ability to synthesize and to analyze visual images has been shown to be positively related to lipreading proficiency in some research but not in others. There is need for an instrument that validly measures lipreading; those instruments available have adequate reliability but give no evidence that they are valid.

Research on instruction in lipreading has included programmed instruction and transfer of training to different speakers. At this point a great deal more information is needed before conclusive statements are justified concerning programmed instruction; however, it does appear that viewers trained by one speaker are able to transfer this training.

Research directed toward determining the desirability of teaching manual language to the acoustically handicapped has dealt with combined methods of communication rather than with manual language alone. It has been shown that the intelligibility of finger spelling is reduced sharply beyond 175 feet and that finger spelling can be supportive of oral language development.

As is the case with manual language, so it is with auditory training—the scientific research studies are few in number and yield fragmentary kinds of results. Little attention has been given the speaker in auditory training research; however, one study has shown that the variables associated with sex of speaker made no significant difference as determined by correct identification of stimuli.

As regards the code factor, careful study has been made of consonant confusions and the cues for identifying vowels. Consonants are found to influence intelligibility of vowels. In cases of conductive loss it has been found that error responses to monosyllables were primarily substitutions rather than omissions. Those with nonconductive types of loss make more consonant and vowel errors than do cases with primarily conductive type losses. Word familiarity also plays a part in intelligibility. As the word becomes less familiar there tend to be more substitution errors. The word substituted is usually a very familiar one. Meaningfulness and length of words are factors known to be important relative to intelligibility as words with more syllables tend to be more intelligible than words with fewer syllables. Meaningful words are more intelligible than nonsense syllables. Phonemic content and number of speech sounds in a word also affect intelligibility. The more closely the context resembles a sentence, the greater the intelligibility.

A study of the desirability of available transmission links for auditory training among teachers dealing with acoustically handicapped children showed that hearing aids were ranked highest and group amplifiers lowest. Teachers using loop-induction systems ranked them the highest.

Direct investigation of the effectiveness of auditory training for hearing handicapped showed that both speech discrimination and intelligibility can be improved through training. Also it has been shown that pure tone audiometric test results improve with training. Short-term auditory training has been found to improve word discrimination and also pure tone frequency discrimination. Attention has been directed recently to the verbotonal method, one which emphasizes the determination of optimal discrete bandwidths for the subject and subsequent training with stimulus material transmitted at these frequency bands. Recent emphasis on infant training programs is apparent in the literature.

Studies involving the receiver in auditory training show that high-frequency loss presents real problems in discrimination. Confusions are similar for both flat loss and high-frequency loss cases. Children with flat losses whose sloping audiograms show good low-frequency response and diminished high-frequency response, profit from auditory training; however, children with profound flat losses do not.

Progress has been made in hearing aid selection procedures, but clinics have not yet accepted any standard test materials or test procedures. Important electroacoustic properties of hearing aids are the flatness of the frequency response and the width of frequency response and, to a lesser extent, level of distortion. Low-frequency response is particularly important for children with residual hearing primarily at the lower-frequency range. New developments in test materials for hearing aid evaluation include the Synthetic Sentence Idenitification test, the Speech Sound Comparison test, the Intermodulation Distortion test, and competing message tests. These are more sensitive than monosyllabic word discrimination tests and SRT measures in determining hearing aid quality. Binaural hearing aids and CROS hearing aids have advantages for some hearing-impaired people in difficult listening situations.

It is desirable for clients to return to the clinic following purchase of a hearing aid for purposes of orientation in the use of their hearing aids. The fact that many do not return poses a problem. Research indicates that the clients feel no need for orientation, are not aware that it is recommended, or delay returning for no apparent reason. Studies show that there is a general disinterest in the idea of returning for orientation purposes. Lack of motivation was the most frequent response given in interviews of clients at a number of hearing facilities. Scheduling difficulties and health-related reasons were mentioned but much less frequently. Questionnaire results reported by the Conference on Hearing Aid Evaluation Procedures show that there is wide variation in following a recommendation for a hearing aid purchase; most clients fail to return after purchasing an aid even though most clinics are equipped to provide rehabilitative training.

The area of sound localization has been studied rather extensively. Signal intensity is a factor in localization. Individuals with interaural differences are found to have difficulty with localization if the differences exceed 21 dB. Subjects with conductive losses seem to have little trouble with sound localization, whereas those with sensorineural losses do have difficulties. Training of individuals with simulated hearing loss shows that improvement can occur; however, data are needed with true cases of hearing loss.

Tactile reception does not as yet provide a substitute for the auditory channel; however, various devices have been constructed to supplement auditory and visual speech reception. Frequency transposition as a technique has been employed as well as unmodified stimulation.

There is a great deal of interest in the utilization of a multisensory approach in aural rehabilitation. The thought is that additional channels of input supplement or reinforce the auditory signal. Both visual and tactual stimuli have been utilized, and both show promise; however, like many other areas, there is a dearth of scientific data to support contentions made.

Manual methods of communication have played a part in aural rehabilitation for centuries. Research indicates that the early learning of finger spelling facilitates the development of oral language skills. A comparison of the Rochester Method of communication and the Oral Method led to greater educational achievement with the former method, but the absolute differences between the groups of children were small.

In the majority of studies it has been found that addition of visual cues to the auditory in such tasks as threshold measurements, discrimination testing, and loudness balance judgments improves performance. These findings are encouraging and warrant close scrutiny in the planning of rehabilitative sessions. Some would say, however, that utilization of multiple channels independently is superior to the simultaneous utilization of multiple inputs.

There is a great amount of data available from studies of the effects of oral training of the acoustically handicapped. Studies of language, pitch of voice, articulation, rate, and related factors, have all shown that a judged improvement occurs with training. Irrespective of the data acquired up to this time, there is still a need for a comprehensive scientific assault on the area of oral output of the severely hard of hearing and deaf.

A few papers have reported training programs for language acquisition. Behavior modification techniques and programmed instruction both have been described.

Numerous instruments have been developed as aids in rehabilitation. Among them are several that make a visible display of speech energy;

several that produce amplification of the acoustic component of speech; one that shows by motion pictures the movement of the articulators; and one that provides for multisensory input through taction, vision, and audition. The extent to which these instruments are useful in developing communication skills in the acoustically handicapped needs further clarification.

Some have viewed the development of gestures among the normal hearing and the hearing impaired. Certain gestures facilitate communication among normal-hearing individuals. These must be learned by the hearing handicapped if indeed they are to be used appropriately. The little research that has been accomplished in this area shows that deaf children develop naturally a rather primitive esoteric system of gestural language with a very restricted vocabulary.

There is no available scientifically derived evidence that specifies the optimal patterns that should be established in carrying out sessions of aural rehabilitation. Content, frequency, duration, and progression of sessions need careful research in order to establish the most meaningful patterns in programs of aural rehabilitation.

Some general findings are available relative to the effects of the clinical milieu in which the handicapped individual finds himself. As regards counseling, it has been shown that parental attitudes differentially affect the emotional development of children as a function of age of child, sex of parent, and congruence of parental attitudes. No scientifically controlled studies were identified relative to effects of counseling the hearing handicapped. The same is true of the area of client characteristics, and clinician-client interaction, and their relationships to success in programs of aural rehabilitation.

RECOMMENDATIONS

As a result of the review and evaluation of literature pertaining to those factors that are important to the concept of aural rehabilitation sessions, the following recommendations are made. Future effort should be directed toward—

1. quantifying the visible component of the spoken oral code
2. determining the transfer of training that occurs in aural rehabilitation from the clinic situation to the real-life situation outside the clinic
3. Further exploration of the speaker characteristics upon lipreadability
4. clarification of differences in lipreading performance as a function of voiced and unvoiced utterances
5. refinement of the categories of sound from a visual point of view
6. complete study of the effects of accent on success in lipreading

7. determining effects of factors such as message length, word familiarity, phonetic and morphemic content, and syntactic structure, and interactions of these factors upon visual reception of oral language
8. more definitive study of the effects of auditory distractions upon the lip-reader
9. the development of a valid and reliable test of lipreading performance
10. The construction of programmed learning materials for aural rehabilitation sessions
11. continued study of personal characteristics of hearing impaired that correlate with success or failure in tasks involved in aural rehabilitation
12. identification of the variables associated with efficient senders and receivers of manual language
13. a more complete description of the code variables of manual language as related to successful transmission
14. determining the relative effects of contextual cues, distracting stimuli, lighting, distance, and angle of view upon performance of the receiver of manual communication
15. deriving data that indicate the social impact on the deaf from having learned manual language
16. an exploration of the amount, type, and usefulness of information in nonverbal visual cues available to hearing-handicapped individuals
17. study of the effects of nonverbal visual cues in relation to lipreading as contrasted with manual communication
18. exploring the personal characteristics and aptitudes of individuals in relation to their success in learning to utilize oral as compared with manual methods of communication
19. further study of speaker variables and their effects upon success in auditory training
20. determination of the optimal verbal and nonverbal materials to be used with certain types of hearing loss in aural rehabilitation
21. continued study of the optimal transmitting systems for use in aural rehabilitation sessions
22. study of factors that are related to success in auditory training
23. determination of the relative importance of nonverbal auditory cues to the hearing handicapped
24. development, evaluation, and classification of auditory training materials, both verbal and nonverbal
25. refinement of newly developed hearing aid evaluation procedures
26. identification of those reasons why adults are reluctant to return for aural rehabilitation upon completion of their hearing and/or hearing aid evaluations

27. scientific investigation of the transmission of verbal and nonverbal materials via cutaneous receptors; the investigation should include basic analyses that deal with (a) effective instrumentation, (b) stimulus characteristics, (c) optimal input locations, (d) personal characteristics, namely, age, sex, degree of auditory deficit, and so forth
28. systematic investigation of the effects of various combinations of stimulus input in aural rehabilitation
29. continued evaluation of the effects of manual communication upon oral language learning, and social and vocational adjustment
30. a comprehensive study of the effects of aural rehabilitative procedures upon the expressive aspect of communication of the hearing handicapped; the study should include definitive investigation of (a) personal characteristics of the individual, (b) methods of training, (c) intelligibility of speech, (d) esthetic quality of speech, and (e) language proficiency
31. gathering evidence concerning the information transmitted by gestures and facial expressions that are beneficial to the hearing-handicapped individual
32. experimental investigation of optimal patterns for aural rehabilitation sessions: the content, frequency, duration, and progression of sessions should be studied in relation to age, severity of hearing loss, and personal characteristics of individuals sustaining hearing impairment
33. determining systematically the progress being made by the acoustically handicapped and the effects of keeping them aware of that progress
34. study of the effects of a counseling program in relation to the handicap associated with the hearing deficit
35. investigation of the relationship of client personality and intellectual characteristics to his trainability
36. study of client-clinician interactions as related to handicap reduction in the hearing impaired
37. evaluating the need for counseling the families of the hearing impaired

References

Alluisi, E. A., Morgan, B., and Hawkes, G. (1965). Masking of cutaneous sensations in multiple stimulus presentation. *Percept. Motor Skills*, 20, 39–45.

Alpiner, J. G. (1965). Diagnostic and rehabilitative aspects of geriatric audiology. *Asha*, 455–459.

Anderson, F. (1960). An experimental pitch indicator for deaf scholars. *J. Acoust. Soc. Amer.*, 32, 1065–1074.

Avery, C. B. (1966). Visual aspects of aural habilitation and rehabilitation. In *Seminar Proceedings—Aural Rehabilitation of the Acoustically Handicapped*. East Lansing: Michigan State University.

Aylesworth, D. L. (1964). The talker and the lipreader in face-to-face testing of lipreading ability. Unpublished Master's thesis, Michigan State University.

Barnlund, D. C. (1968). *Interpersonal Communications: Survey and Studies*. Boston: Houghton Mifflin Co.

Bauer, R. W., Matuza, J. L., and Blackmer, R. F. (1966). Noise localization after unilateral attentuation. *J. Acoust. Soc. Amer.,* 40, 441–444.

Beckmeyer, T. (1963). Application of programmed instruction to remedial reading for the deaf. *Volta Rev.,* 65, 415–417.

Bel'tyukov, V. I., and Masyunin, A. M. (1968). Utilization of residual hearing in work on pronunciation with deaf-mute children. In *Russian Translations of Speech and Hearing* (R. W. West, ed.). *Asha Reports,* 3, 165–176.

Belzile, M., and Markle, D. M. (1959). A clinical comparison of monaural and binaural hearing aids worn by patients with conductive or perceptive deafness. *Laryngoscope,* 69, 1317–1323.

Bennett, D. N., and Byers, V. W. (1967). Increased intelligibility in the hypacusic by slow-play frequency transposition. *J. Aud. Res.,* 7, 107–118.

Berger, K. W. (1964). Binaural hearing—A review. *Audecibel,* 13, 14–17, 31–37.

Bergman, M., Rusalem, H., Malles, I., Schiller, V., Cohan, H., and McKay. E. (1965). Auditory rehabilitation for hearing-impaired blind persons. *Asha Monogr.,* 12, 1–96.

Birch, J. W., and Stuckless, E. R. (1962). The development and evaluation of programmed instruction in language for children with auditory disorders. Title VII Project No. 773, University of Pittsburgh, 62 pages.

Birch, J. W., and Stuckless, E. R. (1963). Programmed instruction and the correction of written language of adolescent deaf students, Title VII, Grant No. 7–48–1110–118, 78 pages.

Birdwhistell, R. L. (1970). *Kinesics and Context; Essays on Body Motion Communication*. Philadelphia: University of Pennsylvania Press.

Black, J. W. (1952). Accompaniments of word intelligibility. *J. Speech Hearing Dis.,* 17, 409–417.

Black, J. W., O'Reilly, P. P., and Peck, L. (1963). Self-administered training in lipreading. *J. Speech Hearing Dis.,* 28, 183–186.

Bode, D. L., Nerbonne, G. P., and Sahlstrom, L. J. (1970). Speechreading and the synthesis of distorted printed sentences. *J. Speech Hearing Res.,* 13, 115–121.

Bode, D. L., and Oyer, H. J. (1970). Auditory training and speech discrimination. *J. Speech Hearing Res.,* 13, 839–855.

Boone, D. R. (1966). Modification of the voices of deaf children. *Volta Rev.,* 68, 686–692.

Borrild, K. (1968). Experience with the design and use of technical aids for the training of deaf and hard-of-hearing children. *Amer. Ann. Deaf,* 113, 168–177.

Boyd, J., and Jamroz, A. (1963). A comparison of group hearing aid systems. *Amer. Ann. Deaf,* 108, 245–250.

Bradley, W. H. (1959). Some relationships between pitch discrimination and speech development. *Laryngoscope,* 68, 422–437.

Brainerd, S. (1969). An investigation of the relation between performance on a filmed lipreading test and analysis of the visual environment. Unpublished Master's thesis, Michigan State University.

Brannon, J. B., Jr. (1961). Speechreading of various speech materials. *J. Speech Hearing Dis.,* 26, 348–353.

Brannon, J. B., Jr., and Kodman, F., Jr. (1959). The perceptual process in speech reading. *Arch. Otolaryng.,* 70, 114–119.

Brehman, G. E. (1965). Programmed discrimination training for lipreaders. *Amer. Ann. Deaf,* 110, 553–562.

Bricker, W. A., and Bricker, D. D. (1970). A program of language training for the severely language-handicapped child. *Except. Children,* 37, 101–111.

Bridges, C. C., Jr., and Huckabee, R. M. (1970). A new visual speech display—its use in speech therapy. *Volta Rev.,* 72, 112–115.

Briskey, R. J., Garrison, M. J., Owsley, P., and Sinclair, J. (1967). Effects of hearing aids on deaf speech. *Audecibel,* 16, 173–188.

Briskey, R. J., and Sinclair, J. (1966). The importance of low-frequency amplification in deaf children. *Audecibel,* 15, 7–10, 12–20.

Brown, A. E., and Hopkins, H. K. (1967). Interaction of the auditory and visual sensory modalities. *J. Acoust. Soc. Amer.,* 41, 1–6.

Burchfield, S. D. (1971). Perception of amplitude compressed speech by persons exhibiting loudness recruitment. Unpublished Doctoral dissertation, Michigan State University.

Burney, P. A. (1972). A survey of hearing aid evaluation procedures. *Asha,* 14, 439–444.

Butler, R. A., and Naunton, R. F. (1967). The effect of stimulus sensation level on the directional hearing of unilaterally deafened persons. *J. Aud. Res.,* 7, 15–23.

Byers, V. W., and Lieberman, L. (1959). Lipreading performance and the rate of the speaker. *J. Speech Hearing Res.,* 2, 271–276.

Calvert, D. R. (1964). A comparison of auditory amplifiers in the classroom in a school for the deaf. *Volta Rev.,* 66, 544–547.

Castle, W. E. (ed.), (1967). A conference on hearing aid evaluation procedures. *Asha Reports,* 2.

Ciliax, D. (1973). Lipreading performance as affected by continuous auditory distractions. Unpublished Doctoral dissertation, Michigan State University.

Cloud, D. T. (1933). Some results from the use of the Gault-Teletactor. *Amer. Ann. Deaf,* 78, 200–204.

Cornett R. O. (1967). Cued speech. *Amer. Ann. Deaf,* 112, 3–13.

Costello, M. R., and Purcell, G. (1968). Perception of defective visual and acoustic verbal patterns. *Int. Audiol.,* 7, 5–8.

Crane N. W., and Evans, B. B. (1962). The talking dictionary. *Volta Rev.,* 64, 125–127.

Dean, L. E. (1934). Experiments in the academic education of adolescent deaf pupils. *Amer. Ann. Deaf,* 79, 292–305.

DiCarlo, L. M., and Brown, W. J. (1960). The effectiveness of binaural hearing for adults with hearing impairment. *J. Aud. Res.,* 1, 35–76.

DiCarlo, L., and Kataja, R. (1951). An analysis of the Utley lipreading test. *J. Speech Hearing Dis.,* 16, 226–240.

Dirks, D., and Carhart, R. (1962). A survey of reactions from users of binaural and monaural hearing aids. *J. Speech hearing Dis.,* 27, 311–322.

Dodds, E., and Harford, E. (1968). Application of a lipreading test in a hearing aid evaluation. *J. Speech Hearing Dis.,* 33 167–173.

Dodds, E., and Harford, E. (1970). Follow-up report on modified ear-pieces and CROS for high-frequency hearing losses. *J. Speech Hearing Res.,* 13, 41–43.

Doehring, D. G. (1968). Picture-sound association in deaf children. *J. Speech Hearing Res.,* 11, 49–62.

Doehring, D. G., and Ling, D. (1971). Programmed instruction of hearing-impaired children in the auditory discrimination of vowels. *J. Speech Hearing Res.,* 14, 746–754.

Donnelly, K. G., and Marshall, W. J. A. (1967). Development of a multiple-choice test of lipreading. *J. Speech Hearing Res.,* 10, 565–569.

Eachus, T. (1971). Modification of sentence writing by deaf children. *Amer. Ann. Deaf,* 116, 29–43.

Egolf, D. B., Rhodes, R. C., and Curry, E. T. (1970). Phoneme discrimination differences between hypacusics and normals. *J. Aud. Res.,* 10, 176–179.

Elfner, L. F., Bothe, G. G., and Simrall, D. S. (1970). Monaural localization: Effects of feedback, incentive, and interstimulus interval. *J. Aud. Res.,* 10, 11–16.

Ellsworth, P. C., and Carlsmith, J. M. (1968). Effects of eye contact and verbal content on affective response to a dyadic interaction. *J. Personal. Soc. Psych.,* 10, 15–20.

Engelberg, M. (1962). Correction of falsetto voice in a deaf adult. *J. Speech Hearing Dis.,* 27, 162–164.

Erber, N. P. (1969). Interaction of audition and vision in the recognition of oral speech stimuli. *J. Speech Hearing Res.,* 12, 423–434.

Erber, N. P. (1971a). Auditory detection of spondaic words in wide-band noise by adults with normal hearing and by children with profound hearing losses. *J. Speech Hearing Res.*, 14, 372–381.

Erber, N. P. (1971b). Auditory and audiovisual reception of words in low-frequency noise by children with normal hearing and by children with impaired hearing. *J. Speech Hearing Res.*, 14, 496–512.

Erber, N. P. (1971c). Effects of distance on the visual reception of speech. *J. Speech Hearing Res.*, 14, 848–857.

Erber, N. P. (1971d). Evaluation of special hearing aids for deaf children. *J. Speech Hearing Dis.*, 36, 527–537.

Falconer, G. A. (1960). Teaching machines for the deaf. *Volta Rev.*, 62, 59–62, 76.

Falconer, G. A. (1961). A mechanical device for teaching sight vocabulary to young deaf children. *Amer. Ann. Deaf*, 106, 251–257.

Falconer, G. A. (1962). Teaching machines for teaching reading. *Volta Rev.*, 64, 389–392.

Fant, L. G., and Roy, H. L. (1961). Programmed lessons for the language of signs. *Amer. Ann. Deaf*, 106, 484–486.

Feldman, S. (1959). *Mannerisms of Speech and Gestures in Everyday Life.* New York: International Universities Press, Inc.

Fisher, C. G. (1968). Confusions among visually perceived consonants. *J. Speech Hearing Res.*, 11, 796–804.

Franks, J. R., and Oyer, H. J. (1967). Factors influencing the identification of English sounds in lipreading. *J. Speech Hearing Res.*, 10, 757–767.

Gaeth, J. H. (1963). Verbal and nonverbal learning in children including those with hearing losses. Cooperative Research Project No. 1001, Wayne State University.

Gaeth, J. H. (1967). "Learning with Visual and Audiovisual Presentation." In *Deafness in Children* (F. McConnell and P. H. Ward, eds). Nashville, Tenn.: Vanderbilt University Press.

Garretson, M. I. (1960). The simultaneous method. *Amer. Ann. Deaf*, 105, 434.

Gault, R. H. (1924). Progress in experiments on tactual interpretation of oral speech. *J. Abnormal Soc. Psychol.*, 19, 155–159.

Gault, R. H. (1926a). Control experiments in relation to identification of speech sounds by aid of tactual cues. *J. Abnormal Soc. Psychol.*, 21, 4–13.

Gault, R. H. (1926b). On the identification of certain spoken words by their tactual qualities. *J. Applied Psych.*, 10, 75–91.

Gault, R. H., and Crane, G. W. (1928). Tactual patterns from certain vowel qualities instrumentally communicated from a speaker to a subject's fingers. *J. Gen. Psych.*, 1, 353–359.

Gay, T. (1970). Effects of filtering and vowel environment on consonant perception. *J. Acoust. Soc. Amer.*, 48, 993–998.

Geldard, F. A. (1940). The perception of mechanical vibration: I. History of a controversy. *J. Gen. Psychol.*, 22, 243–269.

Geldard, F. A. (1954). Hearing through the skin. *Research Rev.*, Office of Naval Research, Department of the Navy, Washington, D.C., 15–20.

Geldard, F. A. (1957). Adventures in tactile literacy. *Amer. Psychol.* 12, 115–124.

Geldard, F. A. (1960). Some neglected possibilities of communication. *Science,* 131, 1583–1588.

Geldard, F. A. (1961). Cutaneous channels of communication. In *Sensory Communication* (W. A. Rosenblith, ed.). Cambridge, Mass.: M.I.T. Press.

Geldard, F. A., and Sherrick, C. E. (1965). Multiple cutaneous stimulation: the discrimination of vibratory patterns. *J. Acoust. Soc. Amer.*, 37, 797–801.

Gengel, R. W. (1969). Practice effects in frequency discrimination by hearing-impaired children. *J. Speech Hearing Res.*, 12, 847–856.

Gengel, R. W., Pascoe, D., and Shore, I. (1971). A frequency-response procedure for evaluating and selecting hearing aids for severely hearing-impaired children. *J. Speech Hearing Dis.*, 36, 341–353.

Gillespie, M. E., Gillespie, M. R., and Creston, J. E. (1965). Clinical evaluation of a "master hearing aid." *Arch. Otolaryng.*, 82, 515–517.

Gilson, R. D. (1968). Some factors affecting the spatial discrimination of vibrotactile patterns. *Percep. Psychophys.*, 3:2B, 131–136.

Giolas, T. G. (1968). Webster, E. J., and Ward, L. M., A diagnostic-therapy setting for hearing-handicapped children. *J. Speech Hearing Dis.*, 33, 345–350.

Goda, S. (1959). Language skills of profoundly deaf adolescent children. *J. Speech Hearing Res.*, 2, 369–376.

Goetzinger, C. P. (1964). A study of monocular versus binocular vision in lipreading. *Report of the Proceedings of the International Congress on Education of the Deaf.* Gallaudet College, June 22–28, Washington D.C.: U.S. Government Printing Office, 326–333.

Goldstein, J. L. (1972). The effects of speaker, training, and transducer on the recognition of tactile differences in combined speech sounds. Unpublished Doctoral dissertation, Michigan State University.

Gray, H. A., Sloan, R. F., Ashley, F. L., Harn, E., and Hanafee, W. (1961). Cinefluorography as an aid to more intelligible speech. *Volta Rev.*, 63, 323–327.

Gray, M. (1964). Sensitivity of the skin to pure-tone frequencies. Unpublished Master's thesis, Michigan State University.

Greenberg, H. J., and Bode, D. L. (1968). Visual discrimination of consonants. *J. Speech Hearing Res.*, 11, 869–874.

Greene, J. D. (1964). An investigation of the ability of unskilled lip-readers to determine the accented syllable of polysyllabic words. Unpublished Master's thesis, Michigan State University.

Guberina, P. (1964). Verbotonal method and its application to the rehabilitation of the deaf. *Report of the Proceedings of the International Congress on Education of the Deaf.* June 22–28, 1963, Gallaudet College, Washington, D.C.: U.S. Government Printing Office.

Haas, W. H. (1970). Vibrotactile reception of spoken English phonemes. Unpublished Doctoral dissertation, Michigan State University.

Haggerty, M. E., Olson, W. C., and Wickman, E. K. (1930). *Manual of directions. Behavior Rating Schedules.* New York: World Book.

Hardick, E. J., Oyer, H. J., and Irion, P. E. (1970). Lipreading performance as related to measurements of vision. *J. Speech Hearing Res.,* 13, 92–100.

Hardy, W. G., Pauls, M. D., and Haskins, H. L. (1958). An analysis of language development in children with impaired hearing. *Acta Oto-Laryng. Suppl.,* 141, 51 pages.

Harford, E., and Barry, J. (1965). A rehabilitative approach to the problem of unilateral hearing impairment: The contralateral routing of signals (CROS). *J. Speech Hearing Dis.,* 30, 121–138.

Harford, E., and Dodds, E. (1966). The clinical application of CROS. *Arch. Otolaryng.,* 83, 455–464.

Harford, E., and Musket, C. H. (1964). Binaural hearing with one hearing aid. *J. Speech Hearing Dis.,* 29, 133–146.

Harris, J. D. (1965). Monaural and binaural intelligibility and the stereophonic effect base upon temporal cues. *Laryngoscope,* 75, 428–446.

Harris, J. D., Haines, H. L., Kelsey, P. A., and Clack, T. D. (1961). The relation between speech intelligibility and the electroacoustic characteristics of low fidelity circuitry. *J. Aud. Res.,* 1, 357–381.

Harris, J. D., and Sergeant, R. L. (1971). Monaural/binaural minimum audible angles for a moving sound source. *J. Speech Hearing Res.,* 14, 618–629.

Harrison, A. (1967). Practical audiology. *J. Speech Hearing Dis.,* 32, 162–169.

Haug, O., Baccaro, P., and Guilford, F. R. (1971). Differences in hearing aid performance. *Arch. Otolaryng.,* 93, 183–185.

Hedgecock, L. D., and Sheets, B. V. (1958). A comparison of monaural and binaural hearing aids for listening to speech. *Arch. Otolaryng.,* 68, 624–629.

Heffler, A. M., and Schultz, M. C. (1964). Some implications of binaural signal selection for hearing aid evaluation. *J. Speech Hearing Res.,* 7, 279–289.

Heider, F. K., and Heider, G. M. (1940). Studies in the psychology of the deaf. *Psych. Monogr.,* 52, 124–133.

Hester, M. S. (1964). Manual communication. *Report of the Proceedings of the International Congress on Education of the Deaf*. Gallaudet College, June 22–28, 1963. Washington, D.C.: U.S. Government Printing Office, 211–227.

Higgins, J. M. (1971). The effects of speaker and pressure variation on the vibrotactile reception of selected spoken English phonemes. Unpublished Doctoral dissertation, Michigan State University.

Hirsh, I. J. (1950). Binaural hearing aids: A review of some experiments. *J. Speech Hearing Dis.,* 15, 114–123.

Hirsh, I. J. (1966). Recent developments in hearing aid use. *Int. Audiol.,* 5, 393–398.

Hirsh, I. J., Reynolds, E. G., and Joseph, M. (1954). Intelligibility of different speech materials. *J. Acoust. Soc. Amer.,* 26, 530–538.

Hochberg, I. (1963). Auditory localization of speech as a function of interaural auditory acuity. *J. Aud. Res.,* 3, 141–147.

Hodgson, W. R., and Murdock, D., Jr. (1971). Effect of the earmold on speech intelligibility in hearing aid use. *J. Speech Hearing Res.,* 13, 290–297.

Holbrook, A., and Crawford, G. H. (1970). Modifications of vocal frequency and intensity in the speech of the deaf. *Volta Rev.,* 72, 492–497.

House, A. S., Goldstein, D. P., and Hughes, G. W. (1968). Perception of visual transforms of speech stimuli: Learning simple syllables. *Amer. Ann. Deaf,* 113, 215–221.

House, H. P. (1969). Hearing standards—fact or fiction? *Arch. Otolaryng.,* 90, 208–213.

Hudgins, C. V. (1953). The response of profoundly deaf children to auditory training. *J. Speech Hearing Dis.,* 18, 273–288.

Hudson, A. (1960). Communication problems of the geriatric patient. *J. Speech Hearing Dis.,* 25, 238–248.

Huizing, H. C., Kruisinga, R. J. H., and Taselaar, M. (1960). Triplet audiometry: An analysis of band discrimination of speech reception. *Acta Oto-Laryng.,* 51, 256–259.

Hutton, C. (1960). A diagnostic approach to combined techniques in aural rehabilitation. *J. Speech Hearing Dis.,* 25, 267–272.

Imai, H., and Hoshi, T. (1966). Hearing therapy for young hard-of-hearing children. *Int. Audiol.,* 5, 242–246.

Jerger, J., Carhart, R., and Dirks, D. (1961). Binaural hearing aids and speech intelligibility. *J. Speech Hearing Res.,* 4, 137–148.

Jerger, J., and Dirks, D. (1961). Binaural hearing aids, an enigma. *J. Acoust. Soc. Amer.,* 33, 537–538.

Jerger, J., Malmquist, C., and Speaks, C. (1966). Comparison of some speech intelligibility tests in the evaluation of hearing aid performance. *J. Speech Hearing Res.,* 9, 253–258.

Jerger, J., Speaks, C., and Malmquist, C. (1966). Hearing-aid performance and hearing-aid selection. *J. Speech Hearing Res.,* 9, 136–149.

Jerger, J., and Thelin, J. (1968). Effects of electroacoustic characteristics of hearing aids on speech understanding, January 1, 1967–March 1, 1968. *Bull. Pros. Res.,* 10–10, 159–197.

Jetty, J. A., and Rintelmann, W. R. (1970). Acoustic coupler effects on speech audiometric scores using a CROS hearing aid. *J. Speech Hearing Res.,* 13, 101–114.

Joergenson, A. (1962). The measurement of homophenous words. Unpublished Master's thesis, Michigan State University.

Johansson, B. (1966). The use of the transposer for the management of the deaf child. *Int. Audiol.,* 5, 362–372.

Johnson, G. F. (1963). The effects of cutaneous stimulation by speech on lipreading performance. Unpublished Doctoral dissertation, Michigan State University.

Jongkees, L. B. W., and Veer, R. A. U. D. (1957). Directional hearing capacity in hearing disorders. *Acta Oto-Laryng.,* 48, 465–474.

Kahn, H. (1964). The utilization of a combined auditory and visual test of discrimination ability with people wearing hearing aids as a measure of communication effectiveness. Unpublished Master's thesis, Michigan State University.

Karlovich, R. S. (1968). Sensory interaction: perception of loudness during visual stimulation. *J. Acoust. Soc. Amer.,* 44, 570–575.

Kasten, R. N., and Lotterman, S. H. (1967). A longitudinal examination of harmonic distortion in hearing aids. *J. Speech Hearing Res.,* 10, 777–781.

Keidel, W. D. (1958). Note on a new system for vibratory communication. *Percep. Motor Skills,* 8, 250.

Keil, J. M. (1968). The effects of peripheral visual stimuli on lipreading performance. Unpublished Doctoral dissertation, Michigan State University.

Kitchen, D. H. (1968). The relationship of visual synthesis to lipreading performance. Unpublished Doctoral dissertation, Michigan State University.

Kringlebotn, M. (1968). Experiments with some visual and vibrotactile aids for the deaf. *Amer. Ann. Deaf,* 113, 311–317.

Kodman, F., Jr. (1969). Attitudes of hearing aid users. *Audecibel,* 18, 76–78.

Kosh, Z. H. (1963). WETA-TV Lipreading Project (unpublished).

Lach, R., Ling, D., Ling, A. H., and Ship, N. (1970). Early speech development in deaf infants. *Amer. Ann. Deaf,* 115, 522–526.

Lawrence, D. L., and Byers, V. W. (1969). Identification of voiceless fricatives by high-frequency hearing-impaired listeners. *J. Speech Hearing Res.,* 12, 426–434.

Leckie, D., and Ling, D. (1968). Audibility with hearing aids having low-frequency characteristics. *Volta Rev., 70,* 83–86.

Leonard, R. (1962). The effects of selected continuous auditory distractions on lipreading performance. Unpublished Master's thesis, Michigan State University.

Leonard, R. (1968). Facial movements of males and females while producing common expressions and sentences by voice and by whisper. Unpublished Doctoral dissertation, Michigan State University.

Levine, E. S. (1960). Psychiatric-preventive and sociogenetic study of the adjustive capacities, human work potentials and total family problems of literate deaf adolescents and adults. *Amer. Ann. Deaf, 105,* 272–274.

Lichtenberg, F. S. (1966). A comparison of children's ability to make speech sound discriminations. *Volta Rev., 68,* 426–434.

Ling, A. H. (1971). Changes in the abilities of deaf infants with training. *J. Commun. Dis., 3,* 267–279.

Ling, D. (1964). Implications of hearing aid amplification below 300 cps. *Volta Rev., 66,* 723–729.

Ling, D. (1969). Speech discrimination by profoundly deaf children using linear and coding amplifiers. IEEE Translations on Audio and Electroacoustics, AU-17, 298–303.

Ling, D. (1971). The hearing impaired pre-schooler: A family responsibility. *Hearing and Speech News,* 39:5, 8–13.

Ling, D., and Doehring, D. G. (1969). Learning limits of deaf children for coded speech. *J. Speech Hearing Res., 12,* 83–94.

Ling, D., and Druz, W. S. (1967). Transposition of high-frequency sounds by partial vocoding of the speech spectrum: Its use by deaf children. *J. Aud. Res., 7,* 133–144.

Ling, D., Ling, A., and Jacobson, C. (1968). Detection and treatment of deafness in early infancy. *Canadian Family Physician,* 14, 47–52.

Lloyd, L. L. (1964). Sentence familiarity as a factor in visual speech reception (lipreading). *J. Speech Hearing Dis., 29,* 409–413.

Lloyd, L. L., and Price, J. G. (1971). Sentence familiarity as a factor in visual speech reception (lipreading) of deaf college students. *J. Speech Hearing Res., 14,* 291–294.

Lott, B. D., and Levy, J. (1960). The influence of certain communicator characteristics on lipreading efficiency. *J. Soc. Psych., 51,* 419–425.

Lotterman, S. H., and Kasten, R. N. (1971). Examination of the CROS type hearing aid. *J. Speech Hearing Res., 14,* 416–420.

Lovering, L. J. (1969). Lipreading performance as a function of visual acuity. Unpublished Doctoral dissertation, Michigan State University.

Lowell, E., and Taaffe, G. (1957). A film test of lipreading. Los Angeles School of Education, University of Southern California, John Tracy Clinic.

Lybarger, S. F. (1966). A discussion of hearing aid trends. *Int. Audiol.*, 5, 376–383.

Lybarger, S. F. (1967). Earmold acoustics. *Audecibel,* 16, 9–19.

Lynn, G., and Carhart, R. (1963). Influence of attack and release in compression amplification on understanding of speech by hypacousics. *J. Speech Hearing Dis.*, 28, 124–140.

Macrae, J. H. (1968a). TTS and recovery from TTS after use of powerful hearing aids. *J. Acoust. Soc. Amer.*, 43, 1445–1446.

Macrae, J. H. (1968b). Recovery from TTS in children with sensorineural deafness. *J. Acoust. Soc. Amer.*, 44, 1451.

Macrae, J. H. (1968c). Deterioration of the residual hearing of children with sensorineural deafness. *Acta Oto-Laryng.*, 66, 33–39.

Macrae, J. H., and Farrant, R. H. (1965). The effect of hearing aid use on the residual hearing of children with sensorineural deafness. *Ann. Otol. Rhinol. Laryng.*, 74, 409–419.

Markle, D. M., and Aber, W. (1958). A clinical evaluation of monaural and binaural hearing aids. *Arch. Otolaryng.*, 67, 606–608.

Markle D. M., and Zaner, A. (1966). The determination of "gain requirements" of hearing aids: A new method. *J. Aud. Res.*, 6, 371–377.

Martin, E. S., and Pickett, J. M. (1970). Masking of F2 transition discrimination in hearing-impaired listeners. *J. Acoust. Soc. Amer.*, 48, 93.

Martony, J. (1968). On the correction of the voice pitch level for severely hard-of-hearing subjects. *Amer. Ann. Deaf,* 113, 195–202.

Mason, M. K. (1943). A cinematographic technique for testing visual speech comprehension. *J. Speech Dis.*, 8, 271–278.

McClellan, M. E. (1967). Aided speech discrimination in noise with vented and unvented earmolds. *J. Aud. Res.*, 7, 93–99.

McConnell, F., ed. (1968). *Proceedings of the Conference on Current Practices in the Management of Deaf Infants (0–3 Years).* The Bill Wilkerson Hearing and Speech Center, Vanderbilt University School of Medicine, June 21–22, 1968. Nashville, Tenn.: U.S. Office of Education Grant.

McConnell, F., Silber, E. F., and McDonald, D. (1960). Test-retest consistency of clinical hearing aid tests. *J. Speech Hearing Dis.*, 25, 273–280.

McCroskey, L. (1967). Progress report on a home training program for deaf infants. *Int. Audiol.*, 6, 171–177.

McDaniel, J. W. (1965). The current status of vocational rehabilitation for disorders of hearing and speech. *J. Speech Hearing Dis.*, 30, 17–31.

McDearmon, J. R. (1967). A method of teaching lipreading using programmed learning principles. *Volta Rev.*, 69, 316–318.

McDonald, E. T., and Frick, J. V. (1957). The frequency and duration of treatment sessions in speech correction. *J. Speech Hearing Dis.*, 22, 724–728.

McGrady, H. J. (1964). The influence of a program of instruction upon the conceptual thinking of the deaf. *Volta Rev.,* 66, 531–536.

Mehrabian, A. (1968). Relationship of attitude to seated posture, orientation, and distance. *J. Personal. Soc. Psych.,* 10, 26–30.

Millen, J. P. (1971). Therapy for reduction of continuous phonation in the hard-of-hearing population. *J. Speech Hearing Dis.,* 36, 496–498.

Miller, A. L. (1968). The evaluation of hearing sensitivity in young children using bands of filtered noise. *J. Commun. Dis.,* 1, 310–315.

Miller, C. A. (1965). Lipreading performance as a function of continuous visual distraction. Unpublished Master's thesis, Michigan State University.

Miller, G. A., and Nicely, P. E. (1955). An analysis of perceptual confusions among some English consonants. *J. Acoust. Soc. Amer.,* 27, 338–352.

Mira, M. (1970). Direct measurement of the listening of hearing-impaired children. *J. Speech Hearing Res.,* 13, 65–73.

Montgomery, G. W. (1966). The relationship of oral skills to manual communication in profoundly deaf adolescents. *Amer. Ann. Deaf,* 111, 557–565.

Morkovin, B. V. (1947). Rehabilitation of the aurally handicapped through study of speechreading in life situations. *J. Speech Dis.,* 12, 363–368.

Morkovin, B. V. (1960). Experiment in teaching deaf preschool children in the Soviet Union. *Volta Rev.,* 62, 260–268.

Morkovin, B. V. (1961). Mechanisms of compensation for hearing loss: Theories and research in the Soviet Union. *J. Speech Hearing Dis.,* 26, 359–367.

Moser, H. M., O'Neill, J. J., Oyer, H. J., Abernathy, E. A., and Showe, B. M., Jr. (1961). Distance and finger spelling. *J. Speech Hearing Res.,* 4, 61–71.

Moser, H. M., O'Neill, J. J., Oyer, H. J., Wolfe, S. M., Abernathy, E. A., and Showe, B. M., Jr. (1960). Historical aspects of manual communication. *J. Speech Hearing Dis.* 25, 145–151.

Mulligan, M. (1954). Variables in the reception of visual speech from motion pictures. Unpublished Master's thesis, Ohio State University.

Myklebust, H. R., and Neyhus, A. I. (1970). *Diagnostic Test of Speechreading.* New York: Grune & Stratton.

Nance, G., and Causey, G. D. (1968). Hearing-aid evaluation: An examination of two procedures. *Bull. Pros. Res.,* 10–9, 119–124.

Neely, K. K. (1956). Effect of visual factors on the intelligibility of speech. *J. Acoust. Soc. Amer.,* 28, 1275–1277.

Neuhaus, M. (1969). Parental attitudes and the emotional adjustment of deaf children. *Except. Children,* 35, 721–727.

Nielsen, H. B. (1970). Measurement of visual speech comprehension. *J. Speech Hearing Res.,* 13, 856–860.

Nielsen, K. M. (1966). The effect of redundancy on the visual recognition of frequently employed spoken words. Unpublished Doctoral dissertation, Michigan State University.

Nordlund, B. (1964). Directional audiometry. *Acta Oto-Laryng.,* 57, 1–18.

Northern, J. L., and Hattler, K. W. (1970). Earmold influence on aided speech identification tasks. *J. Speech Hearing Res.,* 13, 162–172.

Northern, J. L., Ciliax, D. R., Roth, D. E., Johnson, R. J., Jr. (1969). Military patient attitudes toward aural rehabilitation, *Asha,* 11, 391–395.

Oeken, S. W. (1963). Can the hearing of patients suffering from high-tone perceptive deafness be improved by frequency transposition? *Int. Audiol.,* 2, 263–266.

Olsen, W. O., and Carhart, R. (1967). Development of test procedures for evaluation of binaural hearing aids. *Bull. Pros. Res.,* 1-7, 22–49.

O'Neill, J. J. (1951). Contributions of the visual components of oral symbols to the speech comprehension of listeners with normal hearing. Unpublished Doctoral dissertation, Ohio State University.

O'Neill, J. J. (1954). Contributions of the visual components of oral symbols to speech comprehension. *J. Speech Hearing Dis.,* 19, 429–439.

O'Neill, J. J. (1957). Recognition of intelligibility test materials in context and isolation. *J. Speech Hearing Dis.,* 22, 87–90.

O'Neill, J. J., and Davidson, J. L. (1956). Relationship between lipreading ability and five psychological factors. *J. Speech Hearing Dis.,* 21, 478–481.

O'Neill, J. J., and Oyer, H. J. (1961). *Visual Communication for the Hard of Hearing.* Englewood Cliffs, N.J.: Prentice-Hall.

O'Neill, J. J., and Stephens, M. C. (1959). Relationships among three filmed lipreading tests. *J. Speech Hearing Res.,* 2, 61–65.

Owens, E., Talbott, C. B., and Schubert, E. D. (1968). Vowel discrimination of hearing-impaired listeners. *J. Speech Hearing Res.,* 11, 648–655.

Oyer, H. J. (1961). Teaching lipreading by television. *Volta Rev.,* 63, 131–132, 141.

Oyer, H. J. (1964). An experimental approach to lipreading. *Report of the Proceedings of the International Congress on Education of the Deaf,* Gallaudet College, June 22–28, 1963. Washington, D.C.: U.S. Government Printing Office, 322–326.

Oyer, H. J., Donnelly, K. G., Dixon, J., Goldstein, D., Hardick, E. J., Lloyd, L. L., and Mussen, E. F. (1968). Reasons for not returning for aural rehabilitation following audiological evaluation. East Lansing: Michigan State University (unpublished).

Oyer, H. J., and Doudna, M. (1959). Structural analysis of word responses made by hard-of-hearing subjects on a discrimination test. *Arch. Otolaryng.,* 70, 357–364.

Oyer, H. J., and Doudna, M. (1960). Word familiarity as a factor in testing discrimination of hard-of-hearing subjects. *Arch. Otolaryng.,* 72, 351–355.

Palmer, J. M. (1955). The effect of speaker differences on the intelligibility of phonetically balanced word lists. *J. Speech Hearing Dis.,* 20, 192–195.

Perrott, D. R., and Elfner, L. F. (1968). Monaural localization. *J. Aud. Res.,* 8, 185–193.

Pesonen, J. (1968). Phoneme communication of the deaf. *Ann. Academiae Scientiarum Fennicae,* Series B, 151–152.

Pfau, G. S. (1969). Project LIFE PI analysis. *Amer. Ann. Deaf,* 114, 829–837.

Pfau, G. S. (1970a). Reinforcement and learning—some considerations with programmed instruction and the deaf child. *Volta Rev.,* 72, 408–412.

Pfau, G. S. (1970b). Project LIFE: Developing high interest programmed materials for handicapped children. *Educational Technology,* 10, 13–18.

Pfau, G. S. (1970c). Educating the deaf child. *Audiovisual Instruction,* 15, 24–29.

Phillips, N. D., Remillard, W., Bass, S., and Pronovost, W. (1968). Teaching of intonation to the deaf by visual pattern matching. *Amer. Ann. Deaf,* 113, 239–246.

Pickett, J. M. (1963). Tactual communication of speech sounds to the deaf: Comparison with lipreading. *J. Speech Hearing Dis.,* 28, 315–330.

Pickett, J. M. (1968). Sound patterns of speech: An introductory sketch, *Amer. Ann. Deaf,* 113, 120–126.

Pickett, J. M., and Martony, J. (1970). Low-frequency vowel formant discrimination in hearing-impaired listeners. *J. Speech Hearing Res.,* 13, 347–359.

Pickett, J. M., and Pickett, B. H. (1963). Communication of speech sounds by a tactual vocoder. *J. Speech Hearing Res.,* 6, 207–222.

Pollack, I., and Norman, D. A. (1964). A nonparametric analysis of recognition experiments. *Psychon. Sci.,* 1, 125–126.

Postove, M. J. (1962). Selection of items for a speechreading test by means of scaleogram analysis. *J. Speech Hearing Dis.,* 27, 71–75.

Potter, R. K., Kopp, G. A., and Green, H. C. (1947). *Visible Speech.* New York: D. Van Nostrand.

Pronovost, W. (1967). Developments in visual displays of speech information. *Volta Rev.,* 69, 365–373.

Quigley, S. P. (1966). Language research in countries other than the United States. *Volta Rev.,* 68, 68–83.

Quigley, S. P. (no date). The influence of finger spelling on the development of language, communication, and educational achievement in deaf children. Institute for Research on Exceptional Children, University of Illinois.

Rassi, J., and Harford, E. (1968). An analysis of patient attitudes and reactions to a clinical hearing aid selection program. *Asha,* 10, 283–290.

Rea, J. (1968). A factorial study comparing certain features of two methodologies of audiometry: Conventional and Verbotonal. Unpublished Master's thesis, Ohio State University.

Rees, M., ed. (1965). Auditory rehabilitation for hearing-impaired blind persons. *Asha Monogr.,* 12, 96.

Reid, G. (1947). A preliminary investigation in the testing of lipreading achievement. *J. Speech Dis.,* 12, 77–82.

Revoile, S. G. (1968). Speech discrimination ability with ear inserts. *Bull. of Pros. Res.,* 10–10, 198–205.

Rhodes, R. C. (1966). Discrimination of filtered CNC lists by normals and hypacusics. *J. Aud. Res.,* 6, 129–133.

Rhodes, R. C., and Corbett, L. S. (1970). Learning of speech discrimination skills by young hypacusics. *J. Aud. Res.,* 10, 124–126.

Rice, C. G. (1965). Hearing aid design criteria. *Int. Audiol.,* 4, 130–134.

Rintelmann, W., Harford, E., and Burchfield, S. (1970). A special case of auditory localization. *Arch. Otolaryng.,* 91, 284–288.

Roback, I. M. (1961). Homophenous words. Unpublished Master's thesis, Michigan State University.

Roberts, C. (1970). Can hearing aids damage hearing? *Acta Oto-Laryng.,* 69 ,123–125.

Ross, H., and Newby, H. (1965). Speech discrimination of hearing-impaired individuals in noise. *J. Aud. Res.,* 5, 47–72.

Ross, M., and Lerman, J. (1967). Hearing aid usage and its effect on residual hearing. *Arch. Otolaryng.,* 86, 639–644.

Rubenstein, H., and Pickett J. M. (1957). Word intelligibility and position in sentence. *J. Acoust. Soc. Amer.,* 29, 1263.

Rush, M. L. (1966). Use of visual memory in teaching written language skills to deaf children. *J. Speech Hearing Dis.,* 31, 219–226.

Sahlstrom, L. J. (1967). Objective measurement of certain facial movements during production of homophenous words. Unpublished Doctoral dissertation, Michigan State University.

Saleh, H. (1965). Sights and sounds, an auditory training program for young deaf children. *Amer. Ann. Deaf,* 110, 528–534.

Sanders, D. A., and Goodrich, S. J. (1971). The relative contribution of visual and auditory components of speech to speech intelligibility as a function of three conditions of frequency distortion. *J. Speech Hearing Res.*, 14, 154–159.

Sanders, J. W., and Coscarelli, J. E. (1970). The relationship of visual synthesis skill to lipreading. *Amer. Ann. Deaf*, 115, 23–26.

Schultz, M. C., and Kraat, A. W. (1970). A metric for evaluating therapy with the hearing impaired. *J. Speech Hearing Dis.*, 35, 37–43.

Schwartz, J. R., and Black, J. W. (1967). Some effects of sentence structure on speechreading. *Central States Sp. J.*, 18, 86–90.

Scouten, E. L. (1967). The Rochester Method, an oral multisensory approach for instructing prelingual deaf children. *Amer. Ann. Deaf*, 112, 50–55.

Sedge, R. K. (1965). An investigation of the difference between auditory and auditory-visual articulation curves. Unpublished Master's thesis, Michigan State University.

Sheets, B. V., and Hedgecock, L. D. (1949). Hearing aid amplification for optimum speech reproduction. *J. Speech Hearing Dis.*, 14, 373–379.

Shore, I., Bilger, R. C., and Hirsh, I. J. (1960). Hearing aid evaluation: Reliability of repeated measurements. *J. Speech Hearing Dis.*, 25, 152–170.

Shore, I., and Kramer, J. C. (1963). A comparison of two procedures for hearing-aid evaluation. *J. Speech Hearing Dis.*, 28, 159–170.

Siegenthaler, B. M. (1949). A study of the relationship between measured hearing loss and intelligibility of selected words. *J. Speech Hearing Dis.*, 14, 111–118.

Siegenthaler, B. M., and Gruber, V. (1969). Combining vision and audition for speech reception. *J. Speech Hearing Dis.*, 34, 58–60.

Simmons, A. A. (1959). Factors related to lipreading. *J. Speech Hearing Res.*, 2, 340–352.

Smith, K. E, and Hodgson, W. R. (1970). The effects of systematic reinforcement on the speech discrimination responses of normal and hearing-impaired children. *J. Aud. Res.*, 10, 110–117.

Stark, R. E., Cullen, J. K., and Chase, R. A. (1968). Preliminary work with the new Bell Telephone visible speech translator. *Amer. Ann. Deaf*, 113, 205–214.

Steinberg, J. C., and French, N. R. (1946). The portrayal of visible speech. *J. Acoust. Soc. Amer.*, 18, 4–18.

Stewart, J. L., Pollack, D., and Downs, M. P. (1964). A Unisensory program for the limited-hearing child. *Asha*, 6, 151–154.

Stone, L. (1957). Facial cues of context in lipreading. Los Angeles School of Education, University of Southern California, John Tracy Clinic.

Stone, L. J., Fiedler, M. F., and Fine, C. G. (1961). Preschool education of deaf children. *J. Speech Hearing Dis.*, 26, 45–60.

Strizver, G. L. (1958). Frequency discrimination of deaf children and its relation to their achievement in auditory training. *Volta Rev.*, 60, 304–306.

Stuckless, E. R., and Birch, J. W. (1966). The influence of early manual communication on the linguistic development of deaf children, Part I. *Amer. Ann. Deaf,* 111, 452–460 and 499–504.

Stutz, R. (1969). The American hearing aid user. *Asha,* 11, 459–461.

Subar, B. E. (1963). The effects of visual deprivation on lipreading performance. Unpublished Master's thesis, Michigan State University.

Sumby, W. H., and Pollack, I. (1954). Visual contribution to speech intelligibility in noise. *J. Acoust. Soc. Amer.,* 26, 212–215.

Taaffe, G., and Wong, W. (1957). Studies of variables of lipreading stimulus material. Los Angeles School of Education, University of Southern California, John Tracy Clinic.

Tatoul, C. M., and Davidson, G. D. (1961). Lipreading and letter prediction. *J. Speech Hearing Res.,* 4, 178–181.

Tervoort, B. T. (1961). Esoteric symbolism in the communication behavior of young deaf children. *Amer. Ann. Deaf,* 106, 436–480.

Thomas, I. B., and Snell, R. C. (1970). Articulation training through visual speech patterns. *Volta Rev.,* 72, 310–318.

Thomas, I. B., and Sparks, D. W. (1971). Discrimination of filtered/clipped speech by hearing-impaired subjects. *J. Acoust. Soc. Amer.,* 49, 1881–1887.

Thomas, S. (1962). Lipreading performance as a function of light levels. Unpublished Master's thesis, Michigan State University.

Thompson, G., and Lassman, F. (1969). Relationship of auditory distortion test results to speech discrimination through flat versus selective amplifying systems. *J. Speech Hearing Res.,* 12, 594–606.

Thompson, G., and Lassman, F. (1970). Listener preference for selective versus flat amplification for a high-frequency hearing-loss population. *J. Speech Hearing Res.,* 13, 670–672.

Tiffany, W. R., and Bennett, D. R. (1961). Intelligibility of slow-played speech. *J. Speech Hearing Res.,* 4, 248–258.

Tiffany, W. R., and Kates, S. L. (1962). Concept attainment and lipreading ability among deaf adolescents. *J. Speech Hearing Dis.,* 27, 265–274.

Traul, G. N., and Black, J. W. (1965). The effect of context on aural perception of words. *J. Speech Hearing Res.,* 8, 363–369.

University of Oklahoma Research Institute (no date). Effects and interactions of auditory and visual cues in oral communication. Report submitted to Office of Education, Department of Health, Education, and Welfare.

Upton, H. W. (1968). Wearable eyeglass speechreading aid. *Amer. Ann. Deaf,* 113, 222–229.

Utley, J. (1946). A test of lipreading ability. *J. Speech Dis.,* 11, 109–116.

Vernon, M. (1967). Characteristics associated with postrubella deaf children: Psychological, educational, and physical. *Volta Rev.*, 69, 176–185.

Viehweg, R., and Campbell, R. A. (1960). Localization difficulty in monaurally impaired listeners. *Ann. Otol. Rhinol. Laryng.*, 69, 622–634.

VonBekesy, G. (1957a). Sensations on the skin similar to direct hearing, beats and harmonics of the ear. *J. Acoust. Soc. Amer.*, 29, 489–501.

VonBekesy, G. (1957b). Neural volleys and the similarity between some sensations produced by tones and skin vibration. *J. Acoust. Soc. Amer.*, 29, 1063.

VonBekesy, G. (1959). Similarities between hearing and skin sensations. *Psychol. Rev.*, 66, 1–22.

Vos, L. J. (1965). The effects of exaggerated and nonexaggerated stimuli on lipreading ability. Unpublished Master's thesis, Michigan State University.

Ward, W. D. (1960). Recovery from high values of temporary threshold shift. *J. Acoust. Soc. Amer.*, 32, 497–500.

Watson, T. J. (1961a). The use of residual hearing in the education of deaf children, Part II. *Volta Rev.*, 63, 385–392.

Watson, T. J. (1961b). The use of residual hearing in the education of deaf children, Part III. *Volta Rev.*, 63, 435–440.

Wedenberg, E. (1954). Auditory training of severely hard-of-hearing preschool children. *Acta Oto-Laryng. Suppl.*, 110, 1–72.

Willemain, T. R., and Lee, F. F. (1970). Tactile pitch feedback for deaf speakers. *Quarterly Progress Report #99.* Cambridge: Research Laboratory of Electronics, Massachusetts Institute of Technology.

Withrow, F. B. (1965). The use of audiovisual techniques to expand lipreading and auditory experiences of young deaf children. *Amer. Ann. Deaf,* 110, 523–527.

Witter, H. L., and Goldstein, D. P. (1971). Quality judgments of hearing aid transduced speech. *J. Speech Hearing Res.,* 14, 312–322.

Wooden, H. Z. (1966). An audiovisual approach to language instruction of children with severe hearing impairments. *Audiovisual Instruction,* 11, 710–712.

Wooden, H. Z., and Willard, L. L. (1965). Project LIFE Language Improvement to Facilitate Education of hearing-impaired children. *Amer. Ann. Deaf,* 110, 541–552.

Woodward, M. F. (1957). Linguistic methodology in lipreading research. Los Angeles School of Education, University of Southern California, John Tracy Clinic.

Woodward, M. F., and Barber, C. G. (1960). Phoneme perception in lipreading. *J. Speech Hearing Res.,* 3, 212–222.

Woodward, M. F., and Lowell, E. L. (1964). A linguistic approach to the education of aurally handicapped children. Los Angeles School of Education, University of Southern California, John Tracy Clinic.

Wright, H. N. (1967). Head position identification. *J. Speech Hearing Res.*, 10, 438–488.

Wright, W. N., and Carhart, R. (1960). The efficiency of binaural listening among the hearing impaired. *Arch. Otolaryng.*, 72, 789–797.

Yuker, H. E., Block, J. R., and Campbell, W. J. (1960). A scale to measure attitudes toward disabled persons. *Human Resources Study*, 5, 1–14.

Zaliouk, A. (1954). A visual tactile system of phonetical symbolization. *J. Speech Hearing Dis.*, 19, 190–207.

Zerlin, S. (1962). A new approach to hearing aid selection. *J. Speech Hearing Res.*, 5, 370–376.

8
Effects of Training and Counseling

A most logical inquiry to make after having provided the hearing-handicapped individual with rehabilitative sessions is the extent to which the sessions have changed his performance in communication and in related behavior. Supporting the general concept of effects of training and counseling, the constructs that are discussed in this chapter are visual training effects, auditory training effects, tactile training effects, multiple-sensory training effects, and adjustment of hearing-handicapped individuals. As in other instances discussed in preceding chapters, there is only a small amount of scientific data that provide answers to questions concerning each of the above constructs.

Visual Training Effects

Many variables have been found to influence lipreading performance and an extensive literature has developed in this area over the past decade. Application of these findings to lipreading training programs is the next step. Critical review of the literature dealing with rehabilitative procedures shows that very scanty information is available.

In a direct approach to lipreading training Oyer (1961) reported the results of a closed-circuit television program completed by a group of university students interested in aural rehabilitation. Ten weekly lessons included straight drill and such other materials as travelogues. Pretest lipreading scores for a list of 10 monosyllabic words ranged from 5 to 53 words correct with a mean of 28.7 correct. After training, scores ranged from 3 to 66 with a mean of 39.1 words, an average increase of over 10 words.

Black et al. (1963) devised a film training program but utilized a quite different procedure. Six male speakers were filmed as they read lists of words from the Multiple-Choice Intelligibility Test. Each subject practiced a list until he attained a perfect score. To evaluate the effectiveness of training, two new lists were administered as a post-test, one with the same speaker used in training and one with a different speaker. Subjects showed almost as much improvement with a different speaker as they did with the same speaker. This positive transfer was evidenced by the change in mean number of correct responses. Before training, subjects correctly identified 17.5 words, whereas after training they scored 34.0 with the same speaker, and 31.8 with a different speaker.

Both of the above studies suggest that films and television can be useful tools for improving lipreading performance. If the same results can be demonstrated with the hard-of-hearing population, this means of training would seem to be efficient. But questions of program content and related matters should also be considered.

Training that emphasized improving sequential memory was reported by Espeseth (1969). Since lipreading involves processing sequential visual cues, this experiment may be relevant here. Espeseth noted that several sources have found deaf subjects to be relatively poor in their memory span for visual stimuli compared with normal-hearing controls. For example, there is evidence presented by Furth (1961) that the discrepancy arises at age 11 to 12 when the normal hearing first show a noticeably greater visual memory span. Espeseth included in his experiment thirty-six deaf children from 6 to 12 years old who were enrolled in a residential school. Before training, the children were tested on a variety of criterion measures, the primary ones being Visual-Motor Sequencing, a subtest of the Illinois Test of Psycholinguistic Abilities; a Picture Span Test; and a digit span test. Training sessions were scheduled four days a week for a total of forty meetings. Exercises centered upon bead-stringing and flannel-board usage. A control group had meetings twice a week during the same period, but they worked on activities unrelated to memory span. The experimental group was found to show significant improvement on the Visual-Motor Sequencing and Picture Span tests. Although sequential memory has not been shown to relate to lipreading directly, one can speculate that common processes are involved. Whether or not such a congruity exists, an improved visual memory span is important in and of itself.

Auditory Training Effects

Compared to the numerous studies concerned with specific links in the auditory communication process there has been relatively little emphasis on complete training programs. The recent interest in infant programs has altered this balance.

A method of measuring the effects of auditory training based on delayed auditory feedback was proposed by DiCarlo (1958). He reasoned that if severely hard-of-hearing children were using auditory cues as a result of training, then their speech production would be disrupted by delayed auditory feedback in a manner similar to that found with normal-hearing people. To test this hypothesis, DiCarlo measured the speech production of twenty-three children with moderate to profound hearing impairment under conditions of no amplification, under amplification of both 30 dB and 50 dB over speech output intensity level, and finally with 50 dB amplification and delayed auditory feedback at 0.20 seconds. Some of the children had been exposed previously to auditory training and others had not. As he anticipated, those who had been in training were more affected by delayed auditory feedback than those without training. DiCarlo suggested that the amount of disruption could serve as a measure of the effect of auditory training. The more the child learned to depend upon speech sounds as auditory cues, the more disruption he would show.

There are a variety of reports that concern the effects of more generalized training programs for children. In a two-part experiment Lang et al. (1963) studied the effects of an auditory training program, first with preschool children and then with students at a school for hard-of-hearing children. The home training program for preschool children consisted of exposure to pure tones given at increasing intensity levels and varied rhythmic patterns. Training sessions were administered every three to four weeks over a period of twelve to eighteen months. Evaluation of the effects of training was accomplished by comparing pre- and post-training audiograms based on a peep-show technique. Data for eight individual preschool children showed improved threshold acuity of up to 40 dB. Because the training procedure was so successful with this group the investigators carried out a similar program with school-age children. In this case sound stimulation was presented two or three times a week over a period of approximately six months. Improved acuity was found in these cases, but the audiograms did not show as great an improvement as those of the younger children. There was also a very marked change in the active speech in favor of the children who underwent training. Determination of the reliability of the data was accomplished by having threshold findings confirmed by a hearing specialist, who tested the children at the beginning and end of the period using conventional pure tone audiometry.

It is difficult to determine how much real change there was in the thresholds of these children and how much was due to a greater tendency to respond to the pure tone stimulus when it was heard. In any case, the results are rather striking, especially for the younger children, and it may be important to encourage attention to weak stimuli even though acuity has not changed in any fundamental respect.

In recent years attention has turned more and more to the rehabilitation of infants and preschool children. Infant training programs described by the Lings and their colleagues illustrate this trend. Lach, Ling, Ling, and Ship (1970) studied the development of speech in seven deaf children, aged 11 to 32 months, throughout a parent guidance rehabilitation program. Guidance sessions for parents enabled them to carry out infant training at home. Periodic evaluations of the children at the end of three, six, nine, and twelve months yielded data on voice quality, vowel and consonant usage, and number of words produced. Changes occurred in each of the response categories. After twelve months, no child had markedly deviant voice quality, and five of the seven were judged to have normal voices. This contrasts to pretraining when two were very deviant and five were slightly so.

The effects of a parent counseling program on ten infants similar to those in the experiment above were evaluated by A. Ling (1971), who used the Griffiths Mental Development Scale to assess skills in several areas. Activities for the youngest children during the training program included listening, recognition of the source of environmental sounds, and vocal play. At older ages and more advanced ability levels, training material included books, toys and games, rhymes and story-telling. Prior to training, the children were within normal limits on two subtests of the Griffiths Scale, Locomotor and Hand-eye Coordination. Hearing and speech measures were well below all others; with 100 representing the score for average development, the following relations were found in the experimental sample before and after training.

Scale	Before	After
Hearing and Speech	32.3	54.0
Personal-social	82.2	91.1
Performance	87.9	103.8
Hand-eye	97.7	105.0
Locomotor	99.4	107.4

Despite significant improvement in the hearing and speech subtest, the children were still substantially delayed in this area of development.

Gengel (1969) attempted to reduce the size of the difference limen for frequency (DLF) of hearing-impaired children. He also investigated the relationship between hearing level and size of DLF after a period of practice in which children made discriminations of progressively smaller frequency differences. The subjects were twenty-three deaf children, twenty-one hard-of-hearing children, and a normal-hearing control group. Discrimination practice was based on a method of constant stimuli in which a standard frequency was paired with a comparison stimulus and the child judged them to be the same or different. Two standard tones, 250 Hz and 500 Hz, were each paired ten times with each comparison frequency. Over blocks of trials the largest differences between the standard and comparison tones were presented first and the smallest differences were presented last. A comparable procedure was carried out with a group of normal-hearing subjects who were tested once or twice. At the end of three practice sessions there was a marked decrease in the size of the difference limen for frequency for the deaf group. In fact, the DLF at the end of practice was reduced by approximately half. Among the hard-of-hearing children, only the 500 Hz standard comparison showed a decrease in the DLF. When the hard-of-hearing and deaf subjects were considered as a total sample, the children with greater losses had larger DLF's than children with relatively less impairment. The ability to discriminate differences of approximately 4 percent between frequencies indicated that it was possible with training for even the deaf to reach a rather small DLF. This is comparable to the difference required to detect changes in first and second formant frequencies in vowels and to discriminate changes in voice pitch at semitones.

Doehring and Ling (1971) have experimented with programmed training in vowel discrimination for hearing-impaired children. Eight children with severe to profound hearing losses participated in the training series, listening to vowels embedded in monosyllabic words. Although there was evidence that the number of trials required to reach a criterion of learning decreased over the four series of training trials, learning was not reflected in post-test scores when they were compared with pretest results.

Another approach to improving sound discrimination among deaf children was one that emphasized the recognition of various nonspeech sounds (Saleh, 1965). The program developed by Saleh made use of filmstrips centering on the home, farm, city, and so on, with accompanying sound recordings so that the child would be able to associate the visual and auditory stimuli. The analysis of results was subjective, based on the observations of teachers of the deaf. Children were judged to have increased almost 50 percent in the number of correct responses.

Nonspeech auditory stimuli were used by Doehring (1968) in a series of programmed training sessions in which a sample of Saleh's animal sounds and pictures were paired to develop discrimination ability in severely hearing-impaired children. Even the children with the greatest auditory impairment were able to learn the twelve sounds in this restricted set. Older children and those with less severe impairment tended to learn more rapidly.

On the basis of these research reports on programs for young deaf children, there seems no doubt that substantial improvement can occur with auditory training. What appears to be still needed is a coordinated program based on research findings that would allow a deter-

mination of the content and progression of skills that should be introduced to the child. Retention of skills that are developed through
training is also of vital importance. The latter need, particularly, requires longitudinal studies of children who have been exposed to
training very early in childhood and followed throughout their school
years.

Auditory training for the hard-of-hearing adult who has acquired his
handicap in later years should be one major focus of rehabilitation.
However, the research literature reveals that practically no attention
has been paid to older members of the hearing-impaired population.
One experiment by Bode and Oyer (1970) investigated the effects of
the type of response required of the subject, S/N ratio, and the type
of discrimination training material on speech discrimination performance. Thirty-two hard-of-hearing adults with mild sensorineural
hearing losses were divided into four training groups. One group wrote
out responses to the stimulus words and had a signal-to-noise ratio
that varied over the course of the training period. A second group had
multiple-choice material and the S/N ratio varied. The third group had
multiple-choice material with S/N ratio constant, and the last group
wrote out responses and had S/N held constant. During the three-hour
training session subjects were given reports concerning their performance and rest breaks were interspersed. Both before and after training,
three discrimination tests were administered: the W-22 CID Lists, the
Rhyme Test, and the Semi-Diagnostic Test. Percentage of improvement
found in the various discrimination tests was dependent to some extent
upon the particular method of response and the criterion test. For
example, open-set, written responding during training had the greatest
measureable effect on the W-22 test, an open-response test also. Overall, the most improvement was noted on the W-22 list, next on the
Rhyme test, and negligible improvement was seen with the Semi-
Diagnostic material. The percentage change on the three criterion tests
is shown below as a function of the types of training response.

Test	Open-Set (Written)	Closed-Set (Multiple-Choice)	Overall
W–22	9.0	6.4	7.7
Semi-Diagnostic	0.9	2.3	1.5
Rhyme	2.5	4.4	3.5

Closed-set, multiple-choice responding produced greater average
gains over the three criterion tests when the S/N ratio was varied

during the training. When the S/N was constant, written response training was superior, as can be seen in the following table.

Training Response	S/N Varied	S/N Constant
Multiple-Choice	6.5	2.1
Written	3.5	4.8

Hearing Aid Adjustment

Clinical observation suggests that early and continued use of amplification should be recommended as soon as it is determined that the child has a hearing deficit. Empirical evidence tends to support this position. For example, Sortini (1959) followed a preschool group for three years after they had been fitted with individual hearing aids. Questionnaires to parents and reports from teachers provided data to evaluate the effects of amplification. It was found that preschool children adapted more easily than older children to wearing hearing aids and they were reported to show noticeable improvement in many areas of behavior. At age 5 years they were reported to use vowels correctly although consonants were less well pronounced. Personality changes in the direction of better adjustment were given as the primary reason for parental acceptance of hearing aids for their children. Lower incidence of temper tantrums and crying and less fearful response to strangers were mentioned as examples of behavioral change. Only three out of sixty children were not wearing their hearing aids at the end of the third year, and fifty-two wore theirs all the time. Children in the older group adjusted less well. After two years, twelve never wore their hearing aids and only four were full-time users.

Binaural hearing aids were credited with similar effects in a study by Bender and Wiig (1960). Again the results were derived from parents' responses to questionnaires and from telephone interviews. Thirty-three children between the ages of 13 months and 12 years were studied. Progress occurred in the areas of social relationships, vocalization and speech, sound localization, and preference for the binaural hearing aid. Promotion to a higher grade was found in eight cases.

The relative effectiveness of binaural and monaural hearing aids was compared in an experiment by Lewis and Green (1962), who tested the gains in language development and school achievement made by two groups of children aged 5 to 13 years after a year of amplification. Results of a battery of ten language and achievement tests showed no consistent advantage for either the binaural or the monaural group.

Each scored slightly higher on five tests, but only one difference was significant statistically. Children generally preferred the aid with which they had been fitted.

Low-frequency amplification has been found to facilitate speech reception and production in some instances. D. Ling (1964) proposed that hearing aids capable of responding to frequencies well below the usual 300 Hz minimum would benefit children with even small amounts of residual hearing. Preliminary experimental results indicated that children improved in their responses to phonemes with low-frequency formants, and to their own and others' voices. Fundamental pitch, recognition of stress patterns, recognition and reproduction of rhythmic patterns, and amount of spontaneous vocalization and speech were other areas that showed improvement after amplification was introduced. Younger children showed earlier and more noticeable improvement than the older children. More detailed results of low-frequency amplification, down to 100 Hz, have been described by Briskey and Sinclair (1966) and Briskey et al. (1967). Sonograms of speech samples were analyzed at sixty days and succeeding thirty-day intervals up to six months after they were fitted with experimental low-frequency aids. Positive changes were found in at least one variable for eleven of seventeen experimental children. Fundamental pitch was lowered; voices were less breathy when individual words were pronounced; and patterns of resonance became more defined. These experiments emphasize the need for early amplification so that children will adjust to their hearing aids and have the benefit of auditory stimulation during the years when they are developing speech and language skills. Despite the recognized benefits of amplification there has been concern about its effects on residual hearing.

In 1961 Kinney examined records that gave threshold data on children who were hearing aid users. A control group consisted of 146 children who had hearing aids that were considered less powerful than aids used by the experimental group. Experimental subjects included 39 monaurally fitted children and 13 who were binaurally fitted. In the speech range, control subjects showed approximately a 10 percent incidence of further loss amounting to 10 dB to 20 dB. Among monaural users in the experimental group almost half, 48.8 percent, had losses of 20 dB, and 68.2 percent of the binaurally fitted children had averaged losses of 25 dB in both ears. Kinney recommended lower maximum gain and caution in application of binaural amplification.

Barr and Wedenberg (1965) concluded that the progressivity observed in some of the eighty-five children in their study was probably not due to use of a hearing aid. Subjects with endogenous hearing loss and those with exogenous impairment due to meningitis showed deterioration of residual hearing over a fifteen-year period, but exogenous impairment due to rubella or perinatal accidents did not show change in hearing level over an observation period of up to eleven years. Endogenous cases showed erratic deterioration.

An experiment more carefully controlled than those previously mentioned did find damage attributable to hearing aid usage. Ross and Lerman (1967) considered eighteen subjects who had reliable audiograms determined at the time when they were fitted with a hearing aid. Subjects had bilateral hearing losses, were fitted monaurally, and had worn their hearing aids from seven to ten years. Threshold shift in the unaided ear served as an estimate of the effect on residual hearing. If on the average the aided ear shifted more than the unaided ear, this could imply that amplification reduced residual hearing. A relatively greater shift was found in the aided ear at 250, 500, 1000, and 2000 Hz. Nine of the eighteen subjects were responsible for this significant effect; the other nine showed little or no difference between the aided and unaided ear. Relative shift in the aided ear was more strongly correlated with average hearing loss when the aid was fitted and with hours usage per week than it was with maximum power output or duration of use. Similar results were reported by Macrae and Farrant (1965) in a study of two hearing aids, one with average gain of 60 dB and the other, less powerful, with average gain of 48 dB. They found that children who had relatively better hearing at the time of fitting showed a greater shift in their residual hearing. The more powerful aid yielded a positive correlation between amount of shift and hours of use. Macrae, in a later study (1968), studied temporary threshold shift (TTS) and recovery from TTS in four children who used powerful hearing aids. Substantial amounts of TTS were found and recovery was slower than that usually shown by normal-hearing subjects in three of Macrae's subjects. These data suggest that after a child has been fitted with a hearing aid, subsequent checks should be made to determine the effects of amplification on his residual hearing.

Hearing aids are now advocated for a wide range of hearing difficulties. Adjustment to amplification and the benefits derived from amplification have been related to a number of different subject classifications. Siegenthaler and Gunn (1952) used the percent improvement in SRT from unaided to aided test conditions as a measure of the benefit due to amplification. Comparisons were made among subjects with sensorineural losses, conductive losses, and several types of mixed losses. Ranked according to amount of improvement, conductive loss subjects benefited most, mixed cases were intermediate, and sensorineural subjects showed noticeable gains but less than the other groups. Conductive cases showed consistent improvement for all individual users, while members of the sensorineural group were less predictable. Yantis et al. (1966) determined in their experiment that intensity of the speech stimulus is an important variable in the speech discrimination by subjects with sensorineural hearing loss. Discrimination was best at the lower end of the linear range. In a second experiment they found that experienced hearing aid users tended to adjust their gain at levels near the optimum value where PB MAX was obtained. Aided articulation functions showed considerable variability among subjects. This may be a partial explanation of the varied benefits found by Siegenthaler and Gunn (1952).

Bentzen, Griesen, and Jordan (1965) at the Danish State Hearing Center have investigated the effects of age, degree of loss, symmetry of loss, and audiometric configuration on acceptance of binaural amplification. They considered 301 subjects in the age range 15 to 80 years. Those who agreed to try a binaural hearing aid (almost all subjects) were given up to four weeks of instruction at home and in groups. Two months later a follow-up found that 42 percent used their binaural aids full time and 18 percent used only one aid full time or part time. The remainder used the binaural aid some of the time. None of the variables above, such as age or symmetry of loss, was related to acceptance of the binaural hearing aid. In 1967 Jordan et al. conducted a more extensive follow-up of 1147 adults, 63 percent over age 60, all of whom had been fitted with binaural hearing aids. Full-time use was claimed by 31 percent of the sample. Those under 60 years of age tended to have a somewhat higher representation in this group, 36 percent, compared to 27 percent for the over-60 subjects. Type of impairment, symmetry of loss, and audiometric pattern were not related to hearing aid use. A steeply sloping audiogram tended to be associated with part-time use of the binaural aid, and previously inexperienced hearing aid users wore their aids less than those who had already used a monaural aid. Over the total group of binaural and monaural users there were no trends that would allow one to predict adjustment to amplification. A group of 250 subjects over 65 years old were studied by Bentzen et al. (n.d.) to estimate the usefulness of binaural hearing aids for treating presbycusis. All of the subjects were new patients with bilateral loss for whom binaural hearing aids were prescribed. The results of a questionnaire, sent at least three months after fitting, showed that 55.2 percent of the subjects wore the binaural ear-level aid at least part time. Among the remaining subjects, 17.6 percent wore a monaural aid; the others only wore hearing aids occasionally or for short-time intervals.

Campanelli (1968) also studied a group of twenty-seven people over age 50 who were recommended for hearing aid fitting. Seventeen were not wearing an aid at the time of the evaluation. Of this group, two did not follow the recommendation to buy an aid. Those who did buy a hearing aid were divided as to their attitudes; nine reported positively with "good," and six thought their aid only "fair" after a month's use. Most subjects who already were wearing an aid had more positive responses a month later; only one of seven continued to report that the aid was "poor." Campanelli speculated that many of the older subjects came at the instigation of a relative and that they were fatalistic about life generally and hearing aids in particular. After successful adjustment they showed much more positive attitudes.

Children comprise another specific sample that has been investigated. Parents who had participated in the John Tracy Clinic program were contacted for information regarding their children's adjustment to amplification in an experiment carried out by Rushford and Lowell (1960). Information about the child's reaction to his hearing aid and areas of satisfaction and dissatisfaction were tabulated from questionnaire responses made by more than 1500 parents. Three quarters of the children had hearing aids. Satisfaction with their first hearing aid was reported by 43.9 percent of the sample. Children under 2.5 years old and those from 8.5 to 9.4 years accepted hearing aids more readily than other ages. Reasons for rejecting hearing aids included discomfort and lack of value to the child. The greatest satisfaction was expressed by those who purchased the hearing aid early and for those sustaining losses less than 90 dB. The least likely hearing aid user, in the ages studied, was the child with severe loss.

Gaeth and Lounsbury (1966) found some disturbing results in a longitudinal study of children and their hearing aids as they studied a sample of 120 school-age children from 3 to 18 years old through parent interviews, tests with and without the hearing aid, and measurement of acoustic characteristics of the aids. Parents' responses indicated ignorance of battery life expectancy, earmold fit, and feedback problems. Half of the parents were uncertain that the hearing aid helped their children. With liberal criteria of adequate function, only 55 percent of the aids were satisfactory when the child wore it to the clinic for testing, although approximately one third of the parents thought their children were making adequate or good progress in school.

It has been suggested that subjective attitudes of the potential user are possible criteria for hearing aid selection. Several studies have concentrated on the attitudes of hearing aid users after they have had time to adjust to amplification. Kodman (1961, 1969) specifically mentioned the neglect of the client's subjective feelings as a reason for unsuccessful adjustment. He found that the unsuccessful user has many complaints, and that initial experience with amplification is often critical. Successful binaural hearing aid users were reported to be satisfied in 42 percent of the cases compared to 30 percent in an earlier study of successful monaural users. It appears that even though some people wear their aids most of the time they are not completely satisfied. Dirks and Carhart (1962) found that a large sample of monaural and binaural hearing aid users had a similar pattern of response. Satisfied binaural hearing aid users represented 54 percent of all binaural users, and 34.5 percent were dissatisfied. For monaural users, the figures were 43.6 percent satisfied and 42.4 percent dissatisfied.

A rather novel approach to the study of hearing aid characteristics was described by Berger et al. (1968). Rankings of important features of hearing aids were obtained from audiologists, hearing aid users, and from ads found in the yellow pages of telephone directories. Both audiologists and hearing aid users rated performance as the number one concern, but the advertisements emphasized looks. It is gratifying that the hearing aid user and the audiologist agree on priorities even though the method of selection may not satisfy both equally well.

Tactile Training Effects

Even though the tactile transmission of information is not a standard part of rehabilitative programs, there have been demonstrations of successful reception of verbal material through this channel. Nelson (1959) studied the ability of subjects to discriminate among vowel sounds when they were presented cutaneously through electrodes on the dorsal area of the left arm, midway between elbow and wrist. The vowel sounds were embedded in words which were then presented in pairs for comparison. Vowel discrimination was more accurate with a two-electrode unit that divided the frequency range into the bands 100–800 Hz and 800–4000 Hz than it was with a single-electrode unit covering the whole range. Guelke and Huyssen (1959) found that five vowels were recognized accurately 80 to 90 percent of the time after training on their apparatus. Frequencies were transposed downward to the range 100–400 Hz and then transmitted by vibrating reeds placed against the subject's fingers. Poor consonant discrimination was attributed to low speech power, wide frequency distribution, short duration, lack of high frequency cues through the skin, and the idea that consonants are recognized by their effect on vowels.

Direct reception of words and phonemes through a tactual communcation system was found to be quite accurate after a short training period with a Goldman "Shake Table" vibrator, a single vibrator that stimulates the three middle fingers and thumb (Myers, 1960). One of the sophisticated subjects participating in the experiment reached a 95 percent level of correct response to 26 stimuli consisting of 16 words and the numbers 0 through 9. In the second phase of this research, phoneme recognition rose to an average of 91 percent accuracy after eight test and training sessions. When ten-frequency coded vibrators were used by Pickett and Pickett (1963), training on vowel and consonant recognition did not lead to such accurate responding. Two sets of vowels differing on the basis of similarity of formant structure within the set showed markedly different results in terms of correct identification. When there were maximal differences in formant structure among the vowels within a set, two trained subjects were able to reach 60 percent correct identification; but they achieved only 42 percent correct for a set of short vowels with similar formant structure. In other research Pickett (1963) found the ten-channel vocoder useful after limited training for discrimination of durational patterns of vowels, number of syllables in a word, and certain consonants that are confused visually such as /m/ and /b/. Tactual information improved receptive communication without interfering with lipreading, having a particularly positive influence on identification of consonants and syllabic structure.

Perhaps the experiment that comes closest to simulating realistic verbal communication was one reported by Kringlebotn (1968) of Norway. Kringlebotn used a five-frequency vocoder, distributed spatially on the fingers, where each vibrator represented a frequency range in the speech signal. Deaf subjects were trained for multiple-choice identification with up to four alternatives. Stimuli included vowel pairs, word pairs both with and without lipreading, proper names, and nonsense words. Identification scores approached 100 percent for almost all tests. Discrimination of visually homophenous words was found to be aided by vibrotactile cues; combined visual and tactile cues allowed almost perfect identification of difficult meaningless words. Improved articulation also was noted in two deaf subjects after tactile patterns produced by their speech were compared to patterns of their teacher. Kringlebotn suggested that vibrotactile training could serve as a supplement to lipreading and also aid in lipreading and articulation training.

We see that even when experiments have used a closed-response set during training, subjects have had some difficulty correctly identifying consonants and vowels embedded in words. Probably the role of tactile stimuli will be supplementary to visual and auditory cues rather than a substitute for other sensory channels.

Multiple-Sensory Training Effects

Manual Training

The benefits that can arise from combining manual and oral methods of communication have been noted by a number of investigators

(Morkovin, 1960; Hester, 1964; Montgomery, 1966; Stuckless and Birch, 1966; Vernon and Koh, 1970). Evidence for the positive influence of finger spelling and signs usually has been inferred by comparing subjects with manual skills to those without such early experience. Investigators have found facilitating effects on vocabulary, reading, written language, general achievement, and lipreading.

Quigley (n.d.) has provided one of the most extensive studies of the effects of finger spelling on language development, communication, and educational achievement. In the first part of his monograph he described a survey of children (13 years old for the most part) in three experimental schools that used the Rochester Method, *including finger spelling,* and children from three comparison schools that used the Combined Method, some combination of oral and manual methods. The primary difference was the formal use of finger spelling in some schools but not in the others. An initial test battery was administered and repeated annually for the succeeding four years to all subjects. Tests covered finger spelling ability, speechreading, speech intelligibility, general achievement, and written language. By the end of the second year the experimental subjects showed significantly higher scores on most measures involving meaningful language and this advantage continued for the rest of the test period. Speechreading and speech intelligibility were not found to differ in the two comparison groups. A separate analysis of the younger members of the experimental group who averaged about 10 years of age suggested that the earlier finger spelling was introduced the greater the educational benefit. Sample comparisons of test scores in the last test period for all subjects are shown below (Quigley, p. 34).

	Rochester Method		Combined Method		Level of Significance
	Mean	S.D.	Mean	S.D.	Significance
Finger Spelling	84.16	16.04	71.36	20.12	.001
Speech Intelligibility	25.48	19.04	22.21	18.31	——
Stanford Achievement					
Combined Reading	4.91	1.84	4.28	1.42	.02
Combined Arithmetic	6.44	2.12	5.64	1.99	.02
Written Language					
Grammatical Correctness					
Ratio	88.83	8.38	82.75	8.96	.05
Sentence Length	9.74	4.26	9.03	3.98	——
"Cloze" Procedures					
Verbatim	25.92	12.95	23.83	12.79	——
Form Class	66.83	14.99	60.96	14.66	.02

A second part of the monograph detailed the experimental program administered to a group of thirty-two deaf children, half of whom were exposed to the Rochester Method during school hours and in all extraclass activities, and the other half who were in a program at a second school using the Oral Method. The four year preschool program allowed complete control of the communicative environment and thus provided a relatively uncontaminated comparison of the effects of the two methods. The age of the children at the start of the experiment was approximately 3.5 to 4.5 years. Teachers were trained in oral and finger spelling methods for the experimental group and only in the Oral Method for the control group. Children exposed to the Rochester Method were in contact with parents and school personnel, all of whom had been trained in finger spelling. After the children had been four years in the contrasting programs, a test battery was administered to them. Many of the subtests were the same as those administered in the survey of older children. Some of these data are presented below (Quigley, p. 88).

	Rochester Method		Oral Method		Level of Significance
	Mean	S.D.	Mean	S.D.	Significance
Finger Spelling	33.71	21.60	2.34	3.74	.001
Reading					
Stanford Combined	2.27	.49	2.04	.57	.05
Metro Reading	1.96	.54	1.70	.62	.01
Gates Vocabulary	2.21	.81	1.68	.64	.02
Gates Comprehension	2.00	.61	1.74	.59	———
Written Language					
Sentence Length	5.79	1.60	4.49	7.61	.01
Grammatical Correctness					
Ratio	75.53	19.70	89.33	21.82	.05

Ten of the fifteen measures employed showed a significant difference in favor of the experimental group trained under the Rochester Method. Only one measure favored the control group. Analysis of the Grammatical Correctness Ratio in terms of total words written and sentence length suggested that control subjects obtained a higher score because they attempted less complex sentences. Not listed were two measures of lipreading, the Craig Word score and the Craig Sentence score. Subjects in the finger-spelling group were significantly better on the sentence material. On word material they had slightly better scores, but the difference was not significant statistically. Quigley commented on the lack in oral skills that was observed among the subjects. He attributed this partially to differences in quality of instruction. Despite these inconsistencies, the conclusion that finger spelling facilitates development of meaningful language skills and does not detract from lipreading performance seems justified for the types of population that were sampled in this experimental project.

Auditory-Visual Training

Rational arguments can be made both for and against the merits of combined auditory and visual training over single-channel training. An experiment by Hutton (1960) did not find conclusive support for training in phoneme reception with combined sensory channels. Reasoning that auditorily confused phonemes are sometimes visually distinctive, as in the case of /p/ and /t/, and that visually confused phonemes such as /p/ and /m/ are auditorily distinct, Hutton proposed to combine auditory and visual stimuli to improve phoneme intelligibility. Over a two-year period eighteen subjects each underwent sixteen hours of combined sensory training in phoneme recognition. The Semi-Diagnostic Test was administered initially to obtain a base level of performance and to determine error phonemes for the subjects. During training, instructions to notice both the auditory and visual contributions were explicit. The phonemes on which each subject made errors were presented both in isolation and in short words. Drill work progressed from easily contrasted training material to the more difficult levels of connected discourse under poor communicative conditions. Post-training scores on the Semi-Diagnostic Test provided measures of the shift in auditory discrimination, visual discrimination, and the combined sensory discrimination. Hutton found that gains after combined training were observed on the portion of the test measuring combined sensory discrimination. However, for two thirds of the subjects, gains were equally great for one of the single modality subtests. Those with greatest shift in auditory discrimination had negligible improvement in visual discrimination. Similarly the high group in visual discrimination showed only small improvement auditorily. When the single modality dominated, the combined condition was equivalent to the preferred single condition.

Tactile and Visual Training

Research has pointed to the benefits of tactile vibratory stimulation as a supplement to lipreading. An illustration of the supplementary function of vibratory cues was reported by Johnson (1963). Sixteen subjects with primarily sensorineural loss were tested before and after training with a list of 25 monosyllabic words and 25 spondee words. During the training period of ten sessions subjects were able to read lists that included the 50 test words mixed with 100 irrelevant words, half monosyllables and half spondees. Most of the ten sessions called for the subject to read the word as vibratory stimulation was presented through four small speakers resting on the forearm. On two of the training occasions, however, pairs of words were presented for discrimination purposes and subjects responded "same" or "different." Scores before and after training indicated that subjects benefited from exposure to tactile cues. The data, mean percent correct responses, are displayed below.

	Pretest		Post-Test	
	Lipreading	Lipreading + Taction	Lipreading	Lipreading + Taction
Monosyllables	24	25	29	36
Spondees	47	51	56	65
Overall	35	38	42	51

Spondees showed greater intelligibility both before and after training. Lipreading alone improved by 7 percent from pretesting to posttesting and the combined scores advanced 13 percent after training, showing an increment of 9 percent over the post-training score for lipreading alone.

Reference has been made earlier to the facilitating effects of tactual information on lipreading in experimental studies by Pickett (1963) and Klinglebotn (1968). To our knowledge, however, no tactile device has progressed beyond the demonstration stage.

Speech and Language Training

Few experimental training programs for the improvement of speech in deaf children have provided quantitative evaluations or data assessing long-term effects of training. The work of Holbrook and Crawford (1970) stands out as an example of follow-up testing of subjects several months after training was terminated. In their research four adult deaf subjects underwent training to modify vocal frequency. An automatic voice controlling system signaled subjects when their production was within the appropriate range of frequencies. While they were on target a white light remained on; if they deviated from the target range a red light came on. Vocal frequency was successfully modified over a seven-month training period. A post-test three months after training indicated that two subjects maintained their conditioned frequency level and two had shifted partially toward the preconditioned frequency.

Training in language comprehension usually has been administered through programmed instruction. Falconer (1960, 1961, 1962) successfully trained deaf children to recognize fifteen previously unknown nouns. A retention test two weeks after training found no decrement. McGrady (1964) employed programmed instruction to teach four concepts, the generic terms *birds, fish, insects,* and *animals.* Error rates of deaf children were reduced to a level of 3 to 4 percent following training, performance comparable to a normal-hearing control group. No retention measures were reported, however.

A very extensive training program designed to provide deaf children with functional receptive language was developed by Project LIFE (Pfau, 1969, 1970). Spidal and Pfau (1972) have extended the application of Project LIFE instruction to deaf adolescents and adults. Fourteen subjects, ages 16 to 53, had extremely limited communicative skills before training; twelve subjects could not communicate in any symbolic way even with their own families, and reading skill was at the level of recognizing a limited number of nouns. During a six-month training period subjects interacted with programmed language training filmstrips and met with training personnel in small groups for a total of eighteen hours each week. Results were reported by summarizing each subject's gains in language and communicative skills. All subjects progressed beyond the noun recognition stage to the point where they could read and comprehend simple sentences; several reached at least the second-grade reading level. They also could produce sentences orally, in written form, or by signs. When retesting was carried out for material learned earlier in training, no subject failed a previously learned language unit. Their ability and willingness to communicate with others, many for the first time, improved dramatically.

Turning to language production we find several experiments on written language training. Birch and Stuckless (1963) analyzed compositions written by deaf adolescents and then administered programmed instruction that focused on specific errors made by individual subjects. One experimental group completed each written training program only once, while a second group had repeated presentations of each program until errors of that type no longer occurred in their written compositions. A grammar test with a possible score of 70 points was devised by the researchers and served as the main criterion for evaluating training. When the test was administered before training began, a significant difference in performance was found. Scores of experimental group who were to receive repeated presentations of programs were lower than those of other experimental group and a control group. Training was completed in five weeks for subjects with single presentation of programs, and in six months for subjects with repeated presentations. After the grammar test was readministered, the following changes in scores were found: control group improved from 46 to 49 points; the single presentation group from 47.6 to 50.7; the repeated presentation group from 41.3 to 46.0. Differences among the groups were no longer significant. Birch and Stuckless concluded that repeated presentation of programs led to improved grammatical performance but that one presentation of a program did not. Observing the absolute increase in scores, however, the differences among groups is not very large, 4.7 points for the repeated presentation group and 3.0 for the other two groups.

A technique for modifying written sentences of deaf fourth-grade students was described by Eachus (1971). Each of his ten subjects had an overhead projector that displayed his sentences as the child composed them, thus allowing the experimenter to give immediate correction of inappropriate responses. Transparencies depicting objects, people, and places provided stimuli to elicit sentence responses. Over the forty-one experimental sessions Eachus recorded rate and accuracy of response during six successive phases of the study: (1) baseline data, (2) reinforcement by cumulative points awarded for correct responses, (3)reinforcement plus correction of errors by the experimenter written directly on the children's transparencies, (4) neither reinforcement nor correction (extinction), (5) reinstatement of reinforcement and correction, and (6) correction and reinforcement contingent upon production of compound or complex sentences. Both rate and accuracy of response were influenced by the experimental treatments. Compared to the baseline phase where response rate stabilized at approximately 28 sentences per session, the average number of responses in phases two through five ranged from 38 to 48 sentences per session. During phase five, when reinforcement and correction were reinstated, response rate reached the highest level for any session, averaging 57 sentences per child. Phase six required subjects to produce compound and complex sentences, a task that was difficult and time consuming. Rate of responding fell below 20 sentences but then increased gradually over the succeeding four sessions. Accuracy of response was discussed separately for each child. All of the children had substantial increases in percentage of correct sentences during phases two and three relative to their baseline performance. Most subjects achieved an average 90 percent accuracy in these phases although there was variability from session to session. When reinforcement and correction were withdrawn in phase four, accuracy decreased for almost all subjects and in several cases precipitously. This contrasts with the effect on rate of response, which did not change markedly under extinction conditions. In phase five, with treatments reinstated, no subject fell below 92 percent accuracy in any session. Accuracy was again depressed for most subjects in phase six, when reinforcement was contingent upon compound and complex sentence production, but level of correct responding remained well above baseline levels.

If this research had included follow-up testing at some time period after training terminated it would be extremely valuable. Since accuracy of response was affected by cessation of reinforcement and by correction during the experiment, one wonders whether sentence production would be maintained at a high accuracy level. On the other hand, Eachus did remark that while training was in effect samples of classroom work by these children improved in accuracy, indicating positive transfer. Perhaps continued correction and reinforcement by their teachers would be enough to maintain the behavior.

Adjustment of Hearing-Handicapped Individuals

Family Adjustment

Statistics on the marriage pattern of the deaf population have been reported by several authors. Rather different pictures arise depending upon the experimental sample. Vernon (1969) reviewed the literature and found the incidence of marriages among the deaf to be slightly lower than for the hearing population, perhaps because of the higher ratio of men to women. Of those who did marry, 95 percent married other deaf adults; and the marriages appeared to be stable.

Somewhat different patterns were associated with a select group of graduates of a junior high school who lived at home in a large city (Justman and Moskowitz, 1965). In this group 61 percent of the women and 48 percent of the men had married. The mates were deaf in approximately 75 percent of the cases, but 25 percent of the mates had normal hearing.

Northern et al. (1971) noted that 71 percent of their sample had deaf mates, 14 percent married normal-hearing spouses, and 17 percent were single. Survey respondents in this report were members of a Temporal Bone Bank conference in Colorado.

There are marked differences in marriage incidence cited in these studies, perhaps related to the age of the samples when data were collected. The Justman and Moskowitz sample also had a higher percentage of marriages with normal-hearing mates than the other groups.

Only a limited amount of research has focused on the effects of hearing impairment on members of a family unit. Two studies illustrate intrafamily relationships.

Mothers' attitudes toward early independence for children were related to their children's social maturity in a study reported by Gordon (1959). If the mothers favored early independence for normal-hearing children, then their own deaf children showed discrepancies in their intellectual and social maturity. Their social development was below their intellectual ability. It was found also that when mothers had high achievement needs, they tended to approve of later independence in deaf children.

An analysis of the role of hard-of-hearing homemakers as family members was carried out by Oyer and Paolucci (1970). Thirty families with hard-of-hearing homemakers were compared with the same number of control families with normal-hearing homemakers. Measures were obtained of the couples' agreement on family goals, marital tension, dissatisfaction of the homemaker and her role, family members' participation in family tasks and their decision-making power, and parental acceptance of certain behavior in children. Although agreement between husbands and wives on family goals was similar in both groups, mothers' priority rankings of goals differed. Hard-of-hearing women placed more emphasis on the family feeling that home is a place where family members belong. Normal-hearing homemakers emphasized the home as a place to entertain friends. Amount of marital tension did not differentiate the two family groups; but within the experimental families, tension reported by husbands where wives had more severe hearing losses was greater than that reported by husbands of the normal-hearing women. In the hard-of-hearing group family members helped more with family tasks and the mother tended to have more decision-making power.

Other Social Adjustment

Some of the questions that might arise in connection with the social aspects of everyday living have been addressed by a number of investigators. Distinctions should be made between deaf and hard-of-hearing persons and between the person with a mild hearing impairment and a more substantial impairment. Extent of deficit has been a significant variable in the literature.

Horowitz and Rees (1962) studied the effect of age on the attitudes of normal-hearing people toward deaf people. Generally the responses implied a patronizing attitude, noting how deaf people could benefit from contact with a hearing person. There was some recognition of speech difficulties, but also the attitude was that with proper supplementary aids, the deaf person could learn to develop normal speech. The ability of hearing aids to provide adequate compensation and produce normal hearing tended to be exaggerated. There was least consistency in responses concerning the capabilities of deaf people. Children in grades one through six, and particularly the younger ones, were most apt to state that deaf children would have trouble developing speech because they cannot hear their own voices or those of others. Specific knowledge of difficulties and drawbacks associated with hearing aids was most detailed for the adults. College students knew the most about the hearing process and operation of a hearing aid. The investigators were surprised by the well-informed nature of the youngest children with regard to the abilities of deaf children and adults.

The social position of hearing-impaired children integrated in a regular school was investigated by Elser (1959) by means of status scores, friendship scores, reputation scores, and ability to determine who would in fact choose them as friends. On the average, children with hearing losses were not as well accepted as normal-hearing children: they tended to have fewer friends, and their reputation was less positive compared to average scores for the normal-hearing group.

It appears that there may be some critical amount of hearing impairment that must be evidenced before there is any social disruption. Reynolds (1955) tested the personal and social adjustment of children in a junior high school with minimal hearing losses. The California Test of Personality and teachers' ratings of pupil behavior and personality served as comparison measures. There was no evidence of social inferiority on the part of the children who displayed minimal impairment.

A pilot study in England (Rodda, 1966) compared the social adjustment of deaf students in different educational settings. Data showed that when there was high stress, such as occurred in an integrated grammar school, there was more maladjustment. Adolescents in special schools for the deaf had little opportunity for social stress resulting from the necessity of fitting into a normal-hearing situation, and students in the secondary education schools had less pressure to achieve, which might have had favorable impacts on their social position.

The results of several surveys and questionnaires have provided statistical information on the social activities of deaf adults. Vernon (1969) noted the existence of clubs restricted to oral deaf people as an illustration of the inability of many orally trained deaf individuals to communicate with the normal-hearing population. Justman and Moskowitz (1965) derived information from questionnaires sent to graduates of a junior high school who had been out for at least seven years. The older respondents had more deaf friends than hearing friends, and only the younger males who graduated between 1950 and 1958 had more hearing friends. The most frequent leisure-time activities tended to be those not requiring active communication: television, movies, reading, travel, and sports.

Educational Adjustment

Deaf children have been found seriously below the grade level of achievement appropriate for their age. Deaf subjects who were 16 years and older rarely reached the tenth-grade level according to Vernon (1969). A majority, 60 percent, were at or below the 5.3 grade level, and a rather large subgroup, 30 percent, were functionally illiterate. The sample from which these figures were derived consisted of 93 percent of all deaf students age 16 and over. Reading level was summarized for children in school programs for the deaf in the age range 10 to 16 years. In this group at least 80 percent of the 16-year-olds were reading at a grade level below 4.9, and the gain in reading skill of those from 10 years old to those 16 years old was less than one year.

Auxter (1971) administered a battery of physical and sensory tests to youngsters with severe hearing losses in order to identify abilities that discriminated between underachievers and normal achievers in school. Significant differences in performance were found in measures of motor speed, fitness, and tactile and visual reaction times. Auxter suggested remedial programs in motor planning and response speed.

The possibility that early treatment and exposure to training can prevent or ameliorate retardation in educational achievement has attracted several investigators. Their findings have been mixed. Preschool training at two public residential schools was reported to have no permanent effects on later educational development in a study by Craig (1964). Elliott and Vegely (1968) compared the effects of delay in treatment on students at a state school for the deaf with earlier results for private school students. The prior data had supported the idea that more prolonged sensory deprivation resulting from lack of early treatment was associated with poorer school achievement. Stanford Achievement Test scores failed to support this finding in the state school. There was no relationship between test scores and hearing level, age when aid was first worn, or age of enrollment in school. The heterogeneous and transient nature of the student population was presented as a possible reason to doubt that the hypothesis was tested adequately. A summary of six investigations comparing the later achievement of children exposed to manual communication in their early years with those who had none led Vernon (1969) to conclude that the effects of early manual training are positive and lasting. Many of these studies compared deaf children of deaf parents with deaf children of hearing parents. Even though the deaf parents were less well prepared academically, their children were found, in a number of studies, to be more advanced than children of hearing parents in areas such as speechreading, reading written language, overall educational achievement, and percentage of children going to college.

Viewed collectively these results illustrate that some type of early training can benefit the deaf child. The details of an optimum program, however, cannot be determined from the available data.

Two experiments with deaf children have described details of the kinds of activities that occur in the classroom, focusing in particular on teacher-student communication and on visual attending behavior of students. Craig and Collins (1970) trained a number of teachers of the deaf to use a scale for coding communicative interactions according to the purposes of the communication and mode of communication. Later these teachers observed classroom behavior at three schools by sampling ongoing activity during a series of three-second observation intervals. Categories of communication were defined by their purpose; for example, Questioning, Informing, Feedback, and Acceptance of students' behavior were several of the ten categories of teacher response. There were corresponding categories for student initiated remarks. Modes of communication included Finger spelling, Oral, Manual, and Combined among the eleven possible modes. When applied to the classroom, this instrument was found to be reliable for categorizing type and mode of communication. At all three schools teacher initiated remarks accounted for the great majority of student-teacher interactions. Mode of communication, based on data for two schools, was primarily oral at the elementary and intermediate levels. At the high school level a combined mode predominated in the residential school, while the public school program continued in the oral mode.

An experiment by Craig (1970) on visual attending behavior employed a token reinforcement procedure to improve time spent attending to the relevant instructional stimulus in the classroom situation. Baseline attending behavior averaged only 20 to 30 percent. After a tangible candy reinforcement program was initiated, attending rose to between 80 and 90 percent, and this was maintained when a shift to token reinforcement was instituted. Compared to the base level of 45 percent attending in a later phase of the research, social reinforcement led to 67 percent attending, and added tangible reinforcement again produced over 90 percent.

In these experiments some conditions that exist in the regular classroom have been described. Disturbing instances occur in both cases. Communication within the classroom needs to be more equitably balanced between teacher and student and, further, communication should include more acceptance and praise of student performance as well as feedback concerning adequacy of performance. With regard to attention, this has been manipulated successfully as an operant response, a demonstration that can be applied in classrooms generally.

A continuing concern of people who place deaf children educationally is that of integration into a normal-hearing school setting. Some important factors that determined unsuccessful adjustment were brought to light in a study by O'Connor and O'Connor (1961) who interviewed twenty-one deaf students, their parents, school teachers, and the principal. The subjects had been students at the Lexington School for the Deaf before transferring to normal-hearing schools. Half of the students were unsuccessful in the transition. Determining factors were lack of parental support, lack of intelligence, low reading level, and poor teacher and administrative attitudes.

A child described in a case study by Kowalsky (1962) fit well socially and academically into a regular first-grade class. In a more extensive report, Bruce (1960) described the results of personal interviews with fifty-three alumni of Clarke School. At the time of their last assessment before graduation, 70 percent obtained grade-level scores of 8.0 or greater on the Stanford Achievement Test. A quarter of the students had grade levels between 6.0 and 7.9. Half of the alumni went on to an academic high school, for the most part public schools, and of these 85 percent graduated. Of the fifty-three alumni, 87 percent felt that the disadvantages of going to a high school for the deaf were greater than the advantages. The remaining students went to vocational schools (26 percent) or directly sought employment.

Motto and Wawrzaszek (1963) reviewed research related to integration of the hearing handicapped into regular classrooms. Although they found insufficient data on the effects of integration on educational achievement, there was some evidence that gradual transition into the integrated classroom is indicated rather than an abrupt entrance.

Vocational Adjustment

There has been some interest in identifying characteristics of employers who have employed deaf applicants and the particular jobs for which they were hired. Knowledge in this area would help to determine job categories not presently filled by deaf workers for which they are qualified.

In a 1961 report VanDeventer and Scanlon summarized the results of a survey of attitudes of local industrial employers in and around Philadelphia toward hiring persons wearing hearing aids. Out of 1500 employers contacted 476 replied. Replies came from manufacturers, insurance companies, banks, retail stores, public utilities, restaurants, recreational facilities, skilled trades, transportation, and professional and semiprofessional occupations. Employers who had contact with employees who wore hearing aids stated that they were as efficient as other employees, but two thirds of the employers had no contact with an employee or applicant who wore a hearing aid. Only 3.6 percent felt that hearing aid wearers were less efficient, and only 4.3 percent agreed that they missed many instructions. "No objection to hiring a hearing aid wearer" was the most frequent response, 74 percent; 24 percent did not answer; and 1.5 percent did object. The investigators cautioned that employers may have given socially acceptable responses to some extent, wishing to appear unbiased.

Garrett (1964) pointed out some discrepancies in job descriptions that have resulted from different samples of deaf workers and employers. For example, compared to 1956 census data, Garrett's sample showed more than twice as many jobs in the manufacturing category: 59.1 percent in his restricted sample against 25.5 percent nationally. Despite the large percentage difference in the two groups, the trends remained fairly similar, with low incidence of employment in areas requiring communication, such as wholesale and retail trade and public administration, and higher employment rates in manufacturing, which necessitates less communicative skill. Information concerning size of employer and employment of deaf applicants also was reported. Although large size was accompanied by more frequent employment of at least one deaf person, the distribution of deaf employees was such that small employers accounted for more deaf employees than would be expected on the basis of uniform distribution, and large companies accounted for fewer than expected. Interesting comparisons were made between the distribution of occupational categories for which Garrett's sample of employers would hire or have hired a qualified deaf person and the actual current employment distributions of Garrett's sample, the National Survey data, and VRA rehabilitants. In the clerical category 34.9 percent of the employers said they would hire a deaf person. In the samples, Garrett's data showed 33 percent, the National Survey reported 5.2 percent, and VRA data showed 14 percent actually held such positions. This indicates that Garrett's sample of employers was more willing to hire clerical workers than national or VRA figures would indicate. It should be remembered, however, that the sample was not controlled, but consisted of voluntary respondents to a questionnaire. A number of additional articles are available that describe the vocational status of special subgroups of deaf employees (Connor and Rosenstein, 1963; Neyhus, 1964; and Justman and Moskowitz, 1965).

Particular problems faced by deaf applicants in obtaining employment were described by Craig and Silver (1966). They pointed up the need for realistic preparation for employment on the part of the employee and a willingness on the part of the employer to adjust to special characteristics of deaf people. Some barriers to employment might be (1) inadequate written or oral language, (2) inexperience in filling out forms, (3) difficulty in a personal interview situation, (4) level of skills available, and (5) stereotyped attitudes of the employer toward deaf people.

The first four barriers should be overcome during vocational training and counseling before the applicant approaches the employer. Indeed, these are the aims of vocational rehabilitation programs (McDaniel, 1965). McDaniel cited a number of factors that must be assessed: ability to do the job both physically and mentally, intellectual and educational ability to keep the job, personality, work skills, and opportunities for work. It appears that the Scale of Military, Economic and Social Competence of Hearing (Davis and Silverman, 1970) is currently the most promising approach to determining rehabilitation needs and vocational objectives in relation to hearing level. McDaniel (1965) also summarized training programs in Georgia, California, Massachusetts, and Michigan. Citing a 1960 report by Bigman, who obtained data from 1101 deaf persons, he found that deaf employees were more stable in their jobs than those with some residual hearing. Employees who did not use lipreading or hearing aids but depended upon written communication stayed longest at a single job. In conclusion McDaniel stressed the need for a classification system relating to rehabilitation and research and also a widening of opportunities and a breaking down of stereotyped occupations for the deaf.

The Alexander Graham Bell Association and the American University Development, Education, and Training Research Institute cooperated in the development of an interview instrument to assess attitudes toward deaf applicants with minimal skills. A preliminary report in 1968 described intermediate steps in developing the interview questionnaire. The final form was designed for use in a later stage to assess the attitudes of manufacturers, a primary target for expansion of opportunities for deaf applicants. In the final form the test instrument included questionnaire information to determine factors important in hiring personnel, attitudes toward workers with physical handicaps, attitudes toward and reactions to deaf in general and with respect to social and communicative relationships with, and stereotypes about, the deaf. In addition there was a fictitious job application that could represent a real applicant with low-level skills. Response to the simulated hiring situation could be compared with attitudes expressed in the questionnaire. Sample questions included

> In your estimation, at what points in this hiring process are the manual work applicants frequently rejected?

> Suppose you were advising a new personnel officer on how to make hiring decisions about manual workers, what two most important pieces of advice would you give him, and why?

> Suppose a deaf person had come to this plant *yesterday* to apply for an unskilled or semiskilled job. What would probably have happened?

> How favorably or unfavorably do totally deaf workers in manual jobs compare with hearing persons in similar jobs?

Additional items asked the respondent to state his level of agreement or disagreement with various statements about employment of deaf workers and hiring practices for manual workers. Administering such a carefully designed testing instrument to a large sample of employers might prove valuable for counseling and training of minimally skilled deaf persons.

Summary

Scientific evidence concerning the effects of training and counseling the hearing impaired is fragmentary at best.

As regards visual training, it has been shown that lipreading scores of normal-hearing subjects can be improved through sessions of systematic training. Also it has been demonstrated that the effects of lipreading training can transfer from speakers in training sessions to other speakers.

Research on auditory training reveals that experimental efforts have been directed primarily toward children with severe hearing losses. Hearing-impaired children who have been exposed to auditory training have shown greater response to delayed auditory feedback than those who have not had previous training, indicating some reliance on auditory cues. Audiograms and speech output in preschoolers have been shown to improve considerably following auditory training. Recent research on infant training programs can be expected to yield valuable information as the children progress through their late school years. Additionally, auditory training has a positive effect upon auditory discrimination for frequency in children. Nonspeech auditory stimuli have also been used successfully in the development of auditory discrimination learning of young children. Adult hearing-impaired people have increased their auditory skills after a short training period, but the amount of improvement has depended upon the type of training and the type of test material. Training tended to be more effective when the training and test situations were similar.

There is considerable evidence of concern for the adjustment of persons wearing a hearing aid, but little data describing the effects of specific programs of counseling upon adjustment to the hearing aid. In the main, it appears that preschool children adapt rather well to the use of the hearing aid. Progress in the areas of social relationships was noted after children were fitted with individual aids. Language and achievement tests show no difference in performance by children that can be attributed to the use of monaural or binaural hearing aids; both have proved to be effective. Amplification of low frequencies has been found to have a beneficial effect upon speech reception and production. Caution must be exercised in the use of amplification, for preliminary studies indicate that amplification has been associated with threshold shift in the ear receiving amplification. This would suggest frequent checking after a hearing aid has been fitted. Follow-up studies of hearing aid users show that there is less consistent wearing of aids by older persons; approximately half of the parents of children wearing their first hearing aid were satisfied; children under 2.5 years of age and between 8.5 and 9.4 years of age accepted hearing aids more readily than children at ages in between; and the greatest satisfaction was expressed by parents who purchased an aid when their child was very young and by those whose children had hearing losses less than 90 dB. Survey follow-up information also suggests ignorance on the part of the parents as to how the hearing aid was supposed to function. Input from the adult client relative to subjective impressions of hearing aids during the selection process is pointed up as being of some importance in the process of adjustment to the hearing aid.

Several studies have shown that speech stimuli transposed to a tactile modality can be differentiated and learned, at least when there is a limited response set. Vowels seem to provide greater success than do consonants in such a task. Correct perception of words also has been shown to take place following tactile training. There are indications that spatial distribution of signals provides more information than is available from a single source. Tactile information has been shown to improve receptive communication without interfering with lipreading.

In terms of the effects of multiple-sensory inputs during training, careful study has found that finger spelling facilitates language development and educational achievement in children. It seems that the earlier finger spelling is introduced, the greater is the educational benefit. There is evidence that the learning of finger spelling does not detract from lipreading performance. Experimental findings on combining visual and auditory stimuli in paired-associate learning do not show combined conditions to be better than single conditions for all subjects. If one sensory channel dominates, then combined reception does not show an improvement over the preferred channel. Concerning combined tactile and visual conditions, experimental results have shown that hard-of-hearing subjects benefited in a lipreading task from the presence of supplemental tactile stimuli after training.

Modification of vocal frequency in deaf adults has been accomplished by an operant discrimination training program. Effects of training were maintained quite well over a three-month period following training.

Several methods of programmed instruction to improve language comprehension have been investigated. Training has centered on vocabulary, concept formation, and the syntactic and structural aspects of language. Retention of learned material has been excellent in experiments that have included these measures. Training to improve written language production also has been reported and positive transfer to classroom work has been noted.

There seem to be no scientific studies of the effects of counseling the hearing handicapped. However, research has shown general findings relative to adjustment of the hearing-handicapped population. Study of family adjustment has brought to light some characteristics associated with families who have an adult member who is hearing impaired. For example, the incidence of marriage is slightly lower for the deaf population than for hearing individuals. Of the deaf who marry, up to 95 percent marry a deaf mate. Marriages have been stable, showing a low rate of separation and divorce. Hard-of-hearing homemakers with normal-hearing family members have been compared with normal-hearing homemakers on a number of factors. Hard-of-hearing homemakers have a tendency to view the home as a place where family members feel they belong. Normal-hearing homemakers placed relatively more emphasis on the home as a place to entertain friends. Tension felt by husbands of severely hard-of-hearing homemakers is greater than tension felt by husbands of normal-hearing homemakers. Hearing-impaired homemakers receive more help in tasks around the house than do homemakers with normal hearing.

Studies of social adjustment indicate that the hearing impaired have a realistic attitude toward their handicap. Normal-hearing respondents of all ages, from children to adults, overestimate the benefits of the use of hearing aids and show patronizing attitudes. It appears that integrating deaf and hearing students in a school situation may cause a heightened stress among the deaf. The deaf person tends to select other deaf people as friends and also tends to involve himself in leisure-time activities that do not require active participation in communication.

With respect to educational adjustment, deaf children are seriously below the grade level of achievement appropriate to their ages. It appears that early manual training of deaf children has beneficial effects upon achievement. Early training is indicated for the deaf but the exact nature of such training needs further study. In considering integration of deaf children into normal-hearing classrooms, experience suggests that it should be gradual rather than abrupt.

As with the other areas of adjustment, there appears to have been a great deal of concern with the vocational adjustment of the hearing-handicapped person, but there is no scientific data derived from studies of the effects of vocational counseling and training upon vocational adjustment. Survey data on employment rates indicate that there are more than twice as many deaf workers in industrial jobs requiring little communication skill than there are in areas requiring communication. Barriers to employment of deaf workers center about language inability and lack of skill in the interview situation. Some efforts have been made to construct an objective instrument for the assessment of employer attitudes toward minimally trained deaf applicants. Vocational training programs exist and have been described, but systematic evaluation of programs is not available. Only a little is known about the vocational adjustment of the hard of hearing individual. Survey data reflecting attitudes of employers toward hiring persons wearing hearing aids indicated that those employers who had had contact with such employees felt that they were as efficient as employees with normal hearing. Approximately three fourths of the responding employers alleged that they had no objection to hiring a hearing aid wearer.

RECOMMENDATIONS

The following recommendations are made with respect to the effects of training and counseling of the hearing handicapped and as a result of the observed lack of research data dealing with these topics. It is recommended that research efforts be directed toward—

1. study of the effects of lipreading training (a) on subjects in different age ranges, and (b) on subjects with varying degrees of loss
2. study of the effects of auditory training (a) on subjects of varying age and degree of loss, and (b) on receptive and expressive speech and language
3. determination of the part played by various aspects of auditory perception, such as the awareness of sound; recognition of rhythm and auditory patterns; frequency, intensity, and spectral discrimination; and discrimination of speech sounds, in effecting changes in auditory reception.
4. investigation of the effects of tactile training along with and as a supplement to other sensory channels on receptive and expressive performance
5. investigation of optimal materials and procedures to be employed in visual, auditory, tactile, and multisensory training with hard-of-hearing and deaf
6. exploring the relative permanence of visual, auditory, tactile, and multiple-sensory communication training through time in relation to the subect's age, type of hearing loss, and severity of loss
7. determining the shifts in intelligibility and esthetic aspects of speech of the hearing handicapped as a function of auditory, visual, tactile, and combined sensory training
8. the study of measures of transfer and retention following training

References

Alexander Graham Bell Association for the Deaf and The American University Development, Education, and Training Research Institute.

(1968). Assessing the attitudes of industry hiring personnel toward employment of deaf applicants. Washington, D.C.

Auxter, D. (1971). Learning disabilities among deaf populations. *Except. Child.*, 37, 573–577.

Barr, B., and Wedenberg, E. (1965). Prognosis of perceptive hearing loss in children with respect to genesis and use of hearing aid. *Acta. Oto-Laryng.*, 59, 462–473.

Bender, R., and Wiig, E. (1960). Binaural hearing aids for young children. *Volta Rev.*, 62, 113.

Bentzen, O., Frost, E., and Skaftason, S. (Undated). Treatment with binaural hearing aids in presbyacusis. Denmark: OTICON.

Bentzen, O., Greisen, O., and Jordan, O., (1965). Bilateral hearing aid treatment of 300 patients. *Int. Audiol.*, 4, 121–125.

Berger, K., Hoke, J., Lindsay, M., Meyer, W., and Swagerty, T. (1968). Hearing aid preferences. *Audecibel*, 17, 151–160.

Birch, J. W., and Stuckless, E. R. (1963). Programmed instruction and the correction of written language of adolescent deaf students, Title VII, Grant No. 7–48–1110–118, 78 pages.

Black, J. W., O'Reilly, P. P., and Peck, L. (1963). Self-administered training in lipreading. *J. Speech Hearing Dis.*, 28, 183–186.

Bode, D. L., and Oyer, H. J. (1970). Auditory training and speech discrimination. *J. Speech Hearing Res.*, 13, 839–855.

Briskey, R. J., Garrison, M. J., Owsley, P., and Sinclair, J. (1967). Effects of hearing aids on deaf speech. *Audecibel*, 16, 173–188.

Briskey, R. J., and Sinclair, J. (1966). The importance of low-frequency amplification in deaf children. *Audecibel*, 15, 12–20.

Bruce, W. (1960). Social integration and effectiveness of speech. *Volta Rev.*, 62, 368–372.

Campanelli, P. A. (1968). Audiological perspectives in presbycusis. *EENT Monthly*, 47, 3–10, 81–86.

Connor, L. E., and Rosenstein, J. (1963). Vocational status and adjustment of deaf women. *Volta Rev.*, 65, 585–591.

Craig, H. B. (1970). Reinforcing appropriate visual attending behavior in classes of deaf children. *Amer. Ann. Deaf*, 115, 481–491.

Craig, W. N. (1964). Effects of preschool training on the development of reading and lipreading skills of deaf children. *Amer. Ann. Deaf*, 109, 280–295.

Craig, W. N., and Collins, J. L. (1970). Analysis of communicative interaction in classes for deaf children. *Amer. Ann. Deaf*, 115, 79–85.

Craig, W. N., and Silver, N. H. (1966). Examination of selected employment problems of the deaf. *Amer. Ann. Deaf*, 111, 544–549.

Davis, H., and Silverman, S. R. (1970). *Hearing and Deafness*, 3d ed. New York: Holt Rinehart, and Winston.

DiCarlo, L. (1958). The effects of hearing one's own voice among children with impaired hearing. *Volta Rev.*, 60, 306–314.

Dirks, D., and Carhart, R. (1962). A survey of reactions from users of binaural and monaural hearing aids. *J. Speech Hearing Dis.*, 27, 311–322.

Doehring, D. G. (1968). Picture-sound association in deaf children. *J. Speech Hearing Res.*, 11, 49–62.

Doehring, D. G., and Ling, D. (1971). Programmed instruction of hearing-impaired children in the auditory discrimination of vowels. *J. Speech Hearing Res.*, 14, 746–754.

Eachus, T. (1971). Modification of sentence writing by deaf children. *Amer. Ann. Deaf,* 116, 29–43.

Elliott, L. L., and Vegely, A. B. (1968). Some possible effects of the delay of early treatment of deafness: A second look. *J. Speech Hearing Res.*, 11, 833–836.

Elser, R. P. (1959). The social position of hearing-handicapped children in regular grades. *Except. Children,* 25, 305–309.

Espeseth, V. K. (1969). An investigation of visual-sequential memory in deaf children. *Amer. Ann. Deaf,* 114, 786–789.

Falconer, G. A. (1960). Teaching machines for the deaf. *Volta Rev.*, 62, 59–62, 76.

Falconer, G. A. (1961). A mechanical device for teaching sight vocabulary to young deaf children. *Amer. Ann. Deaf,* 106, 251.

Falconer, G. A. (1962). Teaching machines for teaching reading. *Volta Rev.*, 64, 389–392.

Furth, H. G. (1961). Visual paired-associates task with deaf and hearing children. *J. Speech Hearing Res.*, 4, 172–177.

Gaeth, J., and Lounsbury, E. (1966). Hearing aids and children in elementary schools. *J. Speech Hearing Dis.*, 31, 283–289.

Garrett, C. W. (1964). "Quo Vadis": A pilot study of employment opportunities for hearing impaired. *Volta Rev.*, 66, 669–677.

Gengel, R. W. (1969). Practice effects in frequency discrimination by hearing-impaired children. *J. Speech Hearing Res.*, 847–856.

Gordon, J. E. (1959). Relationships among mothers' *n* achievement, independence training attitudes, and handicapped children's performance. *J. Consult. Psych.*, 23, 207–212.

Guelke, R. W., and Huyssen, R. M. J. (1959). Development of apparatus for the analysis of sound by the sense of touch. *J. Acoust. Soc. Amer.*, 31, 799–809.

Hester, M. S. (1964). Manual communication. *Report of the Proceedings of the International Congress on Education of the Deaf,* Gallaudet College. June 22–28, 1963. Washington, D.C.: U.S. Government Printing Office, 211–221.

Holbrook, A., and Crawford, G. H. (1970). Modification of vocal frequency and intensity in the speech of the deaf. *Volta Rev.*, 72 492–497.

Horowitz, L. S., and Rees, N. S. (1962). Attitudes and information about deafness. *Volta Rev.*, 64, 180–189.

Hutton, C. (1960). A diagnostic approach to combined techniques in aural rehabilitation. *J. Speech Hearing Dis.*, 25, 267–272.

Johnson, G. F. (1963). The effects of cutaneous stimulation by speech on lipreading performance. Unpublished Doctoral dissertation, Michigan State University.

Jordan, O., Greisen, O., and Bentzen, O. (1967). Treatment with binaural hearing aids. *Arch. Otolaryng.*, 85, 319–326.

Justman, J., and Moskowitz, S. (1965). Graduates of P.S. #47—A half century report. *Volta Rev.*, 67, 275–280.

Kinney, C. E. (1961). The further destruction of partially deafened children's hearing by the use of powerful hearing aids. *Ann. Otol. Rhinol. and Laryngol.*, 70, 828–835.

Kringlebotn, M. (1968). Experiments with some visual and vibrotactile aids for the deaf. *Amer. Ann. Deaf,* 113, 311–317.

Kodman, F., Jr. (1961). Successful binaural hearing aid users. *Arch. Otolaryng.*, 74, 302–304.

Kodman, F., Jr. (1969). Attitudes of hearing aid users. *Audecibel,* 18, 76–78.

Kowalsky, M. H. (1962). Integration of a severely hard-of-hearing child in a normal first-grade program: A case study. *J. Speech Hearing Dis.*, 27, 349–358.

Lach, R., Ling, D., Ling, A. H., and Ship, N. (1970). Early speech development in deaf infants. *Amer. Ann. Deaf,* 115, 522–526.

Lewis, N. L., and Green, R. R. (1962). Value of binaural hearing aids for hearing-impaired children in elementary schools. *Volta Rev.*, 64, 537–542.

Ling, A. H. (1971). Changes in the abilities of deaf infants with training. *J. Commun. Dis.*, 3, 267–279.

Ling, D. (1964). Implications of hearing aid amplification below 300 CPS. *Volta Rev.*, 66, 723–729.

Macrae, J. H. (1968). TTS and recovery from TTS after use of powerful hearing aids. *J. Acoust. Soc. Amer.*, 43, 1445–1446.

Macrae, J. H., and Farrant, R. H. (1965). The effects of hearing aid use on the residual hearing of children with sensorineural deafness. *Ann. Otol., Rhinol. and Laryngol.*, 74, 409–419.

McDaniel, J. W. (1965). The currect status of vocational rehabilitation for disorders of hearing and speech. *J. Speech Hearing Dis.*, 30, 17–31.

McGrady, H. J. (1964). The influence of a program of instruction upon the conceptual thinking of the deaf. *Volta Rev.*, 66, 531–536.

Montgomery, G. W. (1966). The relationship of oral skills to manual communication in profoundly deaf adolescents. *Amer. Ann. Deaf,* 111, 557–565.

Morkovin, B. V. (1960). Experiment in teaching deaf preschool children in the Soviet Union. *Volta Rev.*, 62, 260–268.

Motto, J., and Wawrzaszek, S. J. (1963). Integration of the hearing handicapped: Evaluation of the current status. *Volta Rev.*, 65, 124–129, 160.

Myers, R. D. (1960). A study in the development of a tactual communication system. Air Force Human Engineering Personnel and Training Research–Symposium, Glen Finch, ed. Washington, D.C.: National Academy of Sciences–National Research Council, Publication 783, 238–243.

Nelson, M. (1959). Electrocutaneous perception of speech sounds. *Arch. Otolaryng.*, 69, 445–448.

Neyhus, A. I. (1964). The social and emotional adjustment of deaf adults. *Volta Rev.*, 66, 319–325.

Northern, J. L., Teter, D., and Krug, R. F. (1971). Characteristics of manually communicating deaf adults. *J. Speech Hearing Dis.*, 36, 71–76.

O'Connor, C. D., and O'Connor, L. E. (1961). A study of the integration of deaf children in regular classrooms. *Except. Children*, 27, 483–486.

Oyer, H. J. (1961). Teaching lipreading by television. *Volta Rev.*, 63, 131–132, 141.

Oyer, E. J., and Paolucci, B. (1970). Homemakers' hearing losses and family integration. *J. Home Econ.*, 62, 257–262.

Pfau, G. S. (1969). Project LIFE PI Analysis. *Amer. Ann. Deaf*, 114, 829–837.

Pfau, G. S. (1970). Project LIFE: Developing high interest programmed materials for handicapped children. *Educational Technology*, 10, 13–18.

Pickett, J. M. (1963). Tactual communication of speech sounds to the deaf: Comparison with lipreading. *J. Speech Hearing Dis.*, 28, 315–330.

Pickett, J. M., and Pickett, B. H. (1963). Communication of speech sounds by a tactual vocoder. *J. Speech Hearing Res.*, 6, 207–222.

Quigley, S. P. (No date). The influence of finger spelling on the development of language, communication, and educational achievement in deaf children. University of Illinois: Institute for Research on Exceptional Children.

Reynolds, L. G. (1955). The school adjustment of children with minimal hearing loss. *J. Speech Hearing Dis.*, 20, 380–384.

Rodda, M. (1966). Social adjustment of hearing-impaired adolescents. *Volta Rev.*, 68, 279–283.

Ross, M. and Lerman, J. (1967). Hearing aid usage and its effect on residual hearing: A review of the literature and an investigation. *Arch. Otolaryng.*, 86, 639–644.

Rushford, G., and Lowell, E. (1960). The use of hearing aids by young children. *J. Speech Hearing Res.*, 3, 354–360.

Saleh, H. (1965). Sights and Sounds, an auditory training program for young deaf children. *Amer. Ann. Deaf*, 110, 528–552.

Siegenthaler, B. M., and Gunn, G. H. (1952). Factors associated with help obtained from individual hearing aids. *J. Speech Hearing Dis.*, 17, 338, 347.

Sortini, A. J. (1959). Importance of individual hearing aids and early therapy for preschool children. *J. Speech Hearing Dis.*, 24, 346–353.

Spidal, D. A., and Pfau, G. S. (1972). The potential for language acquisition of illiterate deaf adolescents and adults. Project LIFE, National Education Association, Washington, D.C.

Stuckless, E. R., and Birch, J. W. (1966). The influence of early manual communication on the linguistic development of deaf children, Part I. *Amer. Ann. Deaf*, 111, 452–460.

VanDeventer, A. J., and Scanlon, J. A. (1961). A survey of attitudes of local industries toward the employability of the hearing aid wearer. *J. Speech Hearing Dis.*, 16, 222–225.

Vernon, M. (1969). Sociological and psychological factors associated with hearing loss. *J. Speech Hearing Dis.*, 12, 541–563.

Vernon, M., and Koh, S. D. (1970). Early manual communication and deaf children's achievement. *Amer. Ann. Deaf*, 115, 527–536.

Yantis, P. A., Millin, J. P., and Shapiro, I. (1966). Speech discrimination in sensorineural hearing loss: Two experiments on the role of intensity. *J. Speech Hearing Res.*, 9, 178–193.

List of Abbreviations

AAOO	American Academy of Ophthalmology and Otolaryngology
ABLB	alternate binaural loudness balance
ASA	American Standards Association
BICROS	bilateral contralateral routing of signals
CHABA	Committee on Hearing, Bioacoustics, and Biomechanics
CID	Central Institute for the Deaf
CID W–22	speech discrimination test (CID)
CNC	consonant-nucleus-consonant
CROS	contralateral routing of signals
DLF	difference limen for frequency
DSS	Developmental Sentence Scoring
EEG	electroencephalography
ERA	evoked response audiometry
GSR	galvanic skin response
HHS	Hearing Handicap Scale
IRI	Index of Response Irregularity
ISO	International Standards Organization
ITPA	Illinois Test of Psycholinguistic Ability
MBFLB	Monaural Bifrequency Equal Loudness Balance Test
MCL	Most Comfortable Loudness (level)
M-R Test	Modified Rainville Test
NSST	Northwestern Syntax Screening Test
N.U.	Northwestern University (Auditory Test No. 1)
PAL	Psycho-Acoustics Laboratory (Harvard University)
PB	phonetically balanced
PB–50 Word Lists	speech discrimination test (PAL)
PBK–50	Phonetically Balanced Kindergarten test—50-word list
PGSR	psychogalvanic skin response
PTA	pure tone average
SAI	Social Adequacy Index
SAL	Sensorineural Acuity Level
SISI	short increment sensitivity index
SL	Sensation Level
S/N	signal-to-noise ratio
SRT	speech reception threshold
SSI	Synthetic Sentence Identification
TIP	Threshold by Identification Pictures Test
TROCA	tangible reinforcement in operant conditioning audiometry
TTR	Type-Token Ratio
USPHS	United States Public Health Service
VAT	Verbal Audiometric Test
VRA	Vocational Rehabilitation Administration
VST	Visible Speech Translation
W–1, W–2	speech reception tests from CID
WIPI	Word Intelligibility by Picture Identification

Name Index

Subject Index